# TUDOR AND STUART DEVON

## THE COMMON ESTATE
## AND GOVERNMENT

*Frontispiece*
Professor Joyce Youings.

# TUDOR AND STUART DEVON

## THE COMMON ESTATE AND GOVERNMENT

Essays presented
to Joyce Youings

Edited by
Todd Gray, Margery Rowe
and Audrey Erskine

UNIVERSITY
*of*
EXETER
PRESS

First published 1992 by
University of Exeter Press
Reed Hall, Streatham Drive
Exeter, Devon EX4 4QR
UK

**British Library Cataloguing in Publication Data**
A catalogue record of this book is
available from the British Library

ISBN 0 85989 384 7

Devon Libraries

Typeset in Stemple Garamond
by Colin Bakké Typesetting, Exeter

Printed and bound in Great Britain
by Short Run Press Ltd, Exeter

. . . whereby the Common Estate and Government hath under the King of this land always been kept & preserved in good estate . . .

JOHN HOOKER alias VOWELL,
*Synopsis Corographicall*, fol. 117

# CONTENTS

# ILLUSTRATIONS AND MAPS

## *Illustrations*

ix

## Maps

# Editors
# and Contributors

FRANK BARLOW is Emeritus Professor of History, University of Exeter.

DAVID DEAN is Lecturer, Goldsmiths' College, University of London.

AUDREY ERSKINE is former Lecturer in Paleography and former Exeter Cathedral Archivist, University of Exeter.

IAN GOWERS is retired Senior Lecturer in History, Liverpool Polytechnic.

ALISON GRANT is Tutor, University of Exeter and Chairman, North Devon Museum Trust.

TODD GRAY is Research Fellow in Cornish Maritime History, Institute of Cornish Studies, University of Exeter.

TOM GREEVES is a freelance cultural environmentalist and Chairman of the Dartmoor Tinworking Research Group.

IAN MAXTED is Devon County Local Studies Librarian.

STEVEN PUGSLEY is a former research student and now publisher.

WILLIAM RAVENHILL is Leverhulme Research Fellow and Emeritus Reardon Smith Professor, University of Exeter.

MARGERY ROWE is County Archivist of Devon.

W.B. STEPHENS is former Reader and sometime Dean of the Faculty of Education, University of Leeds.

MARGARET WESTCOTT is Local Studies Librarian, Westcountry Studies Library.

# Abbreviations

APC: *Acts of the Privy Council*

BL: British Library

CPR: *Calendar of Patent Rolls*

CSPC: *Calendar of State Papers, Colonial*

CSPD: *Calendar of State Papers, Domestic*

DAT: *Devonshire Association Transactions*

DCNQ: *Devon and Cornwall Notes and Queries*

DCO: Duchy of Cornwall Office

DCRS: Devon and Cornwall Record Society

DH: *The Devon Historian*

DNB: *Dictionary of National Biography*

DRO: Devon Record Office

ECA: Exeter City Archives (now in Devon Record Office)

EHR: *English Historical Review*

HLRO: House of Lords Record Office

HMC: Historical Manuscripts Commission

NDRO: North Devon Record Office

PRO: Public Record Office

WCS: Westcountry Studies Library, Exeter

WDRO: West Devon Record Office

County of Devon.

# Preface

The main purpose of this volume is to present to Professor Joyce Youings a collection of contributions from former postgraduates whose work has been associated with or influenced by her; most of them were pupils directly supervised by her. Their essays are a reflection of her great contribution to and encouragement of research in local studies and their wider implications, particularly in her own county of Devon. However, it has also proved possible to combine this presentation with one of a different kind: to give to Professor Youings the first publication of a magnificent screen map of Exeter, with the recent discovery of which she was herself closely involved. This provides a particularly appropriate opening to the volume, in view of her own large share in the study of the history of the city of Exeter in the sixteenth and seventeenth centuries. The first essay, therefore, is an account of the map by Professor William Ravenhill and Mrs Margery Rowe, both of them her longstanding friends and associates; the editors are much indebted to Professor Ravenhill for his investigations in this field which is so particularly his own. The editors would also like to thank Professor Frank Barlow for providing the foreword and Mr Ian Maxted for supplying a bibliography of Professor Youings' publications.

There are many people who have assisted with the production of this volume and the editors would like particularly to thank Professor Christopher Holdsworth, Dr John Critchley, Dr Paul Barnwell, Mrs E.R. Linnell, Professor Charles Thomas, Dr Michael Duffy, and especially Dr Jonathan Barry. The generous financial and other assistance which has been given to this volume is some acknowledgement of Professor Youings' service to the University of Exeter and to local bodies within Devon, and of her research interests overseas. Among those who have contributed are the Department of History and Archaeology, Centre for South-Western Historical Studies, Centre for Maritime Historical Studies, Institute of Cornish Studies, Bridge Trust (Barnstaple), Exeter Civic Society, Devon

& Cornwall Notes & Queries, Devon and Cornwall Record Society, Devon & Exeter Institution, Devon History Society, the Incorporation of Weavers, Fullers and Shearmen of Exeter, Devonshire Association, Victoria County History, Dr H.G. Jones and Virginia and William S. Powell and the North Caroliniana Society. The editors wish to thank Seán Goddard for the maps. For the illustrations the editors are grateful to Mr John Saunders, Ms Julia Chalmers, Mr and Mrs Frank Chesher and particularly the staffs of the Westcountry Studies Library, Devon Record Office and the Royal Albert Memorial Museum, Exeter.

May 1992

For permission to reproduce the illustrations thanks are due to the owner of the screen (1), The British Library and the Royal Albert Memorial Museum (2), the Royal Albert Memorial Museum, Exeter (3, 4), Lord Courtenay (5), Devon Library Services (6, 7, 10, 11, 13, 15, 16, 20), Bedford Settled Estates (8), Ms Julia Chalmers (9), the Devon Record Office (12, 14), Mrs V Chesher (17), North Devon Athenaeum (18) and Dartmouth Town Council (19). The frontispiece photograph of Joyce Youings was provided by Mr John Saunders.

# Foreword

FRANK BARLOW

W.N. Medlicott, when appointed to the Chair of History in the University College of the South West at the end of the War, realized immediately that he needed not only to build rapidly on the sketchy foundations he had inherited but also to assemble a staff which would be worthy of the university status to which Exeter aspired. Among his earliest recruits was Joyce Youings. Medlicott had a shrewd eye for quality, and his typical jest, that he had appointed a woman in order to get the coffee made for his mid-morning departmental meetings, deceived no one. In Joyce he had spotted a young scholar who could play a special and, in his view, indispensable role in his team. Basically he was looking for a Tudor specialist, preferably one who was also interested in local history. With Joyce he found all that, and much besides. She was to become a tower of strength in what was for some years a rather unstable Department.

Born into a long-established Barnstaple business family, Joyce had deep roots in the county. A confirmed member of the Church of England, she had a faith which reinforced her natural equanimity, courage, industry and sense of duty. And with her First-Class Honours degree in History from King's College, London, and her London doctorate, she exemplified the type of product that Medlicott, himself a London graduate, wanted to produce at Exeter. Furthermore, her London Diploma in Education gave promise that not only her research interests but also her zeal for education would be given full play.

Some forty years on, this volume is offered her as an affectionate tribute on her seventieth birthday. Her life has been many-sided. In her youth a vigorous sportswoman, especially on the hockey field (a Green Dragon), she has always been adventurous and ready to meet any challenge. In the University she excelled as a scholar, teacher and administrator. She was a most successful Warden of first Hope then Thomas Halls of Residence.

She served (and not as a token woman) on many university bodies, notably the Publications Committee, and, exceptionally, had two terms, separated by a decade, as its chairman. She was always a staunch supporter of authority and in the History Department a trusty aide to its head. She undertook duties willingly and consistently performed them well. Promoted to Senior Lecturer in 1965 and Reader in 1968, five years later she was awarded one of the first personal chairs to be created in the University, and so became the first woman professor at Exeter.

Her extramural activities were also of great value to the Department and University. She has been, and remains, active in all organizations and societies which promote the study of local history, such as the local section of the National Trust, the Devonshire Association, the Devon and Exeter Institution, the Standing Conference for Devon History, the Centre for South-Western Historical Studies, the Institute of Cornish Studies, the Devon and Cornwall Record Society and the Victoria County History of England; and in most of these she has held important offices. She also remains a devoted alumna of the Institute of Historical Research in the University of London. Her special interest in the maritime history of Devon and Sir Walter Raleigh led to her invitation by the British Academy to deliver the Raleigh Lecture on History in 1989, and brought her into fruitful contact with several American and Canadian universities, where she is always welcome as a visiting lecturer. She has, indeed, a very wide circle of friends and fellow-workers.

Her contribution to historical scholarship has been considerable. By studying late medieval and Tudor economic and social history mainly from a Devonshire standpoint, she has been able to particularize and clarify themes and problems of general interest. And by putting both national and local archives to good use, she has produced a blend of national and local history which exhibits the best qualities of both. Her studies of the disposal of Devon monastic lands after the dissolution of the monasteries is a case in point. Her initial contribution was strikingly original and her findings remain the point of departure for other scholars. If her substantial and scholarly history of Tuckers Hall, Exeter, exemplifies local history at its best, her contribution of a volume on *Sixteenth Century England* to the Pelican Social History of Britain shows that she can tackle wider fields with equal success.

Teaching has always been at least an equal interest. A good lecturer and a devoted tutor, she has exerted a great influence on many generations of undergraduates at Exeter. A striking proof of this is her successful recruitment and supervision of research students. She was an acknowledged expert in her field; she gave her pupils unstinting help; and she would stand no nonsense. A thesis had to be thoroughly researched and properly composed—and it had to be completed. The essays published here are a selection from her pupils' work. Archbishop Lanfranc of Canterbury, one of the greatest and most influential of teachers, once remarked, 'The adornment of a teacher is the honest life of his pupils'. We can be sure that Joyce would echo that and also that her pupils have not let her down. It is, of course, an unfair advantage to be Devonshire born and bred. John Hooker (Vowell), chamberlain of Exeter in 1555, expressed this excellently in his *Synopsis Corographicall*:

> The people ar well Compacte and of good Stature, and be verye stronge and apte to all good excercises, and well inclyned to all honestie and vertue and some to be framed to any action either Civill or martiall whereof theire hathe benne and yet is a Common proverbe Lett a devonshere man come but ones to the Courte and he wilbe a Courtier at the first. In matters of knoledge lerninge and wisedome they be of a deepe Judgement. In matters Civill and for the Common Welth, they be wise pregnant and polytuyque. In matters martiall, they be very valiant and prudent. In all travells and paynes, they be very laboriose: and in all actions ether of the bodye or of the mynde they be very excellent.

Need one say more? He might have had Joyce Youings in mind.

# A Decorated Screen Map of Exeter based on John Hooker's Map of 1587

WILLIAM RAVENHILL and MARGERY ROWE

The illustration chosen to provide the dust-jacket of this book and Plate 1 derives from a four-fold screen,[1] each leaf measuring 190 cm. by 56 cm., on which has been painted a map of Exeter decidedly reminiscent of the kind of town maps which were devised in the late Elizabethan period. It is clearly in the style of the town maps that were made of London c. 1553–9 by an unknown cartographer, Norwich in 1559 by William Cuningham, Cambridge in 1574 by Richard Lyne, Oxford in 1578–88 by Ralph Agas and, more particularly, a close parallel of Exeter 1584–7 by John Hooker.[2] The distinguishing feature of all these maps is the way in which the buildings are all shown in the third dimension, a cartographic device which, although known to the Roman surveyors, appears to have been re-discovered with the Renaissance re-awakening of interest in map-making. This started with the translation of Ptolemy's *Geographia* from Greek into Latin after 1406 in Florence and the subsequent intense interest the humanists took in cartography. Alongside Ptolemy's advocacy for a more realistic representation of space (*sphera in plano*), there was also that other Renaissance re-discovery of visualising space from one controlling view-point, that is linear perspective. It was also a new way for the humanists to structure the three-dimensional physical world by means of two dimensions, a development the articulation of which some scholars have argued cogently was also triggered by Ptolemy's projective geometry. The Renaissance cartography of townscapes became in many instances a merging of these two systems of representing space. Diffusion of the humanistic, artistic and cartographic contexts of the Renaissance spread quickly north of the Alps from Italy to Germany, the Low Countries and Britain where the topographic representation of urban subjects became strongly influenced by a visual sensibility and a penchant for a picturesque composition.

The fact that the map-making at Exeter shared so early with those few other English cities, owes much to the new-found confidence and civic pride which emerged in Exeter after about 1550, as well as to the remarkable character and intellectual stature of one of its citizens, John Hooker. In the middle of the sixteenth century, the rich shire of which Exeter was the county town ranked among the first two or three counties of England in wealth and population.[3] Exeter itself was not only an important economic node but also a provincial capital and since 1537 a county in its own right;[4] its cathedral was the seat of a large diocese and its castle precinct a centre of secular administration for the West Country. Moreover, the city's overbearing and hitherto powerful neighbours the Courtenays had been swept aside. This enabled the navigation of the Exe between the city and the sea to be re-opened.[5] Equally important, if not more so, was the transfer of ownership of the lordship and manor of Exe Island from the Courtenays to the city in 1550.[6] It was, however, not only these geographical and economic aspects which contributed to the early mapping of the city but also the social milieu embodied in the person of John Hooker.

John Hooker's reputation as an archivist and antiquarian is well documented. He was the continuator and editor of Holinshed's *Chronicles* and was lauded by William Camden with the words '*vir eruditus et de antiquitatis studio optime meritus*'. He hailed from a family who were landowners and office holders in the city of Exeter and who bore arms.[7] He received a classical education in the grammar school at Menheniot in Cornwall run by Dr John Moreman and entered Corpus Christi where he became steeped in that college's humanistically-oriented studies. Thence to the University of Cologne and subsequently to the city of Strasbourg which had become the multi-lingual, multi-confessional refuge and rendezvous for many Protestants and humanists. At Strasbourg John Hooker lived in the residence of Peter Martyr, the popular Florentine humanist who had been forced to flee from Italy in 1542 on account of his reforming and heretical teaching. There is a strong likelihood that it was at Strasbourg that John Hooker acquired his interest in and instruction for map-making, as many of the humanists are known to have been cartographically literate. In 1547 both came to England, Peter Martyr on the invitation of Archbishop Cranmer to become Regius Professor of Divinity at Oxford and John Hooker to read Civil Law at Corpus Christi, subsequently returning to Exeter to become a civic official. In 1555 John Hooker was appointed to a newly-created post of City Chamberlain; this involved him in becoming custodian of the official records of Exeter and in seeing to their ordering and preservation. One of the products of this employment was the drafting of legal deeds, and in the case of some of these which involved 'lymitinge and boundeninge' Hooker was able to support them with maps, six of which survive.[8]

John Hooker's effort to map the whole of Exeter is clearly the source and inspiration for the screen but it is not a slavish copy of his surviving engraved map. This has a box in the bottom left corner enclosing the inscription '*Opera et impensis Joannis Hokeri generosi ac huius quaestoris, hanc tabellam sculpsit Remigius Hogenbergius Anno Domini 1587*' (By the labour and expenses of John Hooker Gent. and the City Magistrate, Remigius Hogenberg engraved this map AD1587). Remigius Hogenberg was one of the most eminent among the refugees engraving in England in this period, and to secure his services to do the map of Exeter was no mean achievement on Hooker's part. As City Chamberlain John Hooker would have been the kind of official to whom Christopher Saxton's 'placart' would have provided an entrée when the latter came to the city to organise the mapping of the county. The map of Devon was subsequently engraved by Remigius Hogenberg before 1575 and the fact that he also engraved the map of Exeter in 1584–5 is surely more than a coincidence, which in all probability points not only to official contacts between Saxton and Hooker but also professional ones.[9]

When printed on paper the engraved map survives in three states, and to the best of our knowledge these are unique copies.[10] The successive changes made to the copper-plate are really quite extraordinary. In State A, shown in Plate 2, a blank scale-bar surmounted by a pair of dividers is prominently engraved in the lower right-hand corner. In State B the dividers and scale-bar have been removed from the plate, but not entirely successfully as ghosts are still visible. It is not being extravagant to conjecture that they were removed when it was realized that the map was no longer at a constant scale. To compare this map with a constant-scaled map reveals a distinct foreshortening away from the viewing point. We suggest this is more than likely to be the application of perspective in an attempt to make a picturesque composition, since there is evidence in Hooker's writings that he knew the extent of the city in actual measurements and was familiar with the use of a compass: 'The

Citie . . . conteynethe in circuit or compasse sixteyne hundredth whole
passes after five foote to a passe which accomptinge one thousande passes
to a myle it is a myle and a half aboute and somewhat more.' With regard
to his knowledge of the magnetic compass, the correct orientation by the
use of the words 'northe, southe, weste and easte' was provided in the
four corners of his engraved map. A simile he used in describing the duties
of the Town Clerk also indicated his familiarity with magnetism, 'Like a
skillfull mariner to prick the card and to set the compass and to advertise
and to instruct the master how and in what order he is to keep his course
and make his way',[11] as did the presence on one of his manuscript maps
of a prominently displayed 32–point compass-rose.[12] The use of direc-
tional names on the four corners of an engraved map was a convention
frequently employed in Elizabethan map-making and makes good cartographic sense, but the next alterations to the plate whereby a compass-rose
is placed to fill the blank space left by the removal of the scale-bar on
State C (Plate 3), with the indication for north actually pointing east, make
for a piece of nonsense. Equally reprehensible are the alterations which
misplace St Leonard's church. One wonders what cartographic illiterate
was responsible for such changes which merely add inaccuracies: they
must surely point to tampering with the copper-plate after John Hooker's
death in 1601.

The subject of screens in the western world is apparently neglected,
with neither a strong research effort nor an extensive literature.[13]
Although screens are known to have been in existence in the Orient for
over 2000 years and have been extensively studied by their scholars, the
starting point for us in Europe was apparently the establishment of an
active and regular east-west trade after 1571 with the opening of Nagasaki.
This signalled the beginning of a new commercial and artistic reciprocity.
One result of the exchange of goods was the bringing of screens from their
origin in China via Korea to Japan in the eighth century AD and then to
Europe in the late sixteenth century, where they have continued to exist
and be re-interpreted in a variety of materials and designs. We are aware
of only two other examples of cartographic subjects among the variety of
designs, both of these being in Kobe, Japan: one shows 'Four Cities of
Europe' probably derived from Braun and Hogenberg; the other a World
Map after Ortelius. Both are manifestations of a type of Japanese art called
Namban. This term, meaning literally 'southern barbarian', is applied to
works that combine elements of both Japanese and European cultures. To
return to the West, this is the only screen known to us which portrays a
city map as its main theme.

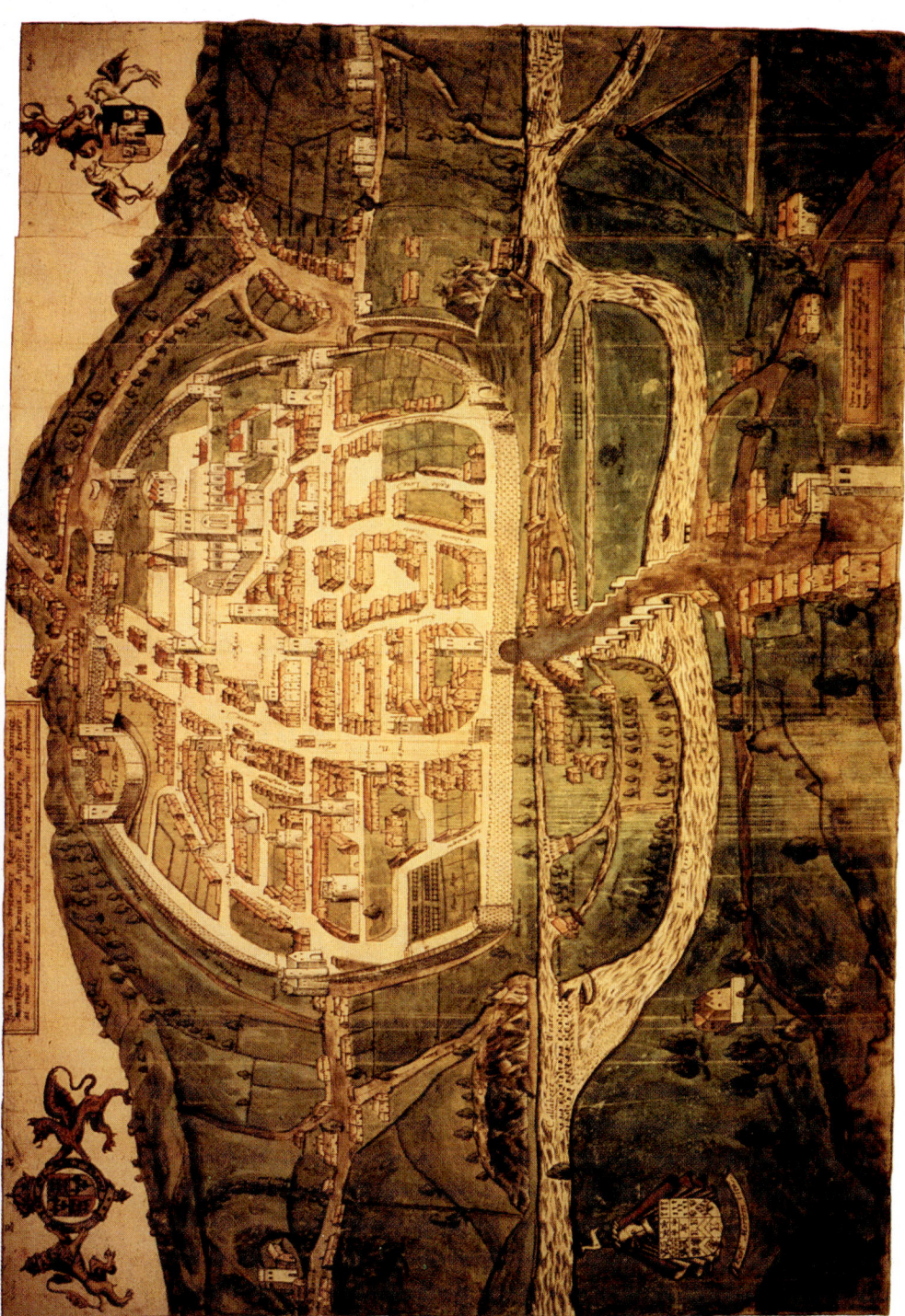

*Plate 2*

John Hooker's map of Exeter, 1587. State A.

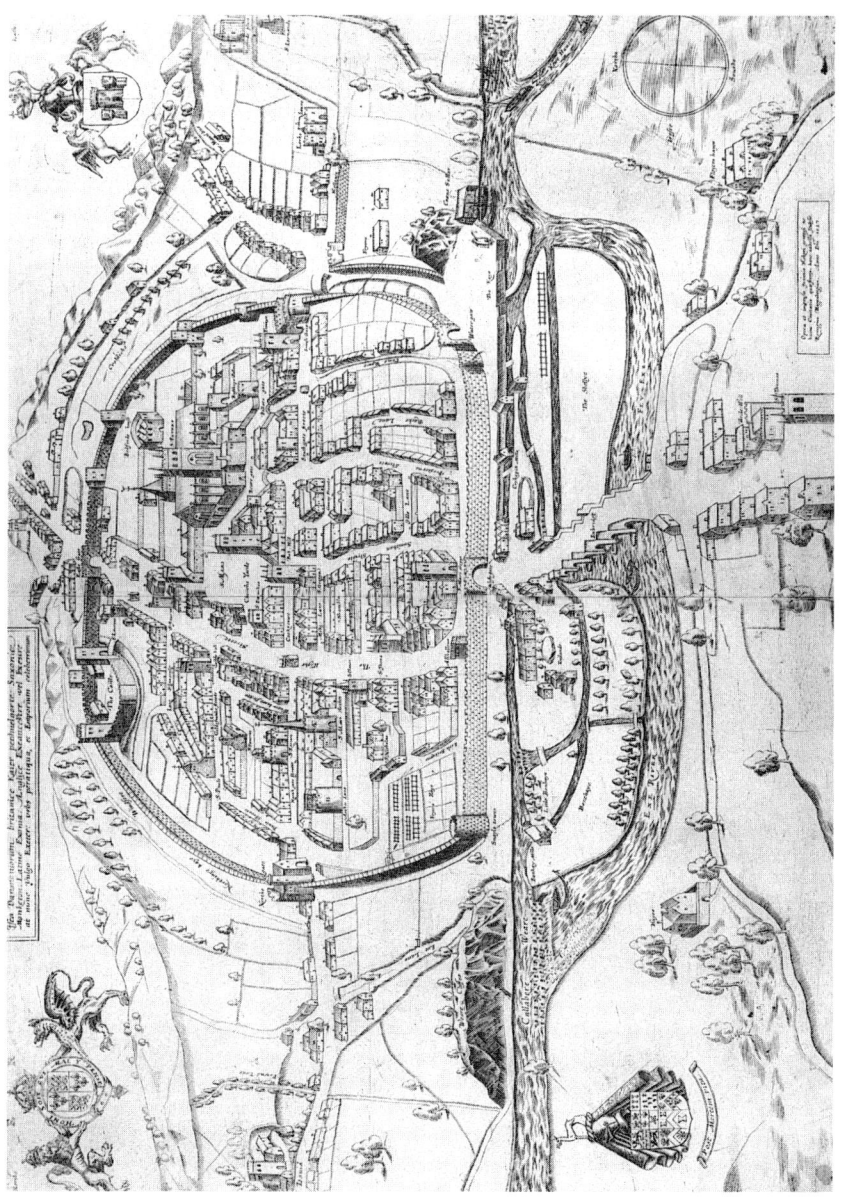

*Plate 3*

John Hooker's map of Exeter. State C.

*Plate 4*
Portrait of John Hooker (1525–1601), nineteenth-century English School copy
after sixteenth-century original.

Another aspect of screens is the material used in their making. Here our attention needs to focus on the heavier, thicker kinds of animal skins, the leathers. The preparation, gilding, varnishing and painting of leather is a specialized subject but it may be sufficient for us to note that the late medieval centre for this craft was Spain whence the skills passed to France and the Low Countries, the latter superseding Spain as the main producer before the end of the sixteenth century.[14] From here knowledge of the craft spread to London where at least two leather gilders are known to have practised in this period. Most frequently such artisans were employed in the making of decorated leather panels which, when scarfed, became a fashionable and insulating form of wall hanging in the more prestigious houses of England. Decorative screens as draught excluders fit into the same context but again would be found only in the possession of the well-to-do.

There are some interesting differences as well as similarities between the screen and the copper-plate-derived Hooker map. One is the angle of view. For the screen the artist has taken a much higher imaginary leap in the air so that the insides of the towers can be seen, but overall the perspective foreshortening is present. The cherubs animating the lower corners present an intriguing problem: one is conspicuously holding a pair of dividers, directing our attention to a divided but unnumbered scale-bar; it pairs with a cherub on the left-hand side grasping a compass with its card showing cardinals, half-cardinals and a fleur-de-lis but not oriented correctly. One may well assume that these elements have been inserted for purely aesthetic reasons; they certainly provide artistic balance. Since, however, they form an intrinsic part of the map itself, being placed within the neat lines, so to speak, their presence could also be interpreted as symbolic as well as aesthetic, reflecting the instrumentation and technique involved in at least an early stage of this map-making process. Many early maps in which the urban form is shown in the third dimension started with a uniform-scaled plan, the street pattern being subsequently adjusted for perspective.

The screen more closely resembles State A than the later states but is, of course, much larger than they are, so that considerably more detail can be shown. For instance, the cathedral is given more flying buttresses and the Gothic decorated window at its west end is accurately represented. Most of the houses also give the impression of being realistically portrayed, in contrast to the many stylised forms of the paper map. From this greater abundance of detail we can be almost sure that the screen is not just an enlarged copy of the smaller Hooker but derived either from a much larger prototype or, less likely, a Hooker providing the outlines with the artist filling in the detail, but, of necessity, on site.

When one extends this kind of analysis, in an attempt to date this artefact with reference to known changes in the contemporary townscape, a most confusing result emerges. For instance, the late medieval covered walkway, part of the Guildhall in the High Street, which is shown clearly on the engraved map, is absent from the screen and so is the 'colonnaded piazza' which replaced it in 1593–5. In view of the immense cost involved in this refurbishment, and its prominence in the line of the street frontage, it would appear most strange for it not to be featured on the screen if it were painted after about 1595. Conversely, the other Guildhall in St Sidwells, destroyed during the Civil War, is not on the screen. This could point to its being painted after 1646, but Hayes Barton, west of the river, which was destroyed on 31 July 1643, is featured whole and upstanding.[15] The mere fact that a feature is left off a map may be less an indication of the date of the map than of the cartographer's practice of generalisation and, in this case, of the artist's selective licence. In that latter context there is also a clear absence of industrial features but a distinct attempt to animate and humanize the piece. People walk the streets, horses draw carts, market stalls are on the cathedral green, cows are being driven across Exe Bridge and even a game of hockey is in progress.

An elaborate and highly decorative border surrounds the actual map-image on all four sides. Investigations thus far point to designs and motifs such as these persisting over long periods, but similarities with those existing in the sixteenth century can with certainty be established. Examples datable to the last decades of that century are comparable with the fruit, the foliage and the half-female, half-pedestal caryatides and strapwork. Art historians to whom photographs of the screen have been shown differ in their opinions with regard to dating the screen by something of the order of a century. Two of their number attribute the decoration to the period around 1600. Two others, while recognizing much that is sixteenth century, also detect elements characteristic of the late seventeenth and early eighteenth centuries: they consider the screen to be a consciously backward-looking object with ornament designed in part to match the period of the map. They link its making with an expression of Bérainesque antiquarianism in England. Jean Bérain (1637–1711) was employed from 1670 by the French Crown as an engraver and in 1674 became 'architecte dessinateur de la Chambre et du Cabinet du Roi' with the duty of providing designs for royal festivities, ballet and the like. He was one of the creators of the Louis XIV style and, more broadly, one of the period's most imaginative and influential designers, whose arabesques and grotesques inaugurated a new movement which led subsequently towards the rococo style. Bérain's particular style came into vogue shortly before 1700 and remained popular for the next quarter of a century, being copied in France and throughout the capitals of Europe.

There is, however, a problem in associating the screen with a nostalgic piece of historicism in Exeter at this later time. Who and what artist around 1700–14 would be moved to re-create an Elizabethan map of Exeter, by then over 100 years old, and would the prototype already referred to have survived until then? There appear to be no known local or contemporary circumstances into which such an unusual endeavour would neatly fit. On the contrary a sixteenth-century context is decidedly more applicable and credible. At the four corners of the screen there are cartouches, each one encompassing a coat of arms. The one in the top-left corner has the arms of Elizabeth I. Does this suggest a date before 1603 for the making of the screen? Separated by unmounted and putto-mounted dolphins in the top-right corner are the arms of the city of Exeter. To balance these, in the lower corners are the arms of the bishop and those of a member of the Cecil family—probably Sir William Cecil, later Lord Burghley.

At this point it should be made known that the extensive city records and those of the bishop, such as survive, have been searched for any references to this screen, utterly without success. Correspondence with Hatfield House and Burghley House, Stamford, have proved similarly unrewarding. That notwithstanding, among these four contexts the one that stands out most positively as having a possible connection with a cartographic screen is Lord Burghley. 'I observe, most honoured Sir, that above all other monuments of the noble arts you take especial pleasure in geographical maps, and that you know how to make good use of them in your office to render unceasing service of all kinds to the state.' It was with these sentiments that Laurence Nowell in 1563 started his letter to Sir William Cecil seeking patronage for the surveying of England and subsequent drafting of a new series of county maps.[16] Nowell's request was not successful, but his letter accurately preserves a true contemporary impression both of Cecil's deep interest in maps and of his ability and necessity to use them as Secretary of State from 1550 to 1572 and as Lord Treasurer from 1572 to his death in 1598. These twin aspects of his close association with Elizabethan cartography resulted in the building-up of a map collection and of his becoming an employer and patron of map-makers. It has been said of his map collection that it was paralleled only by the maps and atlases assembled in the same period for the use of the Spanish Crown. This, however, was not for the mere satisfaction of a collecting obsession, it provided him with the essential adjuncts to the policies he was pursuing and the everyday problems he was being called upon to solve.[17] He appears to have been the kind of statesman who, in addition to having a library of atlases and individual maps to consult, update and use to make decisions with regard to a spatial context, also liked to live surrounded by maps. In his home at Theobalds, a foreign visitor noted in 1592 that covering the walls were numerous 'correct landscapes of all the most important and remarkable towns in Christendom', while beautifying another hall was 'the Kingdom of England, with all its cities, towns and villages, mountains and rivers'.[18] It is not likely that the screen was in this residence, as a more appropriate place for it would have been Exeter House, also at times known as Burghley House and Cecil House, which was in the Strand.

The city of Exeter had good reasons to be eternally grateful to Lord Burghley. Throughout the medieval and Tudor periods the aspirations, commerce and industries of Exeter's merchants had been frustrated and, indeed, physically impeded by the powerful Courtenay family who, as lords of the manor, owned Exe Island. This meander in the river's alluvial flood-plain was ideal for the manipulation and control of the waters of the Exe to provide the water power on which Exeter's fortunes depended. Through the good offices of Sir William Cecil, the City acquired the freehold of Exe Island, which meant the Chamber could develop it as they wished. It became the industrial quarter of the city and remained so until the last few years.

In an age which did not look askance at the acceptance of pensions or gifts by ministers, cities needed to maintain good personal connections in the highest quarters. Exeter made a most auspicious choice. The City's Chamber decided in 1565 that since Sir William Cecil 'hath been our especial friend in our affairs and suits as well for suit for Exiland . . . we grant him an annuity of £5 for life'.[19] This pension was subsequently doubled and it continued to be paid until the end of his life.[20] Nor did that sever the Cecil connection, for on 23 January 1598/9 the Chamber agreed that the same pension should be paid to Sir Robert Cecil for life.[21] In 1608 he was granted the High Stewardship of the City, but the gift of the screen is unlikely to be associated with this award for, had it been so, the arms of James would have been more appropriate as decoration in the cartouche in the top-left corner.

As a token of appreciation for favours rendered, and as a visual reminder of Exeter for favours to come, what more appropriate gift could be devised for Lord Burghley, 'the most cartographically minded statesman of his time'?[22]

## Notes

1. The screen is privately owned.
2. W. Ravenhill, 'Bird's-Eye View and Birds'-Flight View', *The Map Collector* 35 (1986), 36–7.
3. W.G. Hoskins, *Provincial England* (1965), 70–1, *Two Thousand Years in Exeter* (Exeter, 1960), 51–66; Wallace T. MacCaffrey, *Exeter 1540–1640* (1975), 5–25.
4. DRO, ECA Charter xxxiii, Letters Patent of Henry VIII, 23 August 1537.
5. *Statutes of the Realm* 31. Henry VIII, c. 4.
6. DRO, ECA Charter xxxvi, Letters Patent of Edward VI, 22 December 1550.
7. Vernon F. Snow, *Parliament in Elizabethan England, John Hooker's Order and Usage* (1977), 3–27.
8. Cathedral Library, Exeter, John Hooker's MS 3530, fols 37, 43; M 10; DRO, ECA, Letter 619, St Sidwells, *Fee* and Book 52 between pages 30–1.
9. DRO, ECA, Receiver's Book 1584 5, p. 4d: 'paid by Mr Hooker for drawing a Platt of the Cittie in Copper: 30s.'
10. State A, BL Maps C.5.a.3; State B in private hands; State C, DRO, 4292A/BS1. There is some evidence to suggest that a manuscript map by Hooker of the whole city may at some time have been inserted in DRO, ECA Book 52 between pages 2–3; K.M. Constable, 'The Early Printed Plans of Exeter 1587–1724', DAT LXV (1932), 455–73.
11. *John Vowell, alias Hoker, The Description of the Citie of Exeter*, transcribed and edited by Walter J. Harte, J.W. Schopp and H. Tapley Soper from a manuscript in the DRO (DCRS ii and iii, 1919 and 1947) ii. 438–47, iii. 816; see also BL, Cotton MS Titus F. VI, fol. 88. An approximate measure of 8,000 feet compares favourably with the actual figure of 7,710 feet when it is appreciated that Hooker probably rounded off this figure for his narrative.
12. Cathedral Library, Exeter, MS 3530, The Platte of St Sydwells Fee, fol. 37.
13. Janet Woodbury Adams, *Decorative Folding Screens in the West from 1600 to the Present Day* (1982).
14. John W. Waterer, *Spanish Leather* (1971).
15. S.R. Blaylock, 'Exeter Guildhall', in *Devon Archaeological Society Proceedings* 48 (1990), 123–78; S.R. Blaylock and K.A. Westcott, 'Exeter Guildhall' and G.C. Henderson, 'Excavations at Hayes Barton, St Thomas', *Exeter Archaeology* (1985–6), 30–6, 53–4.
16. BL Lansdowne MS 6/54. Latin original translated by R.A. Skelton in *Saxton's Survey of England and Wales*, Imago Mundi Supplement vi (Amsterdam, 1974), 15–16.

17. R.A. Skelton and John Summerson, *A Description of Maps and Architectural Drawings in the Collection made by William Cecil First Baron Burghley now at Hatfield House* (Oxford, The Roxburghe Club, 1971); J.B. Harley, 'The Map Collection of William Cecil, First Baron Burghley 1520–98', *The Map Collector* 3 (1978), 12–19.

18. W.B. Rye, *England as seen by Foreigners* (1865), 44–5. A quotation from the narrative of the visit of Frederick, Duke of Wirtemberg, written by his secretary.

19. DRO, ECA, Act Book iii. 61. There appears to have been a distinction drawn between receiving a gift and being corrupted by one; for in the oath he swore on his appointment as Secretary of State on 20 November 1588, Queen Elizabeth demanded 'This judgement I have of you, that you will not be corrupted by any manner of gifts, and that you will be faithfull to the State'.

20. DRO, ECA, Receiver's Rolls 7–8 Elizabeth; Hatfield Archives, Deeds 277/2, Grant of life annuity of £10 by the City of Exeter, 2 October 1566.

21. DRO, ECA, Act Book v. 438; Hatfield Archives, Deeds 244/11, Grant of an annuity of £10 to Sir Robert Cecil by the City of Exeter, 20 January 1599.

22. J.H. Andrews, *Ireland in Maps* (Dublin, 1961), 5.

## Acknowledgements

The authors are deeply grateful for the welcome and kind hospitality of the owner of the screen who allowed us access for its study and, without the slightest hesitation, gave consent for its photographic reproduction in this volume. They also wish to record their appreciation of the help they have received from art historians associated with the Warburg Institute, the *Burlington Magazine* and the Victoria and Albert Museum and from R.H. Harcourt Williams, Librarian and Archivist to the Marquess of Salisbury at Hatfield House and from Burghley House, Stamford.

# Katherine Courtenay, Countess of Devon, 1479–1527

MARGARET WESTCOTT

At the beginning of December 1527, the town of Tiverton is reported to have witnessed an elaborate funeral.[1] On 2 December the coffin, covered with a pall of cloth of gold decorated with a silver tissue cross and coats of arms, accompanied by mourners wearing black hoods and gowns carrying banners depicting the saints, was brought from the castle, where it had rested since 15 November, to St Peter's Church, and was met by Thomas Chard, abbot of Montacute,[2] his namesake Thomas Chard, abbot of Ford[3] and Simon Rede, abbot of Torre.[4] In a procession in front of the coffin walked local dignitaries from the church and lay administration. On reaching St Peter's the coffin was placed under a richly ornamented canopy on which was set a silver cross and two candlesticks, and after the performance of some funeral ceremonies it was left to lie in state through the night, guarded by attendants. The mourners returned to the castle, where a meal was provided.

The next morning at seven o'clock they all returned to the church for a requiem mass sung by the abbot of Montacute, supported by choristers from Exeter and the surrounding district. Exeter's mayor, John Bythell,[5] and aldermen joined the knights, gentlemen and yeomen at the service, after which the coffin was laid in the vault prepared to receive it, and the mourners again returned to the castle to be entertained to a second meal, more elaborate than that of the previous day, before dispersing to their homes. Eight thousand poor people were said to have received two pence each on condition that they prayed for the soul of the departed.

The lady of the manor, for whom these ceremonies had been arranged, is described in the account as 'the Princess Katherine, youngest daughter of King Edward IV and widow of William Courtenay, Earl of Devon and

Lord of this manor'. The funeral, in fact, marked the end of an era, a period of 15 years when a royal princess lived in Devon, and had occupied a remarkable position as head of the county's principal family and owner of its largest estate. Following the tradition in which she had been born and brought up, she maintained a minor court at her chief residence, Tiverton Castle, and from there her influence was felt thoughout the area. No one could have been left in doubt as to her unique status and importance while she used the proud title 'daughter, sister and aunt of kings' and displayed on her coat of arms not only the emblems of two ancient Devon families but also those belonging to the royal family of England and to some of the most eminent of the aristocracy. The splendid funeral was a fitting conclusion to an eventful life.

Katherine Plantagenet was the sixth daughter of King Edward IV and his queen, Elizabeth Woodville. She was born sometime in 1479, probably at the palace of Eltham.[6] On 28 August of that year her father entered into a treaty with King Ferdinand of Castile for a projected marriage between Katherine, at that time his youngest daughter, and Ferdinand's son Juan.[7] The family already included two sons, Edward and Richard, and four daughters, Elizabeth, Mary, Cecily and Anne. Another daughter, Bridget, was to be born in November 1480, and two other children, Margaret and George, had died in infancy. Entries in the Patent Rolls for 12 July and 5 November 1480[8] record grants of land in Hitchin, Hertfordshire and an annuity of five pounds to Joan Colson, 'nurse to the King's daughter Katherine', and her husband.

Following the death of Edward IV in April 1483, when Katherine was four years old, leaving his young son Edward as his heir, the political uncertainty which had characterized the latter half of the fifteenth century became even more acute. His wife and young family were in a vulnerable position, and Elizabeth Woodville took her second son Richard, duke of York, and her daughters into sanctuary at Westminster. The events which followed are well known. Edward IV's brother assumed the throne as Richard III, the young duke of York joined his brother Edward V in the Tower of London, and both boys disappeared. The eventual fate of Katherine's brothers, the 'Princes in the Tower', still remains a subject of much speculation.

Elizabeth Woodville continued to live in the sanctuary with her daughters and the Act of Parliament of January 1484 which confirmed Richard III as King also included a clause stating that, for various reasons, his brother's marriage was invalid and the resulting children were illegitimate.[9] In the following March, however, Richard III took an oath stating

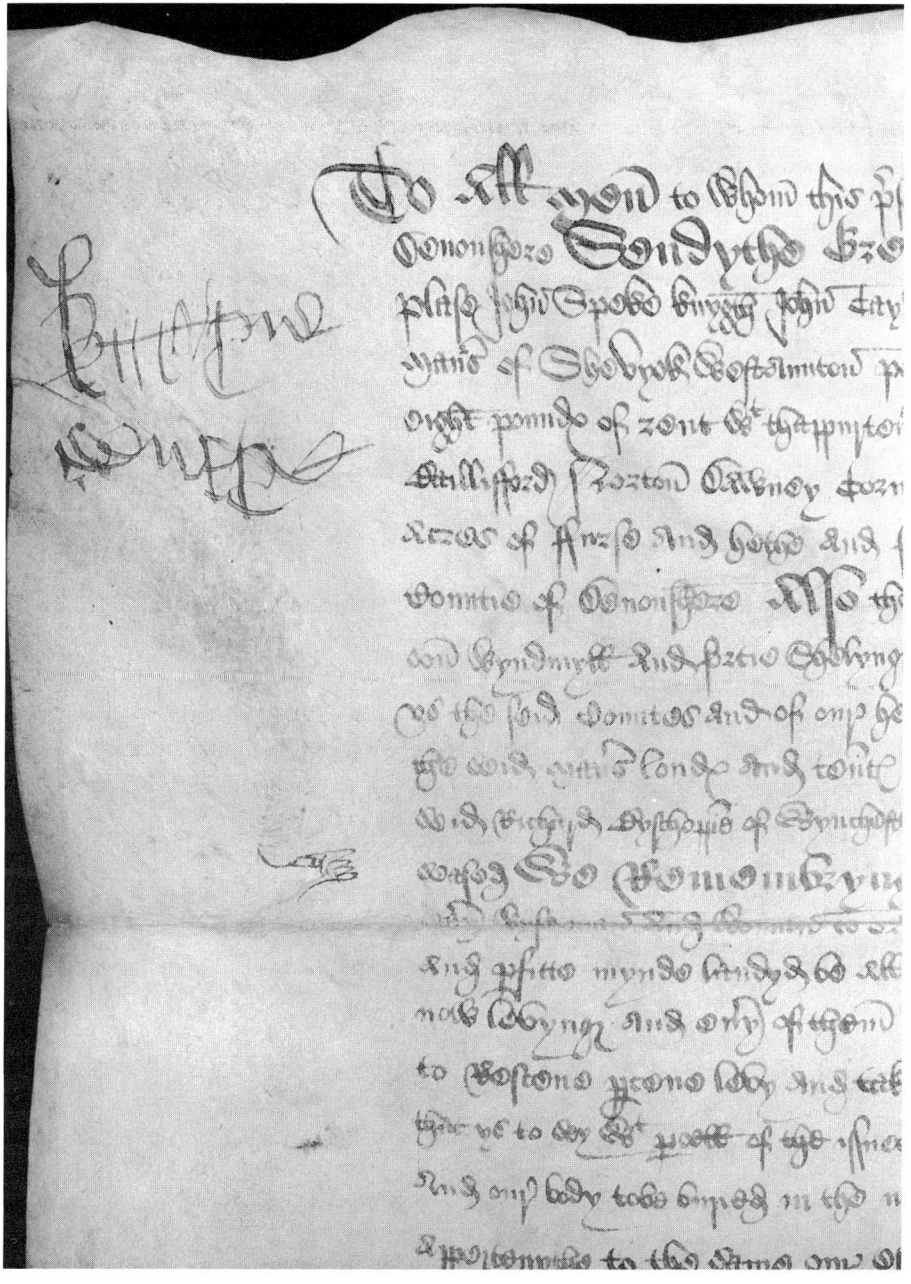

*Plate 5*

Part of the will of Katherine Courtenay, Countess of Devon, 1527, showing her signature.

*Plate 6*

South East view of Tiverton Castle, 1730, engraved for Dunsford's *Historical Memoirs of Tiverton*, 1790.

that if the young princesses came out of the sanctuary and agreed to be 'guided, ruled and demeaned by him' then he would extend his protection to them, ensure that they were treated according to their station and arrange suitable marriages for them in due course, while their mother would be adequately provided for.[10] Elizabeth Woodville was thus persuaded to leave Westminster with her daughters, who appear to have been taken to live in the royal household.[11]

In January 1486, after the battle of Bosworth had led to the death of King Richard III and the succession of Henry Tudor as King Henry VII, Elizabeth of York, Katherine's eldest sister, became the wife of the new King, in an attempt to bring together the warring factions of Lancaster and York. Elizabeth Woodville was restored to her position as Queen Dowager, and the Act of Parliament declaring her marriage invalid and her children illegitimate was repealed.[12] These events seemed to herald a change of fortune for Edward IV's other daughters, now sisters of the Queen of England, although their brother-in-law Henry VII was faced with the problem of settling their futures in situations where their Yorkish blood could pose as little threat to his position as possible. In 1487 Cecily became the wife of John, Viscount Welles, and in 1495 Anne married Thomas Howard, Duke of Norfolk and Earl of Surrey.[13] Mary had already died in 1482 and the youngest daughter, Bridget, became a nun.[14] According to one of Edward IV's biographers, once the Tudors had mounted the throne 'the rest of Edward IV's daughters, for all their surpassing beauty, had to be content with an earl, a viscount and a gentleman, a knight and a nunnery'.[15]

In 1487 Henry VII attempted to arrange a marriage for Katherine with James III of Scotland's second son, James, Marquis of Ormonde,[16] but following the Scottish king's death this plan did not come to fruition. In 1492 she and her sisters were with their mother at the convent of Bermondsey during her last illness, and were mourners at the Queen Dowager's funeral at Windsor.[17] Three years later, some time in 1495, when she was 16 years old, Katherine was married, in the presence of the King and Queen,[18] to Sir William Courtenay, the only son and heir of Edward Courtenay, eighth Earl of Devon.

The Courtenays became the richest and most influential family in Devon in the later Middle Ages and early Tudor period, and are said to have taken their name from the town of Courtenay, in the province of Gastinois, part of the Ile de France.[19] The English branch appears to have begun when Reginald de Courtenay accompanied Eleanor of Aquitaine to England in 1152. The family began a connection with Devon almost immediately when Reginald acquired the wardship and marriage of Hawise, heiress to the barony and honour of Okehampton, the largest in the county. Reginald married his ward, and their son Robert formed an alliance with Mary, the younger daughter of William de Redvers, Earl of Devon. Robert and Mary's great grandson, Hugh de Courtenay, inherited the estates belonging to this earldom and consequently added the second largest honour in the county, that of Plympton, to his Okehampton estates. In 1335 he also won for himself and his heirs the title of Earl of Devon.[20] During the years that followed the family acquired other estates, notably the Bohun inheritance which included the manor of Powderham and the Dauney estates in Cornwall.[21]

When Thomas Courtenay succeeded as fifth earl in 1435 a turbulent period in Courtenay history began, reflecting the climate in the country as a whole with the beginning of the Wars of the Roses, and he and his family helped to provoke lawlessness and violence in Devon.[22] His marriage to Margaret Beaufort, granddaughter of John of Gaunt, tended to ally the Courtenays naturally to the Lancastrian cause. Thus the sixth earl, another Thomas, fought with Henry VI's army in 1460 and 1461, was taken prisoner after the battle of Towton and beheaded at York. His head was one of those substituted for that of Katherine's grandfather, Richard, Duke of York, which had been exhibited above the city gates after the battle of Wakefield.[23] With Edward IV's succession the deceased earl was attainted,[24] one of his brothers, Henry, was executed for treason[25] and the other, John, was killed in the battle of Tewkesbury in 1471,[26] leaving no heir, so that the senior branch of the Courtenay family came to an end. The lands were granted to various loyal subjects by both Edward IV and Richard III, and it was not until the reign of Henry VII that they again reverted to Courtenay ownership.

A junior branch of the family, established at Boconnoc, near Lostwithiel in Cornwall, had begun with the marriage of Hugh Courtenay, the nephew of the third earl, to Margaret, one of the co-heiresses of a Cornish landowner, Sir Thomas Carminow,[27] who had brought with her estates in Devon and Cornwall, centred round the manor of Boconnoc. Sir Hugh Courtenay of Boconnoc was a stout Lancastrian and, like his relative, lost his life at Tewkesbury.[28] During his lifetime he had also contributed to disorder in the county by supporting Earl Thomas in his activities and by engaging in piracy on his own account.[29] His son and heir, Edward Courtenay of Boconnoc, supported the schemes to put Henry Tudor on the throne and fled with him to Brittany, returning in 1485 to take part in the victory at Bosworth, and being rewarded with a knighthood either before or after the battle.[30] The Courtenays had forfeited both lives and estates for the House of Lancaster, so it was only fitting that on 26 October 1485, Edward Courtenay of Boconnoc was created eighth Earl of Devon and had restored to him all the Courtenay estates which had been held by Earl Thomas in 1461.[31]

The inheritance was composed of over 60 manors, eight boroughs and nine hundreds, centred around the honours of Okehampton and Plympton. The majority of the estates lay in Devon, with a few manors in the other south-western counties. There were castles at Okehampton, Plympton, Tiverton and Colyton and the family also owned the boroughs of Chulmleigh, Colyford and Kenn together with the hundreds of Plympton, Tiverton, Colyton, East and West Budleigh, Exminster, Hayridge and Wonford, and certain property in the form of shops, tenements and cellars in the city of Exeter. The Devon manors included Sampford Courtenay, Musbury, Aylesbeare, Topsham and Exminster. There were 16 manors scattered throughout the counties of Somerset, Dorset, Berkshire, Buckinghamshire and Hampshire, and 12 in Cornwall. To these estates Earl Edward added the Boconnoc lands which came to him by inheritance from his father and consequently do not feature in the Letters Patent.[32]

The Earl married Elizabeth, the daughter of Sir Philip Courtenay of Molland, yet another branch of the family,[33] and they had one son, William, who was knighted at the coronation of Elizabeth of York in 1487.[34] It was this Sir William Courtenay who in 1495 married Katherine Plantagenet.

In spite of Edward Gibbon's assertion that 'a daughter of Edward IV was not disgraced by the nuptials of a Courtenay'[35] the marriage cannot be said to have been especially prestigious for the young princess. For her husband's family, however, it must have appeared an advantageous alliance, although in reality, by bringing them into the centre of political affairs, it was to prove something of a disaster. The judgement of Martin Dunsford, Tiverton's early historian, on the marriage, was that 'an incident which appeared at first view likely to raise the Courtenay family to higher honour was big with the most humiliating and destructive events. Had this earl married a lady of inferior rank, and been satisfied with the ample estate, honour and influence of his father, in the remote residence of the castle of Tiverton, himself and family had probably escaped destruction.'[36]

At first all went well for the couple. In November 1495 Sir William's father made some future financial provision for them by putting some of his manors to use, naming several important feoffees, including Prince Henry, Duke of York, the future King Henry VIII.[37] They apparently resided at Court for much of the time during the early years of their marriage, occasional entries concerning them appearing in the accounts of contemporary chroniclers. Sir William had gone with his father on Henry VII's expedition with Maximilian of Austria against the French King Charles VIII in 1492 and was described by Polydore Vergil as an intelligent and virile young man (*filio adolescente animi pariter atque corporis viribus florente*).[38] In 1497 he was in Devon and supported his father and other local nobility in the defence of the city of Exeter against Perkin Warbeck, again being described as a 'man of great force and valiantness'.[39]

On 15 March 1501 a Patent Roll entry records 'a grant during pleasure to the king's servant William Courtenay, knight, son of Edward, earl of Devon, for his daily and diligent attendance on the king's person, an annuity of 50 marks a year at the receipt of the Exchequer'.[40] Sir William accompanied the royal party which met the Duke of Burgundy at Calais in 1500,[41] took part in the jousts celebrating the marriage of Prince Arthur and Katherine of Aragon in November 1501[42] and also in those which took place when the king's daughter Margaret was betrothed to King James IV of Scotland early in 1502.[43]

During these years three children had been born to Sir William and Lady Katherine, two sons, Edward and Henry, and a daughter, Margaret. Up to this time the family appears to have been enjoying a settled life, taking part in Court activities and in favour with the king. This pattern changed, however, when soon after the Scottish betrothal early in 1502 Sir William was charged with conspiracy against Henry VII, together with his wife's cousin, Edmund de la Pole, Earl of Suffolk and others.[44] Contemporary reports suggest that it was suspicion of implication because of his relationship through his wife to the de la Poles, rather than any definite proof, which led to his downfall.[45] In 1503 a Bill of Attainder was passed against the various rebels, including 'William Courtenay, late of Westminster in the county of Middlesex, knight, son and heir apparent of Edward Courtenay, earl of Devon'.[46] The bill stated that Earl Edward was to keep the lands of the earldom of Devon for his lifetime, as he was 'not privy or partner to the offence' of his son, but on his death they were to revert to the Crown. William remained in prison throughout the rest of Henry VII's reign, the only references to him and his family being found in the Queen's Privy Purse Expenses for the period April 1502 to March 1503.[47] These indicate that Elizabeth of York made some provision for her sister Katherine's children, in the form of servants and nurses, food and clothes. They appear to have been in the care of Dame Margaret Cotton at Havering-atte-Bower, in Essex, which at this period was traditionally part of the estates of the Queen or the Queen Dowager.[48] On 6 April 1502, *6s. 8d.* was paid to Robert Bailly and Thomas Ap Howell, late servants to Lord William Courtenay, towards their costs for 'going into the Westcountry to the earl of Devon', probably in connection with his son's recent imprisonment.

In July 1502 Lady Katherine suffered another blow with the death of her eldest son Edward. Twenty pence was paid to Dame Margaret Cotton's servant for his expenses in travelling from Havering to the Queen to ask where the child should be buried, and later payments were made for his funeral expenses and to his nurse and rocker (nursemaid) on their dismissal.

Queen Elizabeth herself died in childbirth in February 1503, Lady Katherine taking part in the funeral ceremonies as chief mourner[49] but after this nothing is heard of her or her children for the rest of her brother-in-law's reign. Presumably they survived with help from the king and the earl of Devon. A contemporary chronicler stated that in October 1508 Sir Richard Carew, Lieutenant of the castle of Calais, brought the Marquis of Dorset[50] and 'Lord William of Devonshire, the Earl of Devonshire's son and heir, which were both of kin to the late Queen Elizabeth and of her blood' out of England, where they had been imprisoned in the Tower of London, to Calais. They were kept prisoners in the castle of Calais as long as King Henry VII lived, and 'should have been put to death, if he had lived longer'.[51]

In 1509 both Henry VII and the earl of Devon died. Henry VIII succeeded to the throne in April 1509 and a new chapter in the Courtenay family fortunes began. The Earl's will was proved at Lambeth on 11 July of that year,[52] and in line with the Bill of Attainder against his son the estates of the earldom of Devon reverted to the Crown, but the Boconnoc inheritance was not subject to forfeiture and from this the Earl made provision for his grandchildren. One hundred marks were to be set aside annually and divided equally for the maintenance of Henry and Margaret Courtenay. Henry's allowance was to continue until he reached the age of 21, and Margaret's until she married, when she was to receive the lump sum of 1,000 marks. The remainder of the Boconnoc estates were to go to his son Sir William 'under condition that he do obtain the king's grace and pardon and be at his liberty'. The Receiver General's accounts for the

Boconnoc estates record the annual payments to Henry and Margaret in the years that followed.[53]

The accession of Henry VIII heralded a return to favour for Sir William and Lady Katherine. The young king seems to have held his aunt in some regard, possibly the relationship had deepened after the death of his mother when he was only 12 years old. In July 1509 he granted to her an annuity of 200 marks.[54] Sir William was released from prison and the couple began negotiations to regain the earldom of Devon and the accompanying estates. As one of the surviving daughters of Edward IV, Lady Katherine was in a strong bargaining position because she had claims on the lands of the earldom of March, which had come into her sister Elizabeth's possession through their father Edward IV's grandmother, the heiress Anne Mortimer,[55] and remained with Henry VII till his death.

In April 1511 the King entered into an agreement[56] with them to reverse Sir William's attainder, create him Earl of Devon and restore the earldom lands to him. In return, they were to renounce all claims to the land of the earldom of March and any other lands purchased by Edward IV. In the following May Sir William was made ninth Earl of Devon, but the negotiations were cut short by another tragedy. Within a month he died, at Greenwich, before the formal investiture could take place. According to the chroniclers he contracted pleurisy, which was an incurable disease in England at the time.[57] The King decreed that Sir William should be buried with the full honours appropriate to an earl,[58] and after his funeral on 9 June 1511 he was interred in the church of the Black Friars in London. In his funeral sermon Dr Standish, the Provincial of the Grey Friars, excused Sir William of 'all infidelity against his sovereign lord the king, adding further that he was falsely accused, counselling all princes and other great lords and estates not to give hasty credence to words without a sure ground'.

Sir William left as his heir his young son Henry, who was ten years old at this time,[59] and his wife, Katherine, only recently reunited with her husband, was a widow, at the age of 32. On 13 July 1511, a month after her husband's death, she made a vow 'for to be chaste in my body and truly and devoutly shall keep me chaste from this time forward as long as my life lasteth, after the rule of St Paul'.[60]

On 6 July 1511 Henry VIII received the feoffment of the lands of the earldom of March,[61] and in February 1512 Lady Katherine received a new grant[62] giving her, in her own right, all the estates of the earldom of Devon for her life. After her death they were to pass to the heirs of herself and Sir William.

Up to the time of her husband's death the circumstances of the Princess Katherine's life can only be gleaned from passing references. Both in her childhood and marriage she had experienced traumatic reversals of fortune which must have affected her attitude to life. Now for the first time she could feel reasonably secure, with the revenues from a large estate enabling her to be independent and to support herself and her children, while her resolution not to remarry helped to remove her from political exploitation. As observed by the chronicler Edward Hall, she had 'long time tossed in either fortune, sometime in wealth, after in adversity, till the benignity of her nephew King Henry VIII brought her into a sure estate according to her degree and progeny'.[63] The fact that she obtained the inheritance of the earldom of Devon in her own right and kept and administered it herself until her death indicates a strong and capable personality. From this time she was usually referred to as 'the Countess Katherine' or 'my lady of Devonshire', and from about this time also she began to use the title 'the excellent Princess Katherine, Countess of Devon, daughter, sister and aunt of kings' in her official documents and on her seal, proclaiming the fact that she was the daughter of Edward IV, the sister of Edward V, and by marriage, Henry VII, and the aunt of Henry VIII. Her coat of arms was made up of her husband's, Courtenay quartering Redvers, and her own royal arms of France, England, Ulster and Mortimer, with the Yorkist crest of a demi-rose with the rays of the sun.[64] She usually used the signature 'Katherine Devonshire'.[65]

During the years which followed, the Countess arranged suitable marriages for her children. Her daughter Margaret was first offered to the Earl of Oxford, who paid a fine for his refusal.[66] In June 1514 Pope Leo X granted a dispensation for her marriage to Henry Somerset, Lord Herbert, the eldest son of the Earl of Worcester[67] and in the Receiver General's accounts of the Boconnoc estates for 1513–14 money was paid over to the Countess for the marriage of her daughter, in fulfilment of Earl Edward's will.[68] There was a tradition that Margaret died at a young age after choking on a fishbone, and was buried in Colyton church, but the tomb there is now believed to be that of Margaret Beaufort, wife of Thomas the fifth earl.[69] In 1520 Margaret Herbert was one of the ladies attending the Princess Mary at Richmond.[70]

With regard to the Countess' son Henry, in the Parliament of 1512 he received the reversal of his father's attainder and restitution in the blood,[71] so that he was able to take the title of Earl of Devon. He appears to have spent much of his time at Court as one of the young men around his cousin the King, increasingly engaged in social and diplomatic activities.[72]

In July 1515 he and his mother received the wardship and marriage of Lady Elizabeth Lisle, daughter and heiress of John Grey, Viscount Lisle, for the sum of £4,000 sterling,[73] which the Countess undertook to meet with payments of 250 marks twice yearly at Candlemas and Midsummer until the debt was cleared.[74] Henry and Elizabeth were consequently married, but sometime before June 1519 she died,[75] and on 25 October of the same year he married his second wife, Gertrude Blount, the daughter of William Blount, Lord Mountjoy.[76]

The Countess Katherine occasionally appears in court records, especially during the early years of her widowhood. For example, in the Revel Accounts for 6 January 1513, payment was made for a garment of cloth of gold for her;[77] and in February 1516 she was one of the godmothers at the christening of her great-niece the Princess Mary, when her son, supported by her son-in-law Lord Herbert, carried the basin.[78] Evidence suggests, however, that she spent most of her time on her estates in Devon. A survey of the houses belonging to her son at the time of his death in 1538[79] records that the castles at Okehampton and Plympton were in a decayed state and not used by the family, but at Tiverton was 'the head and chief mansion house, moated, walled and embattled round like a castle, with all manner of houses of offices and lodgings within the same, well kept and repaired, and fair gardens to the same belonging'. Also attached to the Tiverton estate were the two parks of Ashley and Newpark. In Colyton, at Colcumbe, was 'a fair large house with divers lodgings in the same, well kept and repaired, set standing within the park', and at Columbjohn in Broadclyst 'a fair house with divers lodgings within the same, well kept and repaired'. Thus the Countess had three residences in Devon at the disposal of herself and her household.

In order to run her large and scattered estates she maintained a network of servants and officials. Surviving account rolls[80] show that some of her manors were directly administered by a reeve or a bailiff, while others were let out in their entirety to a farmer. They paid the rent monies to the local receiver for the area, who in turn passed them over to the Receiver General. The administrative organization of the estates was carried out by chief stewards, each having a group of manors in their care, who reported to a central surveyor. The Countess also required an attorney, auditors, and professional experts, while members of the local gentry were retained to give advice from time to time.[81] The Courtenays appear to have commanded loyalty in their retainers, and a large number remained in their service for many years.[82] Some evidence for the organization of the Countess' household can

*Plate 7*

Colcombe Castle, near Colyton, drawn and engraved by T. Bonnor, published by R. Polwhele, 1790.

be found in two surviving household account books.[83] Over all was a treasurer (or comptroller) of the household supervising the financial arrangements, a steward of the household and an almoner also being mentioned. The catering arrangements were organized by the clerk of the kitchen.

In addition to providing details of staff, the accounts are valuable for the insight they give into the routine of the Countess' household in Devon. The first[84] is the account of the steward, summarizing expenses for the year running from Michaelmas 1522 to Michaelmas 1523. He began with a balance of £1,559 5s. 10¼d. in hand. His meat purchases included 49 oxen, four kine, one bull, 499 sheep (described as 'muttons'), with quantities of pork and brawn. A large consignment of fish was made up of 292 dry hakes, 2,645 buckhorn or dried fish, eleven fresh or 'mersant' congers, 328 dry congers, eight salt salmons and 414 milwells or cod. Also mentioned were ling, sturgeons, stockfish, sprats, salt eels, herrings and red herrings. The sea birds puffins were also included in this category, presumably because of their fishy taste; and 69s. 1d. was spent on 12 bushels of salt.

The household consumed 3½ butts of Rhenish wine, 3½ butts of malmsey, one butt of osey (a sweet French wine), together with red and white wine, claret and one bottle of muscadel. Two tuns of cider cost 53s. 4d. and £142 was expended on ale and beer. Among the spices were 3lb. of cloves at 16s., 4lb. of cinnamon at £1 11s., green ginger, mace and saffron. Sugar weighing 443lb. was purchased for £10 9s. 0¼d., 12lb. of almonds for 15s. and 45lb. of marmalade for 18s. 6d. 'Great raisins' weighing 596lb. cost £1 7s. 11d., 17lb. of small raisins 4s. 9d. and 35lb. of prunes 10s. 11d. Other provisions bought included licorice, comfits, caraways, rice, sugar candies and figs.

Other expenses incurred during the year were £10 6s. 8d. for oats for the horses and £3 17s. 7d. on shoeing. A horse was purchased for 46s. 8d. and 13s. 4d. was spent on making and mowing hay. Also bought were 196lb. of soap, wax, tallow candles, torch staves and rushes. The sum of £50 was set aside to reward messengers and servants bringing gifts from local gentry, and £190 for the wages of 70 staff, while over £100 was spent on cloth for servants' liveries. Various sums were required for New Year's gifts, alms, offerings, obits, costs of the law and repairs to the houses and their contents. Riding costs accounted for £30 8s. 3½d., this including £12 11s. 0½d. 'for my lady's hunting', and £18 13s. 8d. was needed for the costs of carriages. Finally, £150 was spent on fresh 'acates', or provisions, and 2s. on gold foil.

After setting out the payments, the steward then listed the stock that was still in hand, and this included the not inconsiderable quantity of 15 oxen and 20 sheep received as presents, as well as 100 salt eels which had been taken in Columbjohn water. In addition there was a number of wool fleeces and sheep fells in store, and 25 horses, geldings and mares on the estates.

The second surviving household account[85] is a more detailed day-to-day survey for the period Michaelmas 1523 to Michaelmas 1524. Although the book is not complete it provides a wealth of information concerning the Countess' household affairs. As might be expected, the provisions bought to feed the household were largely the same as appeared in the previous account, and included meat, fish, wine and spices. Gascon wine was 1s. for a gallon, a box of comfits cost 20d., ginger was 2s. 4d. a pound and cloves 2s. a quarter. Two pounds of pepper cost 4s. 8d., while 4s. was paid to William Wagot for '100 sour oranges, half a hundred sweet oranges, 12 pomegranates and going to the ship'. Also listed were figs, raisins and two pots of apples for Candlemas.

The expenses of the stables included 7s. for 28lb. of oats, 2d. for a key for the stable door and 5d. for a new pail. A smith was paid 12d. on the feast of St Stephen 'for letting of my lady's grace's palfrey's blood'. Payments were made to two men for mowing 25 acres at 6d. an acre, for making the hay, and for two days work in carting it in. Shoeing a palfrey cost 6d.

Other work mentioned for which payment had to be found included the carriage of fish from Exeter to Columbjohn, two days threshing oats, one day frething or vreathing,[86] and the cleaning of the gutter behind the kitchen. A man was paid 4d. for one and a half days' work carrying dung to the garden, and 4d. for two days' work breaking the ground to sow mustard seed. A woman who spent six days weeding the garden at Columbjohn received 7d., another got 16d. for her eight days spent making tallow candles, and 4d. was paid to a poor man for the carriage of white pewter to Colcumbe from Broadhembury. Peter Taylor was paid 15s. for the carriage of wine, beer and other items by boat from Topsham to Colcumbe, and 3s. 4d. was paid to the bailiff of Sampford Peverell for keeping and transporting four swans.

Payments were made for various types of cloth, such as velvet, satin, linen and fine holland, and for shoes, gloves and hose for the Countess. A quarter of a yard and a nail (¹⁄₁₆ of a yard) of tawny velvet and a skein of silk was bought to make a purse for her, together with an ounce of tawny silk for strings and buckram for the lining. A quarter of velvet was needed to mend her kirtle and one of her hats was covered with white sarcenet. A payment of 2s. 6d. was made to Trowe,[87] the skinner of Exeter, for making cuffs for her from 'a skin of pampilion' (fur used for trimming), and the skinner earned another 2s. 8d. for mending her white fur. Other skins used included ermines, coney skins, black lamb skins and budgeskins (lamb's skin with the wool dressed outwards).

Various sums were paid out as rewards to servants bringing presents to the countess. For example, the abbot of Ford sent a boar and two swans on 21 December, and John Veysey, bishop of Exeter,[88] two oxen two days later. Mr Coplestone[89] sent a hare and a pheasant cock and the bishop of Exeter a red deer at the feast of St Thomas. The servant of the abbot of Buckland[90] brought three mersed congers and Mr Chichester[91] sent two kids and five heronshews, or young herons, at Whitsuntide. The abbot of Newenham[92] sent a fresh salmon and Hull[93] of Exeter a box of marmalade to Colcombe. One of the Countess' tenants sent a lamb, and other gifts included conies, conger eels, cygnets, pheasants and partridges, hens, capons, hares, a peacock and a peahen, sugar loaves, ginger and cherries. The bishop of Exeter's servant also received 20d. for bringing a letter of news to the Countess. On 17 May 4d. was paid to Mr Greenaway's servant 'for bringing of strawberries to my lady'. The Countess' reign at Tiverton castle was contemporaneous with John Greenaway's career as a Tiverton merchant,[94] and when he built his chapel in St Peter's church, her coat-of-arms, surmounted by the Courtenay badge of the falcon and the faggot, was placed over the entrance.[95]

Money was also required for the Christmas and New Year festivities. A gallon of honey, and apples and wardens, or pears, were bought 'against Christmas', and oats for fattening the swans cost 17d. The players who performed before Countess Katherine on New Year's Eve and New Year's Day got 13s. 4d., and the waits of Exeter were paid 10s. at Twelfth Night. Two dozen supper lights for Twelfth Night, weighing 5lb., cost 3s. 9d. There were payments for the King and Queen's New Year gifts, and the Countess' New Year gift to her son Henry consisted of two buckles, two pendants, six studs, six oiletts, six aglets and gold and enamel garters.

Various sums were laid out in connection with Philippa the maid's wedding preparations. Materials were purchased for her wedding outfit, including velvet for her dress and kirtle, and the bill for making the outfit and the cost of the wedding ring were also met by the Countess. In addition, Philippa received £6 13s. 4d. as marriage money. Payments were also made for garments for Andrew of the kitchen and for the fools Dick, Mug and Kit, and for mending and washing their clothes.

There are a number of entries for alms and religious offerings given by the Countess. A sum of 20s. was set aside in the Christmas quarter for general alms. In addition, money was given to two soldiers on 25 December, and purses were distributed to poor people on Maundy Thursday during the Mass. Two horseloads of alms meat were sent to prisoners. Offerings were made on All Souls Day, All Saints Day, Christmas Day, Epiphany, Candlemas, Whitsunday and the Feast of the Assumption, and 12d. was recorded as the Countess' offering when she was at Poltimore. On 10 June she gave 8d. as her offering at a requiem mass, probably at the anniversary of her husband's death.[96] In this connection also, Lyne of London, wax chandler, was paid £2 1s. 10d. for a year's supply of wax for Lord William's tomb, and the prior of the Black Friars of London received £5 6s. 8d. for singing services there during the year. On the fourth Sunday in Lent the prior of Exeter's Black Friars was rewarded for preaching before the Countess at Columbjohn and the warden of the city's Grey Friars was similarly paid for his sermon on Good Friday.[97]

There are some entries in connection with the visit of 'the Marquis', presumably the Countess' nephew Thomas Grey, Marquis of Dorset,[98] although various writers[99] have assumed it to be her son Henry as Marquis of Exeter. He did not actually receive the title, however, until June 1525,[100] after the closure of this account. There were payments to the servant who brought news of the Marquis' intended visit to Colcombe, for the carriage of wine, for strawberries and for servants who wrestled before him, and to the bailiff of Sampford Peverell for bringing fish to Columbjohn during the visit.

Other miscellaneous purchases of interest are two pairs of bells for the ravens, a mustard mill from Hooper of Colyton, coloured glass from William Hurst[101] (with payments to a glazier for fetching the glass from Exeter), 28 stone of flocks for stuffing six mattresses, ink, copperas (a form of ferrous sulphate used in making ink), gum and gall, a ream of paper, a gallon of lamp oil and a lady's lantern. Payments were made to English and Company, the King's players, a harper and a tumbler with the King's minstrels, and various other minstrels who performed before the Countess. Another minstrel was rewarded for 'setting and mending of my lady's grace's instrument' and payment made for the making of a butt and frame for a rented lyre.

The Countess gave £200 to her son 'towards his business that my lady should have child' and 88s. to Christopher Say for his expenses in taking four horses to London to her daughter, Mistress Margaret. Various medical expenses were incurred during the year when the Countess was ill, including a payment to Mr Forest[102] for medicines, and a number of disbursements were required when she went on a hunting expedition in Marshwood Park in Dorset. The servant who conveyed letters from the Countess to the King and Cardinal Wolsey received 16s. 8d.

At the conclusion of this household account book were set out the expenses of and provisions used by David Hensley, the clerk of the kitchen, for the period, including a number of lists of the foodstuffs used for each day's menu. For example, on Sunday 26 September he used fresh fish, butter, eggs, three dry lings, three milwells, four congers, four stockfish and 50 buckhorn. On 29 September, Michaelmas Day, in addition to two of the traditional geese, he required a piece of roasting beef, a pig, two capons, eight chickens, butter, eggs, milk and cream and apples for tarts. At Easter the household dined on veal, pigs, chickens, a lamb, beef, mutton and brawn. Also on the menu at various times were apple fritters, frumenty, rabbits, woodcock, pigeons, gulls and cormorants.

These entries appear to show that during her widowhood the Countess Katherine led a comfortable and settled existence on her Devon estates, in contrast to the experiences of her early life. She enjoyed a high standard of living, as befitted her station, with visits from family and friends. She maintained the traditions and observances of her religion and engaged in the pastimes and entertainments current at the time. Her son progressed in favour at Court and received gifts and grants to further his position. Among the offices he held in the West Country were Steward of the Duchy of Cornwall, Warden of the Stannaries and Master Forester of Dartmoor,[103] while on 16 June 1525 he was created Marquis of Exeter by his cousin the King. The Countess' daughter Margaret died before her mother,[104] but Henry had provided her with a grandson,[105] so that the future of the family seemed secure.

The Countess made a will on 2 May 1527,[106] setting out her wishes for the arrangements to be made after her death. She named Henry, Lord Marquis of Exeter 'our dearest and well beloved son' as her sole executor, and directed him to use the revenues from certain of her estates to bury her 'as it shall beseem and become our estate and degree to be'. Her tomb was to be in the 'new chapel lately edified and built in the south side of the Church of St Peter of Tiverton' with all the solemnities due to her station. Historians have differed as to the location of the Courtenay chapel at Tiverton,[107] which contained the tombs of a number of members of the family, but the will implies that she herself requested to be buried in the new Greenaway chapel. All her household servants and those of her son were to be provided with black mourning gowns or coats, and were to be supported for a year after her death, unless taken into service by the Marquis.

Having settled domestic matters, the Countess turned to the spiritual. A sum of £21 was to be set aside to pay the stipends of three honest priests to say three masses daily, either in St Peter's church or in the chapel of our Blessed Lady standing in the churchyard. The priests were also to come together weekly at the Countess' tomb, to say services and hold a requiem mass. After the Gospel at every mass the priest was to pray for the souls of the 'late King of England and France, of famous memory, Edward the Fourth, our father, and Elizabeth his wife, our mother, Late Queen of England, and for the souls of the said Edward Courtenay, and the aforesaid William Courtenay, his son, our late husband, and for the soul of Margaret, late wife of Henry, Lord Herbert, our daughter, and for our soul and all Christian souls, and for the good preservation, health, good and prosperous estate of our said well beloved son, of Henry, Lord Marquis of Exeter and Earl of Devonshire, long to endure, to God's pleasure'. Three poor men living in Tiverton were to be paid 8*d.* a week to sit about the tomb during the masses and pray for the souls of the departed, with preference being given to any family servants who had 'fallen into decay, by casualty of wars or otherwise'. The will was witnessed by Sir George Speke, Humphrey Colles, Richard Haydon and Thomas Spurway, some of the Countess' household officials.

The date of the Countess' death is given as Friday 15 November 1527 and the time as three o'clock in the afternoon.[108] Her body was embalmed and lay in state in the chapel at Tiverton Castle while the funeral arrangements were made. When this took place at the beginning of December, Dr Peter Casely, canon of Exeter, vicar of Broadclyst and of the Pitt portion at Tiverton,[109] took as his text for the funeral sermon the words *Manus domini tetiget me.*

On 2 January 1528, a month after the funeral, an inventory[110] was made listing the contents of the castle at Tiverton which remained in the custody of Thomas Appowell and Davy Henner. The details set out there supply more evidence concerning life at the castle during Countess Katherine's occupancy.

In the castle chapel were vestments made of taffeta, velvet, satin and damask, linen altar cloths, towels and corporis cases for use with the sacrament. For example, the list includes a pair of vestments of blue velvet embroidered with a cross of crimson velvet, one of black velvet with a cross of imagery embroidered in silver and gold, and one of white taffeta with a cross of blue taffeta embroidered with an image of Our Lady and angels. There were four printed mass books and the Countess' matins book, one book being covered with tawny velvet with silver and gilt clasps, and another being covered with black velvet with engraved silver and gilt clasps. The chapel also contained a canopy of needlework to go over the sacrament, two altar cloths of red sarcenet, a little gold pyx of St Gregory decorated with enamel and pearls, a silver and gilt holy water stoup and two silver and gilt cruets. There was a great silver and gilt candlestick, and several chalices and palls. There were manuscript and printed books with the titles 'The Apposteler',[111] *Ortus Vocabulorum, Catholicon* and *Legenda Aurea*,[112] and a law book, together with various statues of the Saints, three timber altars and three great bells.

In the yowry, or ewery, were two gilt basins, and four partly gilt basins and ewers, all having the Countess' arms on them, together with silver and gilt and brass candlesticks, and a quantity of tablecloths, napkins and towels. The pantry contained a collection of gilt salts with covers, including a great salt wreathed with leaves and chased, also a little round gold salt with a chased cover with a red rose enamelled on the top of it, and a square gold salt with a cover in six panels enamelled with red and white. There were two gilt spoons 'one with a crown and the falcon and the faggot' (the Courtenay badge)[113] on the handle, and various other spoons including two white silver spoons made by Thomas Spurway, the receiver-general, out of five little spoons taken at the audit in Cornwall in 1524–5. Among more mundane articles the pantry contained three covered pans, ten bread towels, a case of knives with bone hafts, three chopping knives and nine neck towels.

In the kitchen the servants listed a large collection of items, all sizes and shapes of pots, spice plates, chargers, porringers and saucers, the whole and the broken being accounted for separately, for example 'six dozen and ten whole plates, three dozen and three plates broken, six dozen and six saucers whole, 13 broken'. There were 'two frying pans, a more and a less', two brazen pestles and mortars, three brass skinners and three brass ladles, a dressing knife, two chopping knives, two pair of pot hooks, four gridirons, three iron fire pans, brass pans 'a great furnace of brass to boil the brawn in', two stone mortars and two great pestles of timber, three iron flesh hooks and two axes to hew wood. Among other items in the kitchen were three great troughs to put corn in, a kneading tub, a pair of balances to weigh corn in, a great coffer for fish and a coffer for feathers. In the scullery was a spice coffer and a mustard quern. The buttery held leather pots and cruses, three kits or wooden vessels to receive the dropping of the ale, a tub, a form and a trestle, and a rack to hang cups on. In the laundry was a large and a small pan, a trivet and a chauffer to heat water in.

The stable contained ten great stalls with racks and mangers together with a collection of saddles, pillions, bridles, stirrups and horsecloths. Also resting there was the Countess' black velvet litter with its black satin harness, and the two litter horses, a grey and a bay.

The implements of the household included 40 bedsteads, 16 standing presses, 27 joined stools, 42 plain forms, seven joined table boards ('whereof one is carved and standeth in the cellar'), and other table boards varying in length from 3½ to 8 yards long, together with 26 pairs of trestles. Five coffers bound with plate stood in the tower over the gate, with a number of other coffers also listed. In the storehouse inside the gate was a little turn for the arras man and a frame to hang arras on to dry, and in the armoury two barrels for making chain mail, a hogshead to put mail in, a frame to hang harness on, a pair of tongs and a glazing wheel used for polishing the armour. In the storehouse outside the gate were building materials including 700 slates, various ladders of assorted sizes and 35 pieces of scaffolding timber, and 'in the gate of the place two great guns'.

The steward's stable contained two tubs to put oats in, a coop to put fowls in and a coffer for alms. Other miscellaneous items accounted for were a pair of bellows, a candle mould, a trendle to scald brawn in, a pair of clavichords, and 'the bier which my lady's grace was carried to church upon'. In the garden were a grinding stone and various tools, including five chisels, two staying hooks for a carpenter, two wimbles, a borer, two saws, six planes, a mallet and a square, all stored in a coffer with a key.

At the conclusion of the inventory are recorded the horses kept at the various parks on the Countess' estates. At Ashley Park in Tiverton the stock included a fair bay mare, 18 hands high and seven years old, with her colt, and a great mare that the marquis of Exeter had sent down from London to be put to the stallion. Among the horses at Chulmleigh park were a sorrel mare and the Marquis' roan stallion called Parker, and at Newpark a three-year-old bay colt with a white face, a fair bay colt with a star on the forehead and a grey colt with a blaze on the forehead. Also noted down were a cage for the parrot, an eyrar (or brood) of swans on the North Exe, two eyrars of swans beneath the Exe bridge and three swans at Tiverton.

On the reverse side of the inventory was set down the more valuable items of plate and equipment from the stables, which were to be transported to London for use by the marquis of Exeter, and various items from the chapel which were to be used to furnish the Countess' chantry. The Marquis is said to have erected a tomb in memory of his mother, with the Countess' effigy upon it.[114]

The Countess was in her forty-ninth year when she died, the last of Edward IV's daughters and a representative of the landed aristocracy supporting the traditions of the Catholic Church with its allegiance to Rome. Within a decade this old order had changed. Her nephew King Henry VIII had divorced his wife, broken with the Pope and declared himself Supreme Head of the Church in England. Her son, the marquis of Exeter, was unable to accept the changes and in 1538 was convicted of treason, executed and attainted, with his estates forfeit to the Crown.[115] Cleveland sums up the fate of her grandson Edward Courtenay in the pathetic phrase 'he was kept in prison almost all the days of his life'.[116] He was released by Mary Tudor, but as the great-grandson of Edward IV was still a potential threat, so went into exile, eventually dying in the Italian city of Padua in 1556.[117] He left no direct heir, so with his death the Boconnoc line of the family came to an end, and with it the earldom of Devon, the title remaining in abeyance until restored to the Powderham branch in 1831.[118] His death also removed the Courtenays from the centre of political affairs, a position of doubtful privilege which they had occupied for the sixty years since the young Lord William Courtenay had taken the Princess Katherine as his wife.

## Notes

1. F. Sandford, *Genealogical History of the Kings and Queens of England, 1066–1701* (1707), 419 from College of Arms MS.I.II.23b, and in part in F.J. Snell, *Chronicles of Twyford* (Tiverton, 1892), 34–6; W. Harding, *History of Tiverton* (Tiverton, 1845) i. Bk 2. 71–5.

2. T. Scott Holmes, 'Religious houses', in W. Page (ed.), *Victoria History of Somerset* ii (1911), 115.

3. G. Oliver, *Monasticon Dioecesis Exoniensis* (Exeter, 1846), 340.

4. Oliver, *Monasticon*, 171.

5. Exeter City Library, *Mayors of Exeter from the 13th Century to the Present Day* (Exeter, 1964), 10.

6. F. Madden, 'Children of King Edward IV', *Gentleman's Magazine* ci (Jan.–June 1831), 23–5; D. MacGibbon, *Elizabeth Woodville (1437–1492): Her Life and Times* (1938), 222–3; M.E. Everett Green, *Lives of the Princesses of England* (1849–55), iv. Ch. 1 gives an account of the Princess Katherine's life.

7. T. Rymer, *Foedera* (1727), xii. 110–11, 147–8.

8. *CPR 1476–85*, 203, 221.

9. *Rotuli Parliamentorum* vi. 240–1.

10. H. Ellis, *Original Letters illustrative of English History* (2nd Series, 1827), i. 149–50.

11. R. Holinshed, *Chronicles of England, Scotland & Ireland* (1808), iii. 430.

12. *Rot. Parl* vi. 288.

13. J. Burke, *Extinct and Dormant Peerages* (1831), 562–3; G.E.C., *Complete Peerage* ix. 615–20.

14. C. Ross, *Edward IV* (1974), 6.

15. Ross, *Edward IV*, 249.

16. *Foedera* xii. 328–30.

17. MacGibbon, *Elizabeth Woodville*, 200–2.

18. BL, Add. MS 38, 133 Commonplaces Genealogical and Legal, Henry VII, 1326.

19. E. Cleveland, *Genealogical History of the Noble and Illustrious Family of Courtenay* (Exeter, 1735), 1.

20. *Foedera* iv. 636.

21. M.R. Westcott, 'The Estates of the Earls of Devon, 1485–1538' (unpublished MA thesis, University of Exeter, 1958), 20–30.

22. G.H. Radford 'The Fight at Clyst in 1455', *DAT* xliv (1912), 252–65; 'Nicholas Radford, 1385–1455', *DAT* xxxv (1903), 251–78; 'Margaret Beaufort, Countess of Devon', *DAT* lxvii (1935), 291–8.

23. Cleveland, *Genealogical History*, 228; E. Miller, 'Medieval York', in P.M. Tillot (ed.), *Victoria History of the City of York* (1961), 59–60.

24. *Rot. Parl.* v. 476–82.

25. *CPR 1467–77*, 156.

26. *Complete Peerage* iv. 328.

27. J.L. Vivian, *The Visitations of Cornwall* (Exeter, 1887), 74.

28. *CPR 1467–77*, 374.

29. *CPR 1452–61*, 358, 612, 647, 650. See also C.L. Kingsford, *Prejudice and Promise in Fifteenth-Century England* (Oxford, 1925), 94–7, 103–4, 183–94.

30. *Complete Peerage* iv. 329; W. Metcalfe, *A Book of Knights made between 4 Henry IV and the Restoration of Charles II* (1885).

31. *Rot. Parl.* vi. 273, 298.

32. For more details see Westcott, 'Estates of the Earls of Devon', 294–7.

33. J.L. Vivian, *The Visitations of the County of Devon* (Exeter, 1895), 251.

34. *Complete Peerage* iv. 330; Metcalfe, *Book of Knights*.

35. E. Gibbon, *History of the Decline and Fall of the Roman Empire* (new edn 1912), vi. 473.

36. M. Dunsford, *Historical Memoirs of the Town and Parish of Tiverton* (Exeter, 1790), 94.

37. *Rot. Parl.* vi. 481; *Statutes of the Realm* ii. 611–12.

38. *Angelica Historica of Polydore Vergil, 1485–1537*, edited with a translation by D. Hay (Camden Soc. 3rd Series, 74 1950), 52.

39. E. Hall, *Chronicle of the History of England from Henry IV to Henry VIII* (1809), 484.

40. *CPR 1494–1509*, 223.

41. *Chronicle of Calais in the Reigns of Henry VII and Henry VIII to the year 1540*, edited by J.G. Nichols (Camden Soc. 35, 1846), 4.

42. C.L. Kingsford (ed.), *Chronicles of London* (Oxford, 1905), 251–2.

43. Green, *Lives of the Princesses of England*.

44. *Complete Peerage* xii. 448–53.

45. Hall, *Chronicle*, 496.

46. *Rot. Parl.*vi 544–8.

47. N.H. Nicholas (ed.), *Privy Purse Expenses of Elizabeth of York* (1830).

48. W.R. Powell, 'Havering-atte-Bower', in W.R. Powell, (ed.), *Victoria History of Essex* vii (1978), 9.

49. N.L. Harvey, *Elizabeth of York: Tudor Queen* (1973), 191–5.

50. *Complete Peerage* iv. 418–19.

51. *Chronicle of Calais*, 6.

52. PRO, P.C.C. Wills 15 Bennett.

53. PRO, Ministers Accounts SC6/H8/6186, 6187, 6188.

54. *Letters and Papers, Foreign and Domestic, in the Reign of Henry VIII* i. 77 (158:20).

55. *Complete Peerage* xii. Pt 2, 905; Ross, *Edward IV*, 4, 6.

56. *LPH8* i. 404 (749:23).

57. *Polydore Vergil*, 126; Hall, *Chronicle*, 496.

58. BL, Egerton 2642, 192.

59. A valor of lands taken after the Countess' death in 1527 states that her son was then in his twenty-ninth year: PRO, Close Rolls, C54/396.

60. BL, Lansdowne 978,111. Register of Fitzjames, London.

61. *LPH8* i. 436 (808).

62. *LPH8* i. 521 (1083:2); *Statutes of the Realm* iii. 55–6.

63. Hall, *Chronicle*, 345.

64. G.H. Radford, 'Heraldry in Relation to the Courtenay Tomb in Colyton Church', *DAT* liii (1921), 216–25. This includes a line drawing of the seal. A part of an original seal remains on a grant to John Kayleway making him one of the keepers of the park and chase of Okehampton: BL, Harl. Ch. 43.7. See also Harding, *Tiverton*, 77.

65. E.g., PRO, Ancient Deeds E 210/1,1178 (Appointment of steward of Colyton manor); E 326/8477 (Appointment of a receiver and surveyor for her estates).

66. *LPH8* i. 1285 (2964:80).

67. *LPH8* i. 1530 (3617); *Complete Peerage* xii. Pt 2, 851–2.

68. PRO, Ministers Accounts SC6/H8/6188.

69. G.H. Radford, 'The Courtenay Monument in Colyton Church', *DAT* xxxix (1907), 144–55 and his 'Heraldry in Relation to the Courtenay Tomb'.

70. *LPH8* iii. 323 (896).

71. *LPH8* i. 674 (1471).

72. E.g., *LPH8* i. 361 (641); 394 (726); 496 (986); 1401 (3325) ii. 811 (2611); PRO, Exchequer T.R. Books E 36/218.

73. *LPH8* ii. 176 (660); *Complete Peerage* viii. 61.3.

74. DRO, CR 668.

75. *LPH8* iii. 110 (312); 135 (386).

76. *LPH8* iii. 1538; 1551.

77. *LPH8* ii. 1500; 1502.

78. *LPH8* ii. 435 (1573).

79. PRO, Rentals and Surveys (Miscellaneous Books, Augmentation Office) E 315/384.

80. DRO, CR 525–9; PRO, Ministers Accounts SC6/H8/426, 427, 523, 524, 6174; BL, Additional Charters 13907, 64330, 64331.

81. Westcott, 'Estates of the Earls of Devon', 99–101.

82. Westcott, 'Estates of the Earls of Devon', 300–4.

83. PRO, SP1/28; Exchequer T.R. Books E36/223.

84. PRO, SP1/28.

85. PRO, E36/223. A considerable number of the entries were published in *Western Antiquary* iii (1883/4), 68, 76–7, 79–80, 83.

86. Making brushwood fences: F.T. Elworthy, *West Somerset Wordbook* (1886), 809.

87. M.M. Rowe and A.M. Jackson (eds), *Exeter Freemen 1266–1967* (DCRS Extra Series I, 1973) 65. Robert Trow, skinner, was admitted 1506/7.

88. G. Oliver, *Lives of the Bishops of Exeter* (Exeter, 1861), 120–5.

89. Vivian, *Visitations of Devon*, 224–33.

90. Thomas Whyte: Oliver, *Monasticon*, 381.

91. Vivian, *Visitations of Devon*, 172–84.

92. John Ellys: Oliver, *Monasticon*, 359.

93. A John Hull was admitted as freeman in 1491/92; Rowe and Jackson, *Exeter Freemen*, 61.

94. A.E. Welsford, *John Greenway, 1460–1529: Merchant of Tiverton and London* (Tiverton, 1984).

95. S.R. Blaylock, 'A Survey of Greenway's Porch at St Peter's Church, Tiverton', *Devon Archaeological Society Proceedings* 44 (1986), 92–3, with an illustration of the sculpture. See above, p. 23.

96. His funeral took place on 9 June. See above, p. 22.

97. Oliver, *Monasticon*, 330, 334.

98. *Complete Peerage* iv. 419–20.

99. B.F. Cresswell, *Colyton: the Church and People in Past Times* (Honiton, 1930), 7; A.L. Rowse, *Tudor Cornwall: Portrait of a Society* (new edn 1969), 234.

100. *LPH8* iv. 639 (1431).

101. William Hurst was admitted as freeman in 1503/4: Rowe and Jackson, *Exeter Freemen*, 64, 72. He was mayor of the City in 1524/5 and 1535/6: *Mayors of Exeter*, 10.

102. William Forest, surgeon, was admitted as freeman 1503/4: Rowe and Jackson, *Exeter Freemen*, 64.

103. *LPH8* iii. 1287 (3062:26).

104. The Countess in her will stipulated that prayers should be said for her daughter's soul. See above, pp. 23, 31.

105. Edward Courtenay was born in 1526: *Complete Peerage* iv. 331; Another son, Henry, died young and was buried in Essendon Church, Hertfordshire, near the family home of Bedwell: R. Clutterbuck, *History & Antiquities of the County of Hertford*, (1815–27), iii. 129; E.J.B. Reid, 'Essendon', in W. Page (ed.), *Victoria County History of Hertford* iii (1912), 460–2.

106. DRO, L 1508 M/Family/Test/1. Printed in *Archaeological Journal* x (1853), 53–8.

107. B.F. Cresswell, *Notes on Devon Churches, Deanery of Tiverton* (1920), 7–8, 24–5; Dunsford, *Tiverton*, 314–15; E.S. Chalk, *History of the Church of St Peter, Tiverton* (Tiverton, 1905), 61–4.

108. Sandford, *Genealogical History*, 419.

109. WCS, G.L. Hennessy, Devon Incumbents, 61, 403, 539; J. Foster, *Alumni Oxonienses 1500–1714* (Oxford, 1891), i. 242.

110. PRO, SP1/46, 51–6.

111. Probably an Epistolar, the book from which the epistle was read.

112. *British Museum General Catalogue of Printed Books*, 107.347; 35.479; 133.590.

113. W.H.H. Rogers, *The Ancient Sepulchral Effigies and Monumental and Memorial Sculpture of Devon* (Exeter, 1877), 79–84. The bird is often referred to as an eagle.

114. Sandford, *Genealogical History*, 419.

115. *LPH8* xiii. 451 (1056). For an account of events leading up to his death, see M. and R. Dodds, *The Pilgrimage of Grace, 1536–1537 and the Exeter Conspiracy, 1538* (1915).

116. Cleveland, *Genealogical History*, 245.

117. *Complete Peerage* iv. 331–2; Cleveland, *Genealogical History*, 261.

118. H. Nicolas, *Report of Proceedings on the claim to the Earldom of Devon in the House of Lords* (1832).

# Four Devon Stannaries: A Comparative Study of Tinworking in the Sixteenth Century

TOM GREEVES

'. . . The third Comoditie [of Devon] allso is the nombre of mynes in this Countrie of which some do yelde Golde and sylver some Ledd some Copper and some Iron: but the Cheefe is Tynne . . .

The stannary . . . hath contynued in workinge to the greate increase of the Revenues of the said Erledome or Duchie and the meanetenance of great nombres of housholdes, famylies and inhabitantes bothe of the sayed countrie and of sundry Townes within the Realme but especially of London and of the Merchauntes of the same Who do not onely Worke the same but do also transporte [the same *deleted*] it in to other Countries and nations then which theire is not a better merchandyse . . .'[1]

## 1.   *Introduction*

The late medieval English tin industry of Cornwall and Devon has been described as having a 'kaleidoscopic complexity'.[2] What follows is an exploration of part of this phenomenon within the four stannaries of the county of Devon (Chagford, Ashburton, Plympton and Tavistock)[3] in the early post-medieval period.

The Devon tin industry is documented from the mid-twelfth century,[4] and was particularly active within the sixteenth century. Of special importance, not least because of surviving documentation, was the process of 'coinage' which involved the assay and taxation of tin metal at each of the four stannary towns.

39

The history of tinworking within two of the stannaries—Ashburton and Tavistock—has been set out in articles by Worth[5] and Finberg.[6] Tinworking within Chagford stannary has been partially covered by Ormerod[7] and Broughton.[8] In his paper Finberg included a table, based on payments of coinage duty, showing fluctuations in production between the stannaries from 1381 to 1523.[9] Otherwise, published studies on the Devon stannaries have treated the county as a whole,[10] and no significant attempt has previously been made to compare one stannary with another.

Material spanning the fourteenth to the seventeenth centuries is referred to here, with emphasis placed on the sixteenth century which not only witnessed the peak of the Devon tin industry, but which also was a time of considerable change in the structure of the industry and, perhaps, its technological base (see Section 6, below). Much information has been derived from analysis of the coinage rolls which, for each Midsummer and Michaelmas coinage at each of the four stannary towns, record the names of persons presenting tin metal, the weight of tin they presented, and the amount of duty payable (1s. 6¾d. per hundredweight of 120 or, from about 1550, 100 pounds).[11] Archaeological and documentary data is used to interpret the distribution of blowing mills where tin ore was smelted in the period in question.

## 2.   The Land and the Stannaries

The Devon tin industry exists on account of the ores contained within the granite mass of Dartmoor, the metamorphic aureole of altered sedimentary rocks surrounding it, and the alluvial deposits derived from these, which spread considerable distances from the parent rock (Map 2). From all points of the compass, and especially when viewed from the north, the upland of Dartmoor presents a dramatic contrast to the lush greenery and gentler hills surrounding it. It gives a superficial impression of an integral whole, even an island. Yet within its geological boundaries there is much that distinguishes one part from another.

The districts defined by the stannaries are significantly different in terms of landform, vegetation, distribution of ore deposits, and even climate, all of which must have influenced the development and history of tinworking. The location of the coinage towns themselves must have affected trading potential.

The boundaries of the four stannaries, shown on Map 2, are described in an early seventeenth-century document,[12] and in more detail in a late

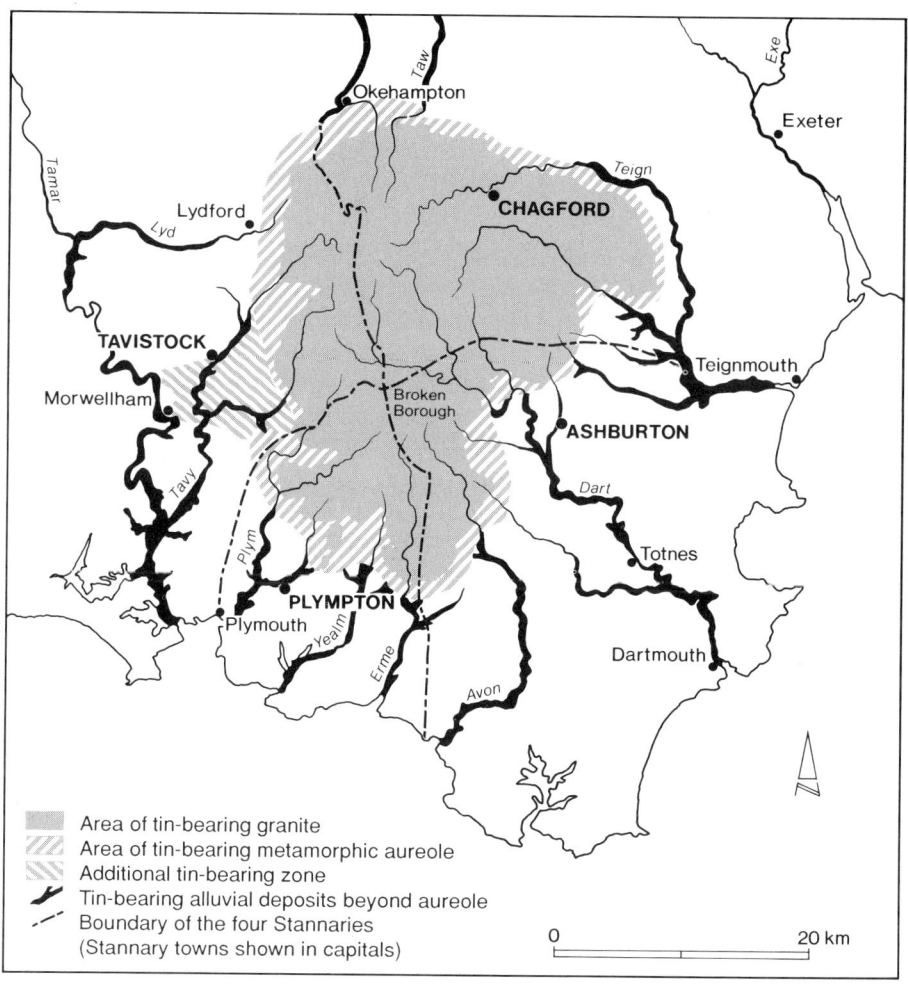

*Map 2.*

Extent of the Devon Stannaries relative to the tin-bearing granite and
metamorphic aureole of Dartmoor.

eighteenth-century copy of another early seventeenth-century manuscript.[13] Each stannary had its own court and was responsible for regis-
tering tinworks and blowing mills within its territory. A statute enacted at
the tinners' Great Court of 1494 decreed that 'the owners of every
blowing house shall bring a certain mark of his blowing house to the court
of the stannary within the precinct where the said blowing house is set
before that any tin shall be marked withall to the intent that all such marks
shall be drawn in a book [which] shall remain in the same court. And all
tin to be blown in the same house to bear the same mark and the mark of
the owner.'[14]

This indicates that the stannary districts must have been defined by this
time. Indeed, it is likely that the boundaries were agreed from 1328 when
Plympton joined the other three towns as a coinage town,[15] and some of
them may be very much more ancient, such as that between Chagford and
Ashburton (which in part follows a Saxon estate boundary),[16] and that
between Chagford and Tavistock, which had no need to be altered in
1328.

It is not yet known whether Plympton stannary was created out of the
territory previously assigned to Ashburton or Tavistock. The arguments
used for the creation of Plympton as a coinage town stressed the decline
and remoteness of Tavistock,[17] which might lead one to conclude that it
was created from Tavistock's area. Certainly Tavistock's production of tin
was at a critically low level in 1303 when its output was only 1½ tons, or
3.7 per cent of the county total, compared to 17½ tons in Chagford and
21½ tons in Ashburton.[18] But this low productivity could be partly
explained by the exclusion of Tavistock from the rich alluvial deposits of
the rivers Plym, Yealm and Erme, if they were then all within Ashburton
stannary. This interpretation is supported by the fact that two men
coining tin at Ashburton in 1303 were Richard Stenylake, almost certainly
from Stanlake on the river Meavy (more or less on the later boundary
between Plympton and Tavistock) and Richard of 'Middelworthi'
(Middleworth), a farm close by.[19] It is therefore more likely that
Plympton was created from territory which once had come under the
jurisdiction of Ashburton.

Map 2 shows the boundaries of the stannaries in relation to the
extent of tin-bearing granite and tin-bearing rocks of the surrounding
metamorphic aureole. It is not known on what basis these boundaries
were agreed, but the fact that they meet at Broken Borough, a pre-
historic cairn very centrally placed, means that each stannary has access
to some of the highest moorland with its valuable peat deposits (for

charcoal) and also to the wooded and deeply dissected valleys of the fringe country.

All four coinage/stannary towns, plus Lydford, had markets from since the twelfth century.[20] As a coinage town, Chagford is the most remote, being about 15 miles (24 km.) distant from the navigable rivers of Exe and Teign, and well away from any major land route. It is not surprising that it had a poor reputation in medieval times for the quality of its supplies.[21] But its stannary district contains the largest tin-bearing zone, more than the equivalent area in Ashburton and Plympton stannaries combined, and includes several of what were historically the richest of Dartmoor tinworks, such as the great Birch Tor and Vitifer complex near Post-bridge,[22] Bradford near Drewsteignton,[23] Rushford Wood[24] and Great Week[25] near Chagford, and Taw Marsh[26] on the north-western limit of the stannary. It also includes the bleakest and highest ground on Dartmoor, much of which is covered by huge deposits of peat which, converted to charcoal, was the prime fuel for the tinners. To the south-east it contains much of Bovey Heathfield, which seems to have been a rich source of alluvial tin in medieval times.[27] Moreover, Chagford stannary represents the eastern limit of tin production in England and so potentially was nearest any land derived market.

Ashburton as a town is relatively well-placed for access to the sea, being only about seven miles (11.3 km.) from the port of Totnes/Dartmouth. It also lies on a major land route passing round the southern edge of Dartmoor. The tin-bearing zone within the stannary is small, like that of Plympton, lending further support to the idea that the latter was created out of a district that was once exclusively Ashburton's. But Ashburton stannary includes important and rich tinworking areas including the Hexworthy/Holne Moor/Ringleshutes complex, and the riches of the river Avon and its tributaries. Brent Moor is included within its area, and this was a major source of peat. In 1566 it was noted that 'there is made in this moore yerely a great quantitye of Turff or Moor cole, which is in effecte the greatest Fewell that the Tenauntes [of Lord Petre] do spend'.[28] The stannary also has important lode deposits relatively close to the town at Owlacombe, Whiddon and Holne Chase.

Plympton is the most conveniently placed of the coinage towns as far as access to the sea is concerned, being practically on the navigable river Plym. The area of the stannary within which lode-bearing deposits of tin are found is small, but this is more than compensated for by the very rich alluvial workings on the rivers Meavy, Plym, Yealm and Erme, unless one argues that the richest pickings here had already been exploited before the fourteenth century. The latter reasoning would appear to be supported by the relatively low level of production within the stannary throughout the sixteenth century (but see Sections 4 and 7, below, for evidence of the importance of the June coinage and a possible link with streamworking). Important tinworks exist within the stannary at Ailsborough in Sheepstor parish,[29] and at Bottle Hill and on Crownhill Down near Plympton itself.[30]

Tavistock stannary, which covers the whole of western Dartmoor roughly west of a line formed by the West Okement, the West Dart and the river Meavy, includes the extensive lode deposits of the rivers Tamar, Tavy and Walkham. The stannary includes Lydford, the site of the tinners' gaol and centre of administration for the Forest of Dartmoor. Until the Dissolution in 1539 the presence of the Benedictine abbey in Tavistock ensured that the town was a good trading centre, well-supplied with goods.[31] The town also had the benefit of the port at Morwellham on the river Tamar, though access to it must always have been relatively difficult, requiring a journey of four miles (6.4 km.) over hilly ground.

## 3. County Production

In the mid-fifteenth century, production of tin in Devon stood at around 125,000 pounds per annum (56 tons),[32] which was about one-sixth of Cornish output (Tables 1 and 2). Thereafter there was a steady increase for the remainder of the century so that by 1500 production had increased nearly threefold to approximately 325,000 pounds per annum (145 tons), about one-third of Cornish output. A rapid increase within the next 20 years resulted in a peak of production in Devon being reached in 1521 with nearly 627,000 pounds (280 tons) recorded, representing about one half of Cornish output.[33] In other words, although Cornish production had been rising over the same period, nearly doubling in 75 years, the proportional fivefold increase in Devon was much more spectacular. The value of this Devon tin was considerable, in 1523 amounting to £9,400, some seven times the rental of the wealthiest layman, the earl of Devon.[34]

For the rest of the sixteenth century, total Devon output declined at a similar rate to the preceding increase, so that by 1600 production figures were more or less what they had been in 1450. But, as shall be seen, this crude statistic masks considerable variation in the fortunes of the different stannaries and significant changes in the structure of the industry. The decline in total output continued into the seventeenth century, reaching a nadir from 1629 onwards when it was less than at any time since the late thirteenth century.[35] Table 1 shows the overall county figure between 1450 and 1650. Table 2 shows county production at June and September for ten selected years between 1456 and 1642.[36]

## 4. *Production in the Stannaries*

On the evidence of the statute of 1494 requiring the registration of blowing house marks (which were stamped on the ingots of tin) in the court of the stannary in which they were located (see Section 2, above), we can be reasonably confident that the coinage rolls give a consistent picture of the differences in production of tin metal between the stannaries. Tin blown in a particular mill (i.e., blowing house) would obviously have to be presented for coinage in the town where its mark had been recorded.

Tables 2–8 relate to a sample of ten individual years spanning 1456–1642, for which good coinage data are available. Table 4 includes seven additional years from the late-fourteenth century onwards, for which figures have been derived from a table published by Finberg.[37] Table 3 shows production per stannary in pounds. This demonstrates immediately how misleading the pattern for the county as a whole (Tables 1 and 2) can be. Tavistock stannary most closely follows the county trend. That for Ashburton is similar, but is exaggerated: its decline at the end of the sixteenth century is more extreme, and its peak of production in September 1523 is 35,000 pounds (15.6 tons) greater than its nearest rival, Tavistock. Moreover, this difference is greater than the total production for Plympton at that coinage. Chagford and Plympton were both much less dramatically affected by the county trend, with more modest and consistent levels of production.

Analysis of the coinage rolls also hints at seasonal factors at work. Coinages were held only twice a year in the period in question, at Midsummer (June) and Michaelmas (September). We know from other sources that sixteenth-century blowing mills, where tin was smelted, 'did usuallie go for the moste parte yearelie betweene Eastor and Michaelmas'.[38] The evidence from the coinage rolls shows that in most cases the largest amounts of tin metal were presented in September, which suggests that most smelting would have been carried out in July and August. This seems to have been a well-established pattern in both counties. Between 1445 and 1449 total production in Devon in September was between five and twenty times what it had been in June.[39]

Table 3 shows that this pattern was particularly marked in Ashburton and Tavistock, but less so in Chagford where, notably, in 1595 nearly twice as much (30,602 pounds) was presented in June than in September. This may have been due to exceptional exploitation of rich lode deposits, perhaps at Birch Tor and Vitifer, or at Bradford tinwork. In Plympton, at the peak of the industry, the June coinages for 1523 and 1531 recorded larger quantities than in September. This possibly reflects an increase in streamworking activity on alluvial deposits in Plympton stannary at this time, as abundant supplies of water would have been needed. Water was more likely to be available in the spring months than in the summer (see also Table 6 and Section 7, below).

Table 4 shows yearly production for each stannary as a percentage of the county total, from the late-fourteenth century onwards. The hypothetical 'average' of 25 per cent is shown on each graph. Immediately one can see how relatively poor Plympton's production is, at mostly less than 15 per cent of the county total. Only in the 1380s did it rise above 25 per cent. Chagford was dominant until the mid-fifteenth century, with over 40 per cent of the county total. Its relative revival around 1600 is also indicated. Starting from a low base in the 1380s, Ashburton flourished during the peak of the industry (mid-fifteenth to mid-sixteenth century) but, as already noted, its decline was rapid in the second half of the sixteenth century. In sharp contrast to the other three stannaries, Tavistock played an increasingly major role right through the period, starting at less than 20 per cent in the 1380s and 1390s, but rising to between 40 and 50 per cent of the total by the beginning of the seventeenth century, and to over 80 per cent in 1642.

## 5. *Blowing Mills and the Smelting of Tin*

Of all the structures associated with tinworking, the most important are the knocking and blowing mills where ore was crushed and smelted.[40] County-wide, we now know of more than 100 mills which date before about 1750,[41] and about 45[42] of these can be reasonably considered as candidates for blowing mills operating in the period in question (Map 3). Most of them will date to before 1650, but recent archaeological evidence from the blowing mill at Upper Merrivale in Tavistock stannary suggests that several of the larger well-preserved mills may be late-seventeenth century in date in their last phases.[43] Given the uncertainty of dating these sites, all are considered here. There remains, *a priori*, a likelihood that most of the mill sites known from either documentary or field evidence will date to the sixteenth century as the period of greatest activity.

Blowing mills, which often combined knocking (i.e. stamping) with smelting, are clearly the most significant sites on account of their function as producers of precious tin metal ready for coinage. In terms of distribution of these mills, pride of place must go to Chagford stannary: 17 blowing mills are known from within its area, representing 38 per cent of the county total. They are listed below, with their parishes in brackets. Dates are given for known or possible documentation:

1. Blackaller (North Bovey)—1527[44]
2. Blackaton (Widecombe)—1566[45]
3. Blackaton Brook/Lovebrook/Yeo (South Tawton)—*c.* 1530[46]
4. Bradford (Drewsteignton)—1687, 1692, 1696–7[47]
5. Brimley/Burnt House (Bovey Tracey)
6. Casely/Caseleigh Smitha (Lustleigh)—?1434, ?1598–9, 1613[48]
7. Challacombe (Manaton)
8. Ford (Throwleigh)—1559–60[49]
9. Outer Down (Chagford)
10. Pizwell (Lydford)
11. Ramsley/Prospect (South Tawton)[50]
12. Riddon (Lydford)
13. South Hill (Chagford)—?1491, ?1495–6, ?1505–6[51]
14. Stannon Brook (Lydford)
15. Taw River (Belstone)—1535, 1538–9, ?1608[52]
16. Teignhead Farm/Blacksmith's Shop (Lydford)
17. Thornworthy (Chagford).

These Chagford mills have a well-spread distribution throughout the stannary, the only major stream without one being the East Okement. Given the apparent prosperity of Chagford stannary in about 1600, many of the mills may date to this period, though one should not forget Chagford's productive years of the late-fourteenth to the mid-fifteenth century (see Table 4). The mill at Blackaton, Widecombe, which had been abandoned at some time before 1566, provides key evidence for declining production in the mid-sixteenth century, at least in that specific locality. But the decline was not general, for part of the same survey recorded of Natsworthy ('Nottisworthy'), near Widecombe: 'ther be Mynes of Tynne within this manor'.[53]

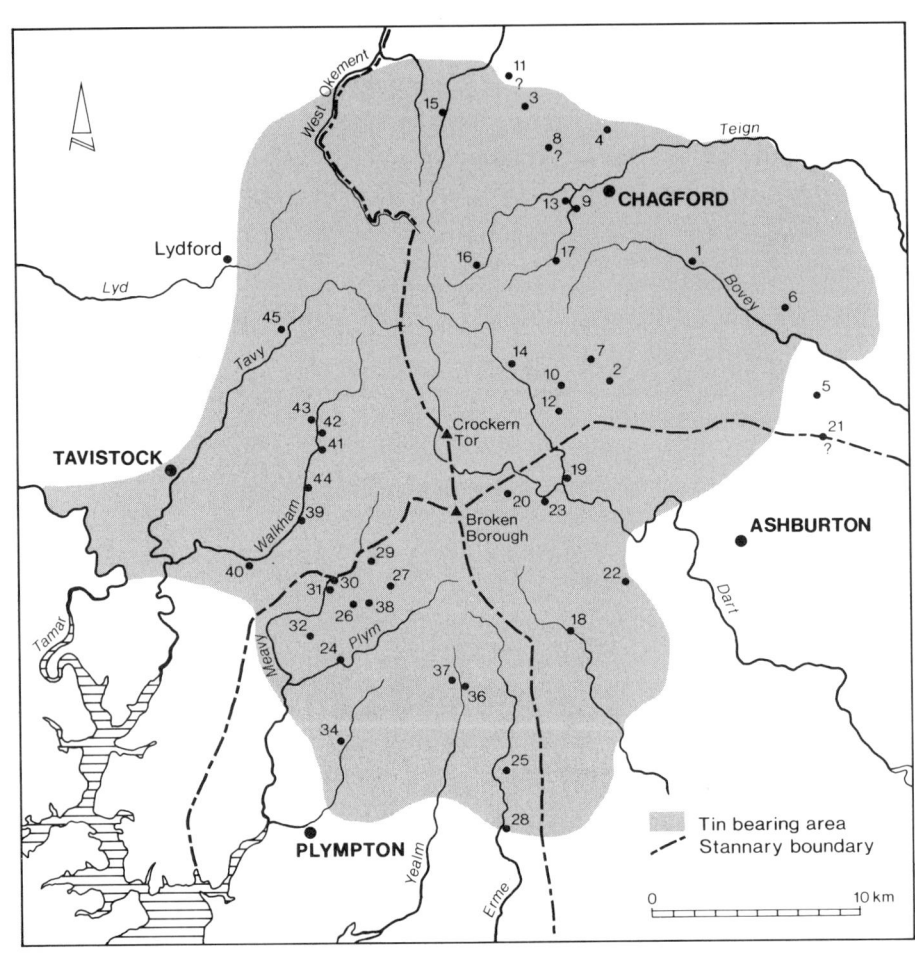

*Map 3*

Distribution of tin blowing mills in Devon, with stannary boundaries and the limits of ground containing lode tin. NB—nos 33 (Plympton) and 35 (Sheepstor), both within Plympton stannary, are not marked because reasonably precise locations for them are not known.

In sharp contrast, only six definite blowing mills are known from the whole of Ashburton stannary, representing 13 per cent of the county total:

18. Avon Dam (Dean Prior)
19. Dartmeet (Widecombe)—1514 'lately built'[54]
20. Gobbett (Lydford)
21. Ilsington—1557[55]
22. Runnaford Combe/Rotherford alias Ronaford(e) (Buckfast-leigh)—1619, 1622–3, 1630, 1651–2[56]
23. Week Ford, Lower (Lydford)—1521?, 1608, 1730, 1737.[57]

This surprisingly small number of known blowing mills may reflect the rapid decline of the stannary in terms of production from the second half of the sixteenth century onwards (see Tables 3 and 4). Further evidence for this decline is contained in a survey of Lord Petre's estate in 1566 which noted, under a heading 'Myneryes of Tynne and Moore Cole' that 'there ys in Brent Moore . . . certayne myneryes of Tynne, the greatest parte of which be wrought and spent to thuttermoste, and those that remayne ar thought to be of smalle value'.[58] But other blowing mills must remain to be discovered, given the fact that in the first half of the sixteenth century more tin was being smelted in Ashburton stannary than any other. For example, in 1523 nearly 40 per cent of the county total was coined at Ashburton (see Table 3). A lease[59] dated 1 January 1514 of a newly-built blowing mill at Dartmeet is not at all surprising given the importance of the stannary at this time. Christopher Prous and Richard Hamelyn, the tenants, can hardly have failed in their investment.

Given the relative unimportance of Plympton stannary in terms of output for all of the period in question, it is perhaps surprising that as many as 15 blowing mills have been recorded (33 per cent of the county total) within its area:

24. Brisworthy Burrows/Brightisworthy (Meavy)—1560[60]
25. Butterbrook (Harford)
26. Colleytown (Sheepstor)
27. Combeshead/Harthill (Sheepstor)—1571, 1581, 1584[61]
28. Ivybridge/Meyes/Lewes Burys Blowyng Myll (Ivybridge/Har-ford)—early sixteenth century, 1550, 1555[62]
29. Keaglesborough (Walkhampton)—1565, 1577, 1584[63]
30. Longstone 1 (Sheepstor)
31. Longstone 2 (Sheepstor)—1623, ?1658[64]
32. Lovaton (Meavy)—early sixteenth century[65]

33. Plympton—1680, 1719, 1730, 1751[66]
34. Portworthy/Fernhill/Millond alias Southdowne (Shaugh Prior)—1546–8, 1550, 1570[67]
35. Sheepstor—1680, 1719, 1730, 1751[68]
36. Yealm Steps Lower (Cornwood)
37. Yealm Steps Upper (Cornwood)
38. Yellowmead (Sheepstor)—1502.[69]

So far, the reference to Yellowmead in 1502 is the earliest-known documentary mention of a specific smelting site in Devon. Six other mills are documented in the sixteenth century. Two (Plympton and Sheepstor) have only late references, but are included here because of the likelihood of their having had precursors.

The sites of only seven tin blowing mills are known from Tavistock stannary, representing 15.5 per cent of the county total. All except the one at Will are located along the river Walkham:

39. Eggworthy (Walkhampton)
40. Little Horrabridge/Fylly (Walkhampton)—sixteenth century, 1528[70]
41. Merrivale, Lower (Walkhampton)
42. Merrivale, Middle (Walkhampton)
43. Merrivale, Upper (Peter Tavy)
44. Parktown (Walkhampton)
45. Will (Peter Tavy).

This is clearly an incomplete record, and many other blowing mills must have existed within the stannary[71] given its increasing importance throughout the period in question. The three Merrivale mills and the one at Eggworthy are well-preserved structurally. As mentioned above, preliminary results from current excavations by the Dartmoor Tinworking Research Group at Upper Merrivale indicate that this particular mill is likely to be late-seventeenth or even early-eighteenth century in its final smelting phase.[72] The implication is that the other mills may, in their last phases, belong to a similar period. If so, there remains a major gap in our knowledge of sixteenth-century blowing mills within Tavistock stannary. Only the mill at Horrabridge is so far documented, though even here the references are actually to a knocking mill on the site.[73] The concentration of six known blowing mills along the river Walkham is unparalleled elsewhere on Dartmoor, but demonstrates what may have been the situation on other rivers too. Much archaeological and documentary research needs to be continued.

Thus in terms of field and documentary evidence we are left with the strange anomaly that the two most productive stannaries for much of the sixteenth century (Ashburton and Tavistock) have so far revealed the smallest number of blowing mill sites. Put another way, in 1523 the production of these two stannaries amounted to 68 per cent of the county total, yet their known blowing mills spanning roughly the period 1450–1700 represent only 29 per cent of the total number of blowing mills yet recorded within the county.

## 6. *Ingot Weight and Technology*

The coinage rolls often give the weights of individual pieces of tin, and so it is possible to calculate the average weight of ingots smelted at the blowing mills. Table 5 shows the weight of pieces coined at June and September for each stannary from 1456–1642. In the late-fourteenth century, Devon ingots appear to have weighed about 100 pounds each.[74] From the mid-fifteenth century to the mid-sixteenth century, Devon ingots consistently weighed an average of between 100 and 125 pounds, with no significant difference between the stannaries. By the 1590s Chagford had taken the lead in producing ingots of an average weight of 200 pounds. The other stannaries had increased their average weight to about 150 pounds by then, but it was not until 1610 that they caught up with Chagford. Thereafter, some very large pieces of tin, weighing up to 300 pounds or more, boosted the average in each stannary to between 200 and 245 pounds. For example, in June 1610 Henry Trend's 23 pieces presented at Chagford averaged 301 pounds per piece.[75] In June 1625 the 34 pieces presented at Plympton by William Strode averaged 257 pounds in weight, the heaviest of them being 359 pounds.[76] Two years later, the average weight of his 31 pieces was 268 pounds, the heaviest being 339 pounds. At Tavistock in September 1627 John Tapson presented two pieces, one of 342 pounds and the other of 276 pounds.[77] In September 1628 Jasper Badge presented a single piece of tin at Tavistock weighing 317 pounds and in the following year presented another piece weighing 346 pounds.[78]

These enormously heavy blocks of tin correspond more to Cornish practice than that of Devon. Since the end of the fifteenth century Cornish ingots had weighed, on average, about twice those of contemporary ingots in Devon, even when the latter increased in weight. For example, the average weight of Cornish pieces presented for coinage at Lostwithiel between 1577 and 1607 was 328 pounds.[79] By the early seventeenth century individual Cornish ingots frequently weighed 400 pounds or more.[80]

The reason for the difference between the two counties is not yet known. Nor do we know why Chagford should have moved ahead of the other Devon stannaries in the late sixteenth century in terms of weight, nor the reasons for the increase itself. It is tempting to suggest that the answer lies in a combination of tradition, of technological improvement in the smelting process, and of increasing Cornish influence on the declining Devon industry.[81]

## 7.  The Pattern of Coinage

The detail and quantity of information contained within the coinage rolls allows the opportunity for extensive investigation of the process of change. What follows is a preliminary analysis of selected rolls, exploring variation between the stannaries, principally over the period 1456–1642.[82]

Hatcher has claimed that the Devon stannaries 'remained very much the province of the small-scale operator',[83] in sharp contrast to Cornwall where, in the early fourteenth century, huge quantities of tin (commonly more than 50 thousandweights per person) were presented for coinage by a few individuals.[84] While acknowledging this to be broadly true, the detail of the Devon coinage rolls shows that there was considerable inter-stannary variation both in numbers of people presenting tin (Tables 6 and 7) and in the average weight of tin coined per head (Table 8).

The most comprehensive figures are set out in Table 6 which shows for each stannary the number of persons presenting tin metal at each coinage, grouped according to the weight of tin presented. Table 7 shows what percentage of the total number of persons these groups represent. Both tables demonstrate that until the mid-sixteenth century the Devon stannaries were indeed very much the preserve of the small producer. At no time was it common for individuals to be presenting more than two thousand pounds of tin (10–20 individual ingots) at any one coinage.

In September 1523 641 persons out of 709 presented less than one thousand pounds within the county. Indeed, for the years under scrutiny, until the mid-sixteenth century the number of persons presenting less than one thousand pounds of tin metal was mostly around 90 per cent of the total number of presenters. The range was from a high of 94.6 per cent in September 1470 to a low of 83.9 per cent in June 1531. Between 1595 and 1629 this figure was usually between 70 and 80 per cent, though dropping as low as 63.6 per cent in June 1610. Tavistock's dominance as the home of the 'traditional' small producer is sharply emphasized by the percentage figures for September 1531 and 1550. At both these coinages, 40 per cent of all those presenting tin in Devon were doing so at Tavistock, with less than one thousand pounds per head. From 1595 this figure rose to 53.6 per cent (September 1595) and then 66.7 per cent (September 1629 and 1642), reflecting the fact that Tavistock was the maintainer of long-established Devon practice.

In contrast, the process of change which so affected Chagford in the late sixteenth century can be seen to have already begun in 1531 or even 1523, when those presenting less than one thousand pounds were reduced to less than nine and twelve per cent of the county total respectively.

Both Chagford and Plympton usually had fewer than one hundred persons presenting tin, even in the peak years, compared with a maximum of 275 at one Ashburton coinage (September 1523), and about 250 at two separate Tavistock coinages (September 1523 and 1531). The stannaries usually had more persons presenting tin in September than in June, which may indicate that a significant proportion of tinners were seasonal summertime workers. Exceptions are Plympton (1523, 1531, 1642), Ashburton (1550, 1625, 1629) and Tavistock (1625). The seventeenth-century exceptions are less surprising given the decline of the industry. Plympton's difference at the peak of the industry supports the idea that winter or early springtime streamworking, when plentiful supplies of water could be expected, may have accounted for a large proportion of the stannary's production.

Table 8 shows for each stannary the average weight of tin presented for coinage per head. Here we see clearly that Ashburton and Tavistock, despite the latter's increasing importance in the early seventeenth century, did remain strongly influenced by the small-scale producer presenting less than one thousand pounds weight per head, and often only a few hundred pounds on average. In sharp contrast, something very significant happened in Chagford at the end of the sixteenth century where, despite falling production, a much reduced total of persons presented an average of between four and nearly eight thousand pounds each. In Plympton stannary a similar but less marked phenomenon occurred.

## 8. *People and Influence*

Hundreds of names are recorded on the coinage rolls, and detailed analysis of these must await further study. However, it is obvious that those presenting the largest quantities of tin for coinage in the individual stannaries must have been among the most influential persons within the complex networks of the tin industry. Considered here are some of the key figures of the period of greatest change: the late sixteenth century and early seventeenth century.

By 1595 total output in the county was approximately 53 per cent of the level it had been in 1550. But the individual stannaries had coped with this period very differently. Tavistock, the leader, was still producing 78.5 per cent of its total for 1550. Chagford, usurping Ashburton's second place, coined 72 per cent of what it had in 1550. The other two stannaries showed a very different picture. Ashburton's rapid decline is revealed by the fact that it managed to coin only 28 per cent of its mid-century (1550) figure. Plympton, too, had witnessed an even more severe decline in output, with less than a quarter (24 per cent) of what had been presented for coinage there 45 years previously.

For Chagford and Plympton especially, the influence of a few persons at the end of the sixteenth century and in the early seventeenth century was dramatic. In effect, a mere handful of people appear to have been controlling the production of tin in the stannaries in the 1590s and early 1600s, which has interesting implications regarding ownership and/or occupation of blowing mills of that period.

In Chagford, despite falling output, the amounts of tin presented by individuals had increased substantially. In June 1595 a total of only four persons presented 30,602 pounds, averaging 7,650 pounds per head. The people responsible were William Barnes/Barons (13,635 pounds), Gregory Trend (8,084 pounds), John Trend (7,479 pounds) and Richard Downman (1,404 pounds). William Barons and William Stockman (presenting at Tavistock) between them presented more than 40,000 pounds (18 tons) of tin metal for coinage in 1595, equivalent to more than a quarter of all tin produced in Devon that year. Their role within the industry has been discussed elsewhere.[85]

William Strode (1562–1637) was active in Plympton stannary at this time. He was a member of a family with a long involvement with tin, but whose members rarely appear in the coinage rolls.[86] He married Maria, daughter of Thomas Southcote of Bovey Tracey who owned tin mills in Widecombe and Ilsington.[87] He was a JP in 1592, sheriff of Devon in 1594 and an MP in 1597. He received a knighthood in 1598. From 1601–25 he was MP for the borough of Plympton, and Recorder of Plymouth. He was also the friend, business adviser, and executor of the will of Sir Francis Drake. He owned Newnham House near Plympton as well as Meavy Barton and a house in Exeter.[88]

It is clear that some of his wealth must have been derived from tin. Between 1591 and 1596 he received shares in several tinworks from his uncle Philip Strode.[89] His importance in the tin industry of this period is shown by the fact that in five separate years between 1610 and 1629 he presented between one-sixth and one-twelfth of the total coined in Devon, and dominated production in Plympton stannary where he was by far the largest producer. For example, in 1610 he coined 64 per cent of the Plympton total, in 1625 81 per cent, in 1627 82 per cent, in 1628 85 per cent and in 1629 86 per cent.[90]

Tavistock was the most productive stannary in 1595, producing 46.5 per cent of the county total, and one would expect the key figures there to have had considerable influence. The third largest amount coined at Tavistock in September 1595 (2,967 pounds) was presented by Benedict Peterfield, who was to dominate Tavistock production in the early seventeenth century, and whose pattern of involvement in the industry was similar to that of William Strode. From 1595 until 1627 he presented increasingly large quantities of tin at Tavistock.[91] His 13,000 pounds in 1627 represented not much less than one-fifth of the Devon total that year. Thereafter he presented less for coinage, but it continued to be an increasingly large proportion of the county's total, so that in 1642 he accounted for about half of all tin coined in Devon.[92] In 1614 he was described as a 'Tinner & Owner of Blowing House' when he was accused with others of selling uncoined tin.[93] He had shares in tinworks in the Bickleigh area of south-west Devon.[94]

The man who presented the greatest amount of tin for coinage within the county in 1610 was Henry Trend, with a total of 12,409 pounds coined at Chagford.[95] This represents 46 per cent of the Chagford total and 8.5 per cent of the Devon total for the year. Interestingly, the average weight of his 23 ingots coined in June of that year was 301 pounds apiece, which suggests that he was involved in new smelting technology or perhaps employing Cornish tinners for whom ingots of that weight were commonplace (see above, Section 6). He remained important in Chagford throughout the 1620s, but nothing else is yet known of him.

As a final example of influence on the tin industry of the late sixteenth and early seventeenth centuries, it is worth noting the Atwell/Atwill family who were presenting tin consistently at Tavistock. The family home was at Welltown, Walkhampton (Plate 9), and it may well be that wealth from tinworks contributed to the lavish modernisation of the property at this time.[96] Richard Atwill, gent., was a jurate at Crockerntor in 1600.[97] The exact family relationships have not yet been clarified, but

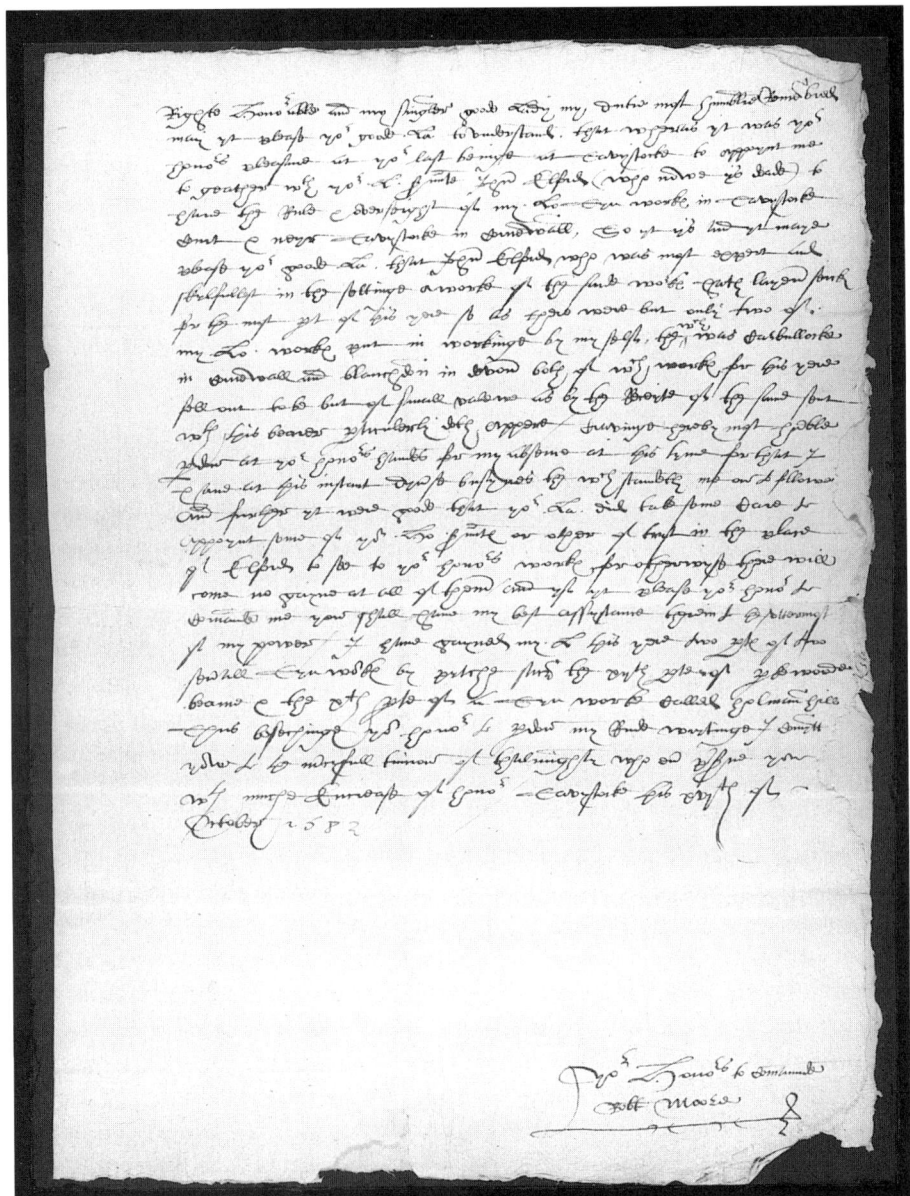

*Plate 8*
Letter from Robert Moore to the Countess of Bedford, 1582, concerning the
oversight of the Earl's tin works in Tavistock.

*Plate 9*

Welltown farmhouse in Walkhampton, home of the Atwell family.

five members (John, Pasco, Philip, Richard and Roger) appear in the coinage rolls for Tavistock stannary from 1595 to 1642. If their totals are combined we find that in 1625 Atwells presented 19.2 per cent of all tin coined at Tavistock, in 1627 27.0 per cent, in 1628 17.9 per cent, in 1629 18.8 per cent, in 1641 no less than 40 per cent and in 1642 19.1 per cent.[98] In September 1641, of eight persons presenting tin at Tavistock, five were Atwells.

Their importance as a group is increased by the fact that Tavistock was the dominant stannary in the first half of the seventeenth century and that from 1625 onwards was always producing at least 50 per cent of the county total (over 80 per cent in 1642).

## 9.   *Conclusion*

The complexity of the Devon tin industry is beginning to be revealed by examining detailed differences between the stannaries over a two hundred year period. Ashburton experienced a spectacular but still puzzling decline in its fortunes in the second half of the sixteenth century. Plympton also suffered, but had never really been prosperous, even during the peak of the industry. Chagford appears consistently innovative, being progressive in its adoption of increased ingot size (as a result of new technology, or borrowing from Cornwall), and also being the first to be dominated by a few persons presenting very substantial quantities of tin. Tavistock, in contrast, appears staunchly traditional, maintaining—right to the collapse of the industry in the 1640s—the Devon pattern of the small producer presenting less than one thousand pounds of tin, even when very power-ful individuals such as Benedict Peterfield were operating within its boundaries.

Explanation and interpretation of these phenomena is more difficult. Much probably depends on the richness or otherwise of notoriously fickle tin lodes. Although we know of more than 800 tinworks of the period in question,[99] we still know practically nothing about production from indi-vidual works.

Much still needs to be explored. Several more blowing mills must remain to be discovered by systematic fieldwork, especially within Ashburton and Tavistock stannaries. Comparison with Cornwall should also be fruitful, particularly with the eastern stannaries of Foweymore and Blackmore centred on Liskeard and Lostwithiel, which most closely resemble their Devon counterparts. For example, at Midsummer 1595 more tin was presented at both Chagford and Tavistock than in either of the two nearest Cornish stannaries.[100]

Ultimately we shall hope to reveal and understand the tinners themselves rather better, but fulfilment of this ambition must await further study.

## *Notes*

1. John Hooker alias John Vowell, 'Synopsis Corographical' (*c.* 1598–9) (DRO, Z19/18/9, fols 32, 34). An inaccurate transcript is given in W.J. Blake, 'Hooker's Synopsis Chorographical of Devonshire', DAT xlvii (1915), 347–8.
2. J. Hatcher, *English Tin Production and Trade before 1550* (Oxford, 1973), 149.
3. The four Devon stannaries were always listed in this order in the coinage rolls, and the same sequence is used here.
4. G.R. Lewis, *The Stannaries: A Study of the Medieval Tin Miners of Cornwall and Devon* (Truro, repr. 1965).
5. R.N. Worth, 'The Ancient Stannary of Ashburton', DAT viii (1876), 311–22.
6. H.P.R. Finberg, 'The Stannary of Tavistock', DAT lxxxi (1949), 155–84.
7. G.W. Ormerod, 'On the Traces of Tin Streaming in the Vicinity of Chagford', DAT i (1866), 110–15.
8. D.G. Broughton, 'Tin Working in the Eastern District of the Parish of Chagford, Devon', *Proc. Geologists' Assoc.* 78 (1967), 447–62.
9. Finberg, 'The Stannary of Tavistock', 171.
10. E.g., R.H. Worth, 'The Stannaries', *Trans. Plymouth Inst.* xv (1910), 21–45.
11. Differences in duty and in weights between Cornwall and Devon are not yet explained. See T.A.P. Greeves, 'The Devon Tin Industry 1450–1750: An Archaeological and Historical Survey' (unpublished PhD thesis, University of Exeter, 1981), 282–3 for a discussion of the evidence for units of weight used.
12. J.V. Somers Cocks, 'The Stannary Bounds of Plympton and Tavistock', *DCNQ* xxxii (1971), 76–9.
13. Greeves, 'The Devon Tin Industry', 391–4; D. Brewer, *A Field Guide to the Boundary Markers on and around Dartmoor* (Exeter, 1986), 40–1.
14. PRO, E101/267/10, spelling modernized.
15. Finberg, 'The Stannary of Tavistock', 164–5.
16. M. Swanton and S. Pearce, 'Lustleigh, South Devon: Its Inscribed Stone, its Churchyard and its Parish', in S. Pearce (ed.), *The Early Church in Western Britain and Ireland: Studies presented to C.A. Ralegh Radford*, BAR 102 (Oxford, 1982), 141–2.
17. Finberg, 'The Stannary of Tavistock', 164–5.
18. Worth, 'The Stannary of Ashburton', 315.
19. Ibid.
20. H.P.R. Finberg, *Tavistock Abbey: A Study in the Social and Economic History of Devon* (repr. 1969), 169. Plympton was not created a coinage town until 1328.
21. Finberg, 'The Stannary of Tavistock', 163.

22. D.G. Broughton, 'The Birch Tor and Vitifer Tin Mining Complex', *Trans. Cornish Inst. Engineers* 24 (1968/9), 25–49.
23. Greeves, 'The Devon Tin Industry', 96–101.
24. PRO, SC2/166/23/CP 1517.
25. Broughton, 'Tin Working in . . . Chagford', 453–62.
26. DRO, DD 32193b; F.M. Osborne, *The Church Wardens' Accounts of St Michael's Church, Chagford 1480–1600* (privately published, 1979), *passim*.
27. PRO, C1/17/185, C1/962/19, C1/971/24–25, C3/121/50; DRO, CC211/27; C. Vancouver, *General View of the Agriculture of the County of Devon* (1808), 69, 258–9, 292–3.
28. DRO, 123M/E31, fol. 29.
29. DRO, DD 4349; DD 1357; DD 4350; J. Webster, *Metallographia: An History of Metals* (1671), 290–2. The tinwork is spelt Yealesborough or Ellesbowrre, with variants.
30. WDRO, 72/990 *passim*; Greeves, 'The Devon Tin Industry', 313; A.K. Hamilton Jenkin, *Mines of Devon Volume I: The Southern Area* (Newton Abbot, 1974), 125–6, 129.
31. Finberg, 'The Stannary of Tavistock', 162–3.
32. All figures of tin presented for coinage have been converted to pounds weight, rather than hundredweights or thousandweights for which there is uncertainty about their exact values—see n. 11, above.
33. Hatcher, *English Tin Production*, 155–60.
34. J.E. Kew, 'The Land Market in Devon 1536–1558' (unpublished PhD thesis, University of Exeter, 1967), 76.
35. Hatcher, *English Tin Production*, 155–60; Greeves, 'The Devon Tin Industry', 374–7. No production figures are available for Devon 1304–70.
36. Ibid., 78, for Midsummer and Michaelmas coinage figures 1445–9.
37. Finberg, 'The Stannary of Tavistock', 171.
38. PRO, E134/32 and 33 Eliz/Mich. 24.
39. Hatcher, *English Tin Production*, 78.
40. The term 'blowing mill' is used here in preference to 'blowing house' which is rarely found in contemporary Devon records; see Greeves, 'The Devon Tin Industry', 171.
41. T. Greeves, 'Blowing and Knocking—The Dartmoor Tin Mill before 1750', *Dartmoor Magazine* 23 (Summer 1991), 18–20.
42. The 45 mills listed here are taken from the list given in Greeves, 'Blowing and Knocking', 19–20. Nos 42 and 110 in the latter should have been asterisked as blowing mills and are included here. Nos 72, 73, 79, 90 and 95 are not included as they are finds of tin slag from contexts unlikely to be of actual mills. No. 82 is not included as it is an unfinished mouldstone.
43. S. Gerrard and T. Greeves, *Excavation of Upper Merrivale Tin Blowing and Stamping Mill, Peter Tavy, Dartmoor, Devon—Interim Report No. 1—1991 Season* (1991).
44. Northamptonshire RO, Ex.61/12.
45. 'Sumtyme a Blowynge house': H. French and C.D. Linehan, 'Abandoned Medieval Sites in Widecombe-in-the-Moor', DAT xcv (1963), 175–6.
46. PRO, E134/32 and 33 Eliz/Mich. 24.

47. DRO, Letters and Accounts relating to DD 35531–50.
48. DRO, 1837Z Add. Z7/41–41b.
49. PRO, CP25(2)/105/1289/42(382).
50. DRO, South Tawton Tithe Apportionment 931 and 980.
51. S. Rowe, *A Perambulation of the Antient and Royal Forest of Dartmoor and the Venville Precincts* (3rd edn, 1896), 303; W. Crossing, *Guide to Dartmoor* (1912), 258; E. Hemery, *High Dartmoor—Land and People* (1983), 773.
52. T. Greeves, 'Taw River', in C. Blick (ed.), *Early Metallurgical Sites in Great Britain—BC 2000 to AD 1500* (1991), 23–30.
53. DRO, Z17/3/19.
54. DRO, 48/14/40/3.
55. DRO, Cal. Deeds Enrolled 466. This site may be within Chagford stannary.
56. DRO, DD 79,83; DRO/Z12/7/3, 4a and 4b.
57. DCO, Dartmore Proceedings 1203–1735, fol. 29; DRO, Accessions List—Widecombe Documents in possn E.J. Eales; S. Moore and P. Birkett, *A Short History of the Rights of Common upon the Forest of Dartmoor and the Commons of Devon* (Plymouth, 1890), 44 *re* Oakbrookfoot.
58. DRO, 123M/E31, fol. 28.
59. DRO, 48/14/40/3.
60. WDRO, 72/1033.
61. BL, Add. 21605; Walkhampton Manor Ct. Roll (inf. L. Govier).
62. PRO, C1/1252/34–5; *CPR* E VI, iii 435; DRO, Cal. Deeds Enrolled 420.
63. Walkhampton Manor Ct. Roll May 1565 (inf. L. Govier); BL, Add. 21605.
64. D.J. Hawkings, *Water from the Moor* (Exeter, 1987), 34–5.
65. PRO, C1/1252/34 and 35.
66. DCO, Inrolment Bk 2/1673–1702, fol. 69; DCO, Inrolment Bk 3 (1702–15), 220; DCO, Biographical Note of Duchy Officials, 397; DCO, Misc. Papers prepared for binding by Richard Gray; DCO, MS Papers Relating to Rights of Tinners 1700–1750.
67. WDRO, 72/279 and Notes and Extracts, 110, 130, 155–6.
68. As for n. 66, above.
69. DCO, Ministers' Accounts (Copies), Cornwall and Devon 18, 19, 23 Henry VII, vi. 93.
70. DRO, DD 22524; WDRO, 1196/7.
71. A mill called 'Toker's Blowing Mill' recorded in 1527 (Finberg, *Tavistock Abbey*, 164) was just possibly on the Devon side of the river Tamar, within Tavistock Stannary, but was more probably within Stoke Climsland parish in Cornwall, and is not included here.
72. Gerrard and Greeves, *Excavation of Upper Merrivale Tin . . . Mill*.
73. A mouldstone at the site proves its status as a blowing mill.
74. P.Q. Karkeek, 'The Shipping and Commerce of Dartmouth in the Reign of Richard II', *DAT* xiii (1881), 190.
75. PRO, E101/281/1.
76. PRO, E101/283.
77. Ibid.
78. Ibid.

79. H.M. Whitley, 'The Great Coinage Hall of Lostwithiel', *DCNQ* vii. Pt 7 (1913), 225–32.
80. Greeves, 'The Devon Tin Industry', 232.
81. T. Greeves, 'Adventures with Fiery Dragons—The Cornish Tinner in Devon from the 15th to the 20th Century', *J. Trevithick Soc.* xix (1992) 2–5.
82. The main sources for this section are coinage rolls for 1456, 1470, 1523, 1531, 1550, 1595, 1610, 1625, 1629 and 1642.
83. Hatcher, *English Tin Production*, 76.
84. Ibid., 75–82.
85. T.A.P. Greeves, 'The Great Courts or Parliaments of the Devon Tinners 1474–1786', DAT 119 (1987), 156.
86. Greeves, 'The Devon Tin Industry', 82–95.
87. DRO, Cal. Deeds Enrolled 466; R.N. Worth, 'Some Devonian Items', DAT xxviii (1896), 337.
88. WDRO, 72/279 Notes and Extracts.
89. WDRO, 72/990/68.
90. PRO, E101/281/1, E101/283.
91. PRO, E101/279/9, E101/281/1, E101/283.
92. PRO, E101/287/1.
93. PRO, STAC 8/20/25.
94. WDRO, 73/1034.
95. PRO, E101/281/1.
96. B. Cherry and N. Pevsner, *Devon* (2nd edn, 1989), 887.
97. H.P.R. Finberg, 'An Unrecorded Stannary Parliament', DAT lxxxii (1950), 297.
98. PRO, E101/283, E101/287/1.
99. Greeves, 'The Devon Tin Industry', Appendix 1.
100. R.N. Worth, 'The Ancient Stannary of Ashburton', 317.

## Sources for tables

Table 1—T.A.P. Greeves, 'The Devon Tin Industry 1450–1750: An Archaeological and Historical Survey' (unpublished PhD thesis, University of Exeter, 1981), 374–9.
Tables 2, 3, 5–8—PRO, E101/265/19 and 23 (1456); PRO, E101/266/20–21 (1470); H.P.R. Finberg, 'The Stannary of Tavistock', DAT lxxxi (1949), 173–82 (1523); PRO, E101/272/3–4 (1531); PRO, E101/273/16–17 (1550); PRO, E101/279/9 (1595); PRO, E101/281/1 (1610); PRO, E101/283 (1625, 1629); PRO, E101/287/1 (1642).
Table 4—As for Table 2 and Finberg, 'The Stannary of Tavistock', 171.

TABLE 1

*Annual production of tin metal in Devon 1450–1650.*

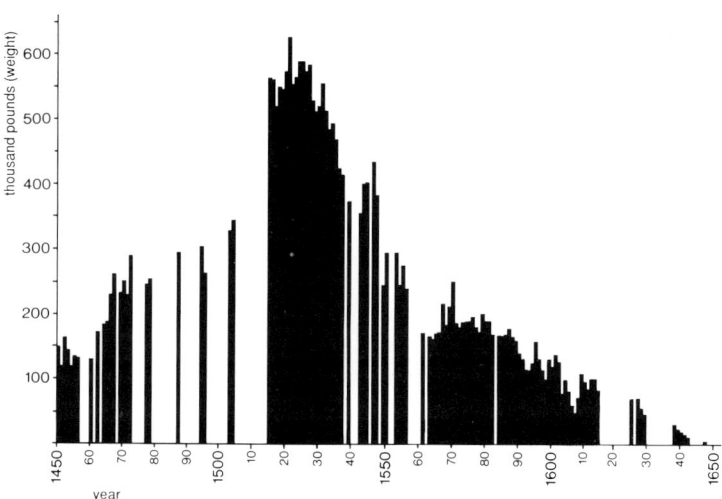

TABLE 2

*County production of tin metal in Devon 1456–1642, at June and September coinages.*

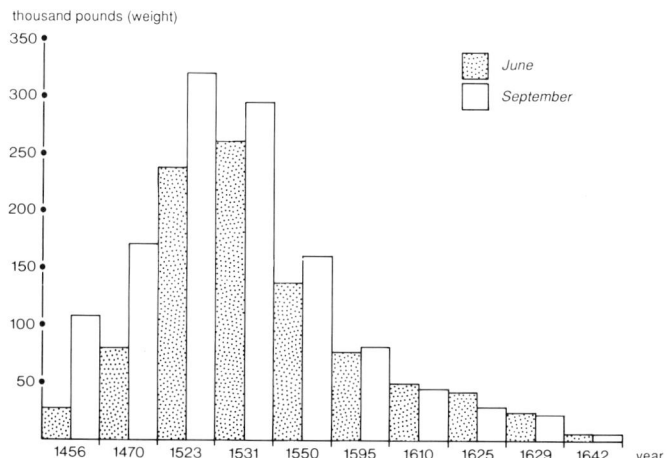

TABLE 3

*Production of tin metal in each Devon stannary 1456–1642, at June and September coinages.*

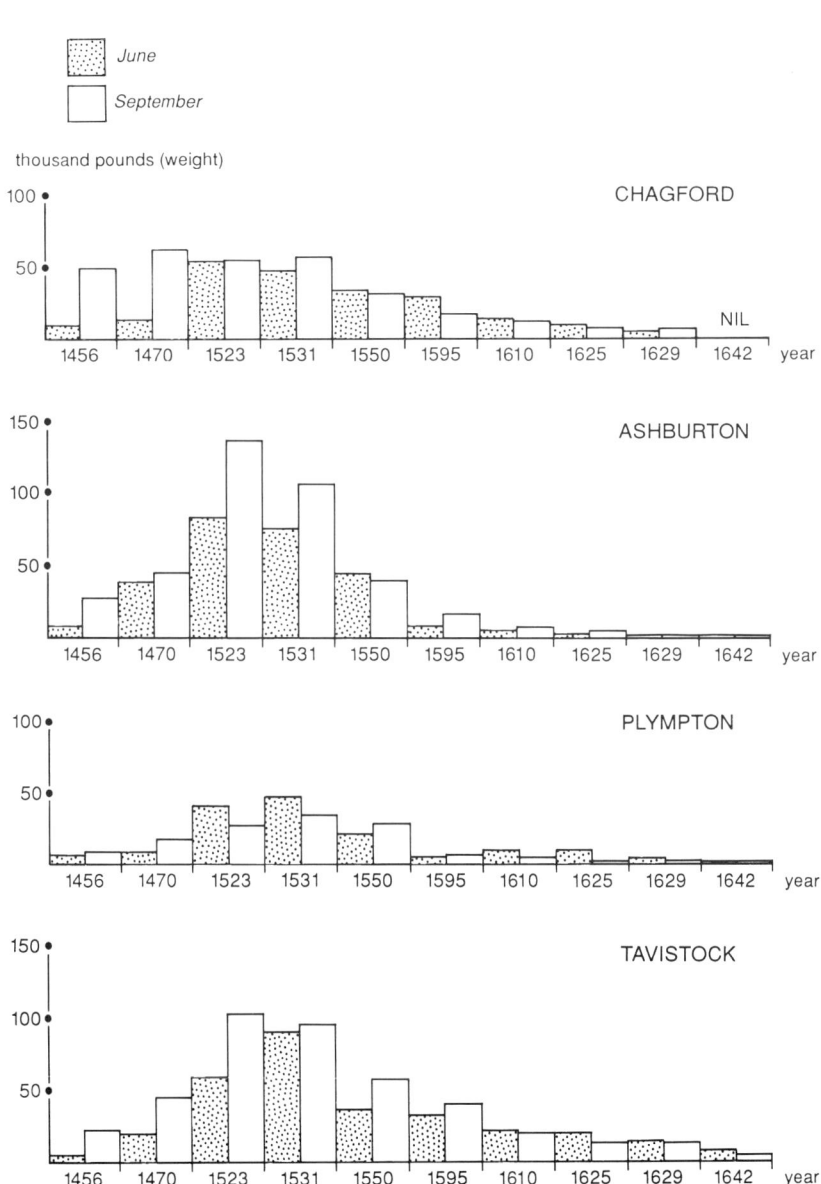

## TABLE 4

*Annual stannary production of tin metal, as percentage of county total 1385–1642.*

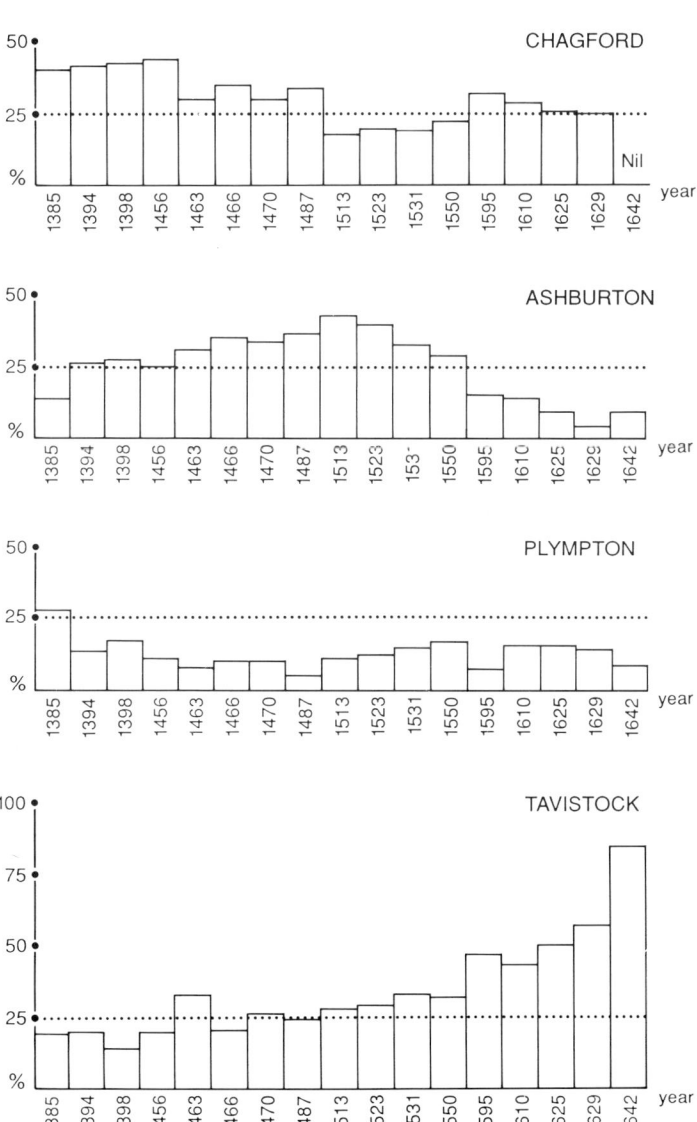

TABLE 5

*Average weight of pieces (ingots) of tin presented for coinage in each Devon stannary 1456–1642, June and September.*

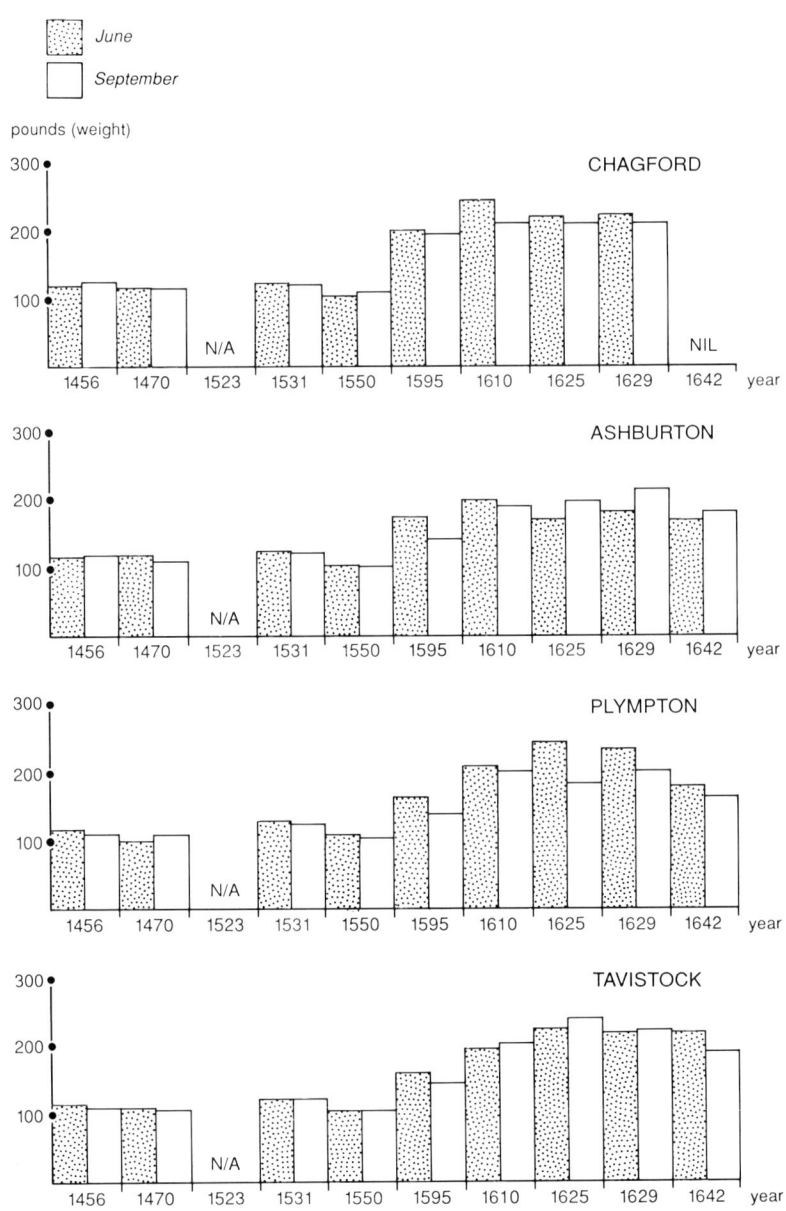

TABLE 6

*Numbers of persons presenting tin for coinage in each Devon stannary 1456–1642, June and September, per each thousand pounds weight.*

J=June  S=September

### 1523

| weight in pounds (1,000s) | | Under1 | 1–2 | 2–3 | 3–4 | 4–5 | 5–6 | TOTAL PERSONS PRESENTING |
|---|---|---|---|---|---|---|---|---|
| CHAGFORD | J | 57 | 12 | 2 | 1 | 1 | 1 | 74 |
|  | S | 79 | 7 | 4 | 1 | 1 | 0 | 92 |
| ASHBURTON | J | 134 | 17 | 3 | 1 | 0 | 0 | 155 |
|  | S | 242 | 27 | 1 | 3 | 2 | 0 | 275 |
| PLYMPTON | J | 93 | 7 | 0 | 0 | 0 | 0 | 100 |
|  | S | 85 | 3 | 0 | 0 | 0 | 0 | 88 |
| TAVISTOCK | J | 136 | 8 | 3 | 1 | 0 | 0 | 148 |
|  | S | 235 | 13 | 2 | 3 | 1 | 0 | 254 |
| TOTALS | J | 420 | 44 | 8 | 3 | 1 | 1 | 477 |
|  | S | 641 | 50 | 7 | 7 | 4 | 0 | 709 |

### 1531

| weight in pounds (1,000s) | | Under1 | 1–2 | 2–3 | 3–4 | 4–5 | 5–6 | 6–7 | 7–8 | 8–9 | 9–10 | TOTAL PERSONS PRESENTING |
|---|---|---|---|---|---|---|---|---|---|---|---|---|
| CHAGFORD | J | 28 | 6 | 1 | 2 | 2 | 0 | 0 | 0 | 1 | 0 | 40 |
|  | S | 51 | 6 | 2 | 3 | 1 | 0 | 0 | 0 | 0 | 1 | 64 |
| ASHBURTON | J | 85 | 16 | 0 | 4 | 0 | 0 | 1 | 0 | 0 | 0 | 107 |
|  | S | 163 | 13 | 3 | 4 | 1 | 0 | 1 | 0 | 0 | 0 | 185 |
| PLYMPTON | J | 73 | 7 | 3 | 0 | 0 | 1 | 1 | 0 | 0 | 0 | 90 |
|  | S | 74 | 6 | 2 | 0 | 0 | 0 | 0 | 0 | 0 | 0 | 82 |
| TAVISTOCK | J | 144 | 16 | 2 | 1 | 0 | 1 | 0 | 1 | 0 | 0 | 165 |
|  | S | 235 | 10 | 2 | 1 | 1 | 0 | 0 | 0 | 0 | 0 | 249 |
| TOTALS | J | 337 | 45 | 6 | 7 | 2 | 2 | 1 | 1 | 1 | 0 | 402 |
|  | S | 523 | 35 | 9 | 8 | 3 | 0 | 1 | 0 | 0 | 1 | 580 |

### 1456

| weight in pounds (1,000s) | | Under1 | 1–2 | 2–3 | 3–4 | 4–5 | TOTAL PERSONS PRESENTING |
|---|---|---|---|---|---|---|---|
| CHAGFORD | J | 17 | 3 | 0 | 0 | 0 | 20 |
|  | S | 54 | 13 | 2 | 0 | 1 | 70 |
| ASHBURTON | J | 19 | 1 | 0 | 0 | 0 | 20 |
|  | S | 38 | 4 | 3 | 0 | 0 | 45 |
| PLYMPTON | J | 24 | 0 | 0 | 0 | 0 | 24 |
|  | S | 37 | 0 | 0 | 0 | 0 | 37 |
| TAVISTOCK | J | 7 | 0 | 0 | 0 | 0 | 7 |
|  | S | 58 | 2 | 0 | 0 | 0 | 60 |
| TOTALS | J | 67 | 4 | 0 | 0 | 0 | 71 |
|  | S | 187 | 19 | 5 | 0 | 1 | 212 |

### 1470

| weight in pounds (1,000s) | | Under1 | 1–2 | 2–3 | 3–4 | 4–5 | TOTAL PERSONS PRESENTING |
|---|---|---|---|---|---|---|---|
| CHAGFORD | J | 47 | 1 | 0 | 0 | 0 | 48 |
|  | S | 104 | 14 | 0 | 0 | 0 | 118 |
| ASHBURTON | J | 50 | 5 | 2 | 0 | 0 | 57 |
|  | S | 119 | 3 | 0 | 0 | 1 | 123 |
| PLYMPTON | J | 18 | 2 | 0 | 0 | 0 | 20 |
|  | S | 49 | 1 | 0 | 0 | 0 | 50 |
| TAVISTOCK | J | 66 | 1 | 0 | 0 | 0 | 67 |
|  | S | 145 | 4 | 1 | 0 | 0 | 150 |
| TOTALS | J | 181 | 9 | 2 | 0 | 0 | 192 |
|  | S | 417 | 22 | 1 | 0 | 1 | 441 |

*Table 6 continued*

J=June
S=September

**1550** — weight in pounds (1,000s)

| | | Under1 | 1–2 | 2–3 | 3–4 | 4–5 | 5–6 | TOTAL PERSONS PRESENTING |
|---|---|---|---|---|---|---|---|---|
| CHAGFORD | J | 16 | 11 | 2 | 0 | 1 | 1 | 31 |
| | S | 29 | 7 | 4 | 0 | 0 | 0 | 40 |
| ASHBURTON | J | 89 | 5 | 1 | 0 | 1 | 0 | 96 |
| | S | 78 | 4 | 0 | 1 | 2 | 0 | 85 |
| PLYMPTON | J | 48 | 2 | 1 | 0 | 0 | 0 | 51 |
| | S | 75 | 3 | 1 | 1 | 0 | 0 | 80 |
| TAVISTOCK | J | 94 | 5 | 1 | 0 | 0 | 0 | 100 |
| | S | 144 | 10 | 1 | 0 | 0 | 0 | 155 |
| TOTALS | J | 247 | 23 | 5 | 0 | 2 | 1 | 278 |
| | S | 326 | 24 | 6 | 2 | 2 | 0 | 360 |

**1595** — weight in pounds (1,000s)

| | | Under1 | 1–2 | 2–3 | 3–4 | 4–5 | 5–6 | 6–7 | 7–8 | 8–9 | 9–10 | 10–11 | 11–12 | 12–13 | 13–14 | TOTAL PERSONS PRESENTING |
|---|---|---|---|---|---|---|---|---|---|---|---|---|---|---|---|---|
| CHAGFORD | J | 0 | 1 | 0 | 0 | 0 | 0 | 0 | 1 | 1 | 0 | 0 | 0 | 0 | 1 | 4 |
| | S | 0 | 1 | 0 | 0 | 1 | 1 | 1 | 0 | 0 | 0 | 0 | 0 | 0 | 0 | 4 |
| ASHBURTON | J | 8 | 1 | 1 | 0 | 0 | 0 | 0 | 0 | 0 | 0 | 0 | 0 | 0 | 0 | 10 |
| | S | 10 | 2 | 0 | 0 | 0 | 0 | 0 | 0 | 1 | 0 | 0 | 0 | 0 | 0 | 13 |
| PLYMPTON | J | 18 | 0 | 0 | 0 | 0 | 0 | 0 | 0 | 0 | 0 | 0 | 0 | 0 | 0 | 18 |
| | S | 24 | 1 | 0 | 0 | 0 | 0 | 0 | 0 | 0 | 0 | 0 | 0 | 0 | 0 | 25 |
| TAVISTOCK | J | 33 | 3 | 1 | 2 | 0 | 0 | 0 | 1 | 0 | 0 | 0 | 0 | 0 | 0 | 40 |
| | S | 60 | 7 | 1 | 1 | 0 | 0 | 0 | 0 | 0 | 0 | 0 | 1 | 0 | 0 | 70 |
| TOTALS | J | 59 | 5 | 2 | 2 | 0 | 0 | 0 | 2 | 1 | 0 | 0 | 0 | 0 | 1 | 72 |
| | S | 94 | 11 | 1 | 1 | 1 | 1 | 1 | 0 | 1 | 0 | 0 | 1 | 0 | 0 | 112 |

## Table 6 continued

**1629** weight in pounds (1,000s)

| | | Under1 | 1–2 | 2–3 | 3–4 | 4–5 | 5–6 | TOTAL PERSONS PRESENTING |
|---|---|---|---|---|---|---|---|---|
| CHAGFORD | J | 0 | 1 | 0 | 1 | 0 | 0 | 2 |
| | S | 2 | 0 | 1 | 1 | 0 | 0 | 4 |
| ASHBURTON | J | 2 | 0 | 0 | 0 | 0 | 0 | 2 |
| | S | 1 | 0 | 0 | 0 | 0 | 0 | 1 |
| PLYMPTON | J | 1 | 0 | 0 | 1 | 0 | 0 | 2 |
| | S | 1 | 1 | 0 | 0 | 0 | 0 | 2 |
| TAVISTOCK | J | 11 | 3 | 0 | 0 | 0 | 1 | 15 |
| | S | 18 | 1 | 0 | 0 | 0 | 1 | 20 |
| TOTALS | J | 14 | 4 | 0 | 2 | 0 | 1 | 21 |
| | S | 22 | 2 | 1 | 1 | 0 | 1 | 27 |

**1642** weight in pounds (1,000s)

| | | Under1 | 1–2 | 2–3 | 3–4 | TOTAL PERSONS PRESENTING |
|---|---|---|---|---|---|---|
| CHAGFORD | J | 0 | 0 | 0 | 0 | 0 |
| | S | 0 | 0 | 0 | 0 | 0 |
| ASHBURTON | J | 2 | 0 | 0 | 0 | 2 |
| | S | 3 | 0 | 0 | 0 | 3 |
| PLYMPTON | J | 2 | 0 | 0 | 0 | 2 |
| | S | 1 | 0 | 0 | 0 | 1 |
| TAVISTOCK | J | 6 | 0 | 0 | 1 | 7 |
| | S | 10 | 0 | 1 | 0 | 11 |
| TOTALS | J | 10 | 0 | 0 | 1 | 11 |
| | S | 14 | 0 | 1 | 0 | 15 |

J=June
S=September

**1610** weight in pounds (1,000s)

| | | Under1 | 1–2 | 2–3 | 3–4 | 4–5 | 5–6 | 6–7 | TOTAL PERSONS PRESENTING |
|---|---|---|---|---|---|---|---|---|---|
| CHAGFORD | J | 0 | 0 | 0 | 1 | 1 | 0 | 1 | 3 |
| | S | 1 | 1 | 1 | 1 | 0 | 1 | 0 | 5 |
| ASHBURTON | J | 8 | 2 | 0 | 0 | 0 | 0 | 0 | 10 |
| | S | 10 | 2 | 0 | 0 | 0 | 0 | 0 | 12 |
| PLYMPTON | J | 2 | 0 | 1 | 0 | 0 | 0 | 1 | 4 |
| | S | 4 | 0 | 1 | 0 | 0 | 0 | 0 | 5 |
| TAVISTOCK | J | 18 | 8 | 0 | 1 | 0 | 0 | 0 | 27 |
| | S | 26 | 5 | 0 | 0 | 1 | 0 | 0 | 32 |
| TOTALS | J | 28 | 10 | 1 | 2 | 1 | 0 | 2 | 44 |
| | S | 41 | 8 | 2 | 1 | 1 | 1 | 0 | 54 |

**1625** weight in pounds (1,000s)

| | | Under1 | 1–2 | 2–3 | 3–4 | 4–5 | 5–6 | 6–7 | 7–8 | 8–9 | TOTAL PERSONS PRESENTING |
|---|---|---|---|---|---|---|---|---|---|---|---|
| CHAGFORD | J | 2 | 0 | 2 | 1 | 0 | 0 | 0 | 0 | 0 | 5 |
| | S | 4 | 1 | 0 | 0 | 1 | 0 | 0 | 0 | 0 | 6 |
| ASHBURTON | J | 5 | 0 | 0 | 0 | 0 | 0 | 0 | 0 | 0 | 5 |
| | S | 2 | 1 | 1 | 0 | 0 | 0 | 0 | 0 | 0 | 4 |
| PLYMPTON | J | 2 | 0 | 0 | 0 | 0 | 0 | 0 | 0 | 1 | 3 |
| | S | 3 | 0 | 0 | 0 | 0 | 0 | 0 | 0 | 0 | 3 |
| TAVISTOCK | J | 18 | 6 | 0 | 0 | 0 | 1 | 0 | 0 | 0 | 25 |
| | S | 12 | 4 | 0 | 1 | 0 | 0 | 0 | 0 | 0 | 17 |
| TOTALS | J | 27 | 6 | 2 | 1 | 0 | 1 | 0 | 0 | 1 | 38 |
| | S | 21 | 6 | 1 | 1 | 1 | 0 | 0 | 0 | 0 | 30 |

TABLE 7

*Percentage of persons presenting tin at each Devon coinage 1456–1642, June and September, per each thousand pounds weight per stannary.*

J=June
S=September

**1523** — weight in pounds (1.000s)

| | | Under1 | 1–2 | 2–3 | 3–4 | 4–5 | 5–6 |
|---|---|---|---|---|---|---|---|
| CHAGFORD | J | 11.9 | 2.5 | 0.4 | 0.2 | 0.2 | 0.2 |
| | S | 11.1 | 1.0 | 0.6 | 0.1 | 0.1 | 0 |
| ASHBURTON | J | 28.1 | 3.6 | 0.6 | 0.2 | 0 | 0 |
| | S | 34.1 | 3.8 | 0.1 | 0.4 | 0.3 | 0 |
| PLYMPTON | J | 19.5 | 1.5 | 0 | 0 | 0 | 0 |
| | S | 12.0 | 0.4 | 0 | 0 | 0 | 0 |
| TAVISTOCK | J | 28.5 | 1.7 | 0.6 | 0.2 | 0 | 0 |
| | S | 33.1 | 1.8 | 0.3 | 0.4 | 0.2 | 0.2 |
| TOTALS | J | 88.0 | 9.3 | 1.6 | 0.6 | 0.2 | 0 |
| | S | 90.3 | 7.0 | 1.0 | 0.9 | 0.5 | 0.2 |

**1531** — weight in pounds (1.000s)

| | | Under1 | 1–2 | 2–3 | 3–4 | 4–5 | 5–6 | 6–7 | 7–8 | 8–9 | 9–10 |
|---|---|---|---|---|---|---|---|---|---|---|---|
| CHAGFORD | J | 7.0 | 1.5 | 0.2 | 0.5 | 0.5 | 0 | 0 | 0 | 0.2 | 0 |
| | S | 8.8 | 1.0 | 0.3 | 0.5 | 0.2 | 0 | 0 | 0 | 0 | 0.2 |
| ASHBURTON | J | 21.4 | 4.0 | 0.5 | 1.0 | 0 | 0 | 0.3 | 0 | 0 | 0 |
| | S | 28.1 | 2.2 | 0.8 | 0.7 | 0.2 | 0 | 0.2 | 0 | 0 | 0 |
| PLYMPTON | J | 19.7 | 1.7 | 0.3 | 0 | 0 | 0.3 | 0 | 0 | 0 | 0 |
| | S | 12.8 | 1.0 | 0.5 | 0 | 0 | 0 | 0 | 0 | 0 | 0 |
| TAVISTOCK | J | 35.8 | 4.0 | 0.5 | 0.3 | 0.2 | 0.3 | 0 | 0.3 | 0.2 | 0 |
| | S | 40.5 | 1.7 | 0.3 | 0.2 | 0.5 | 0.6 | 0 | 0.3 | 0 | 0.2 |
| TOTALS | J | 83.9 | 11.2 | 1.5 | 1.8 | 0.5 | 0.6 | 0.3 | 0.3 | 0.2 | 0 |
| | S | 90.2 | 5.9 | 1.4 | 1.4 | 0.6 | 0 | 0.2 | 0 | 0 | 0.2 |

**1456** — weight in pounds (1.000s)

| | | Under1 | 1–2 | 2–3 | 3–4 | 4–5 |
|---|---|---|---|---|---|---|
| CHAGFORD | J | 23.9 | 4.2 | 0 | 0 | 0 |
| | S | 25.5 | 6.1 | 0.9 | 0 | 0.5 |
| ASHBURTON | J | 26.8 | 1.4 | 0 | 0 | 0 |
| | S | 17.9 | 1.9 | 1.4 | 0 | 0 |
| PLYMPTON | J | 33.8 | 0 | 0 | 0 | 0 |
| | S | 17.5 | 0 | 0 | 0 | 0 |
| TAVISTOCK | J | 9.9 | 0 | 0 | 0 | 0 |
| | S | 27.4 | 0.9 | 0 | 0 | 0 |
| TOTALS | J | 94.4 | 5.6 | 0 | 0 | 0 |
| | S | 88.3 | 8.9 | 2.3 | 0 | 0.5 |

**1470** — weight in pounds (1.000s)

| | | Under1 | 1–2 | 2–3 | 3–4 | 4–5 |
|---|---|---|---|---|---|---|
| CHAGFORD | J | 24.5 | 0.5 | 0 | 0 | 0 |
| | S | 23.6 | 3.2 | 0 | 0 | 0 |
| ASHBURTON | J | 26.0 | 2.6 | 1.0 | 0 | 0.2 |
| | S | 27.0 | 0.7 | 0 | 0 | 0 |
| PLYMPTON | J | 9.4 | 1.0 | 0 | 0 | 0 |
| | S | 11.1 | 0.2 | 0 | 0 | 0 |
| TAVISTOCK | J | 34.4 | 0.5 | 0.2 | 0 | 0 |
| | S | 32.9 | 0.9 | 1.0 | 0 | 0 |
| TOTALS | J | 94.3 | 4.6 | 0.2 | 0 | 0 |
| | S | 94.6 | 5.0 | 0.2 | 0 | 0.2 |

## Table 7 continued

J=June
S=September

| 1550 weight in pounds (1,000s) | | Under1 | 1-2 | 2-3 | 3-4 | 4-5 | 5-6 |
|---|---|---|---|---|---|---|---|
| CHAGFORD | J | 5.8 | 4.0 | 0.7 | 0 | 0.4 | 0.4 |
| | S | 8.1 | 1.9 | 1.1 | 0 | 0 | 0 |
| ASHBURTON | J | 32.0 | 1.8 | 0.4 | 0 | 0.4 | 0 |
| | S | 21.7 | 1.1 | 0 | 0.3 | 0.6 | 0 |
| PLYMPTON | J | 17.3 | 0.7 | 0.4 | 0 | 0 | 0 |
| | S | 20.8 | 0.8 | 0.3 | 0.3 | 0 | 0 |
| TAVISTOCK | J | 33.8 | 1.8 | 0.4 | 0 | 0 | 0 |
| | S | 40.0 | 2.8 | 0.3 | 0 | 0 | 0 |
| TOTALS | J | 88.9 | 8.3 | 1.9 | 0 | 0.8 | 0.4 |
| | S | 90.6 | 6.6 | 1.7 | 0.6 | 0.6 | 0 |

| 1595 weight in pounds (1,000s) | | Under1 | 1-2 | 2-3 | 3-4 | 4-5 | 5-6 | 6-7 | 7-8 | 8-9 | 9-10 | 10-11 | 11-12 | 12-13 | 13-14 |
|---|---|---|---|---|---|---|---|---|---|---|---|---|---|---|---|
| CHAGFORD | J | 0 | 1.4 | 0 | 0 | 0 | 0 | 0 | 1.4 | 1.4 | 0 | 0 | 0 | 0 | 1.4 |
| | S | 0 | 0.9 | 0 | 0 | 0.9 | 0.9 | 0.9 | 0 | 0 | 0 | 0 | 0 | 0 | 0 |
| ASHBURTON | J | 11.1 | 1.4 | 1.4 | 0 | 0 | 0 | 0 | 0 | 0.9 | 0 | 0 | 0 | 0 | 0 |
| | S | 8.9 | 1.8 | 0 | 0 | 0 | 0 | 0 | 0 | 0 | 0 | 0 | 0 | 0 | 0 |
| PLYMPTON | J | 25.0 | 0 | 0 | 0 | 0 | 0 | 0 | 0 | 0 | 0 | 0 | 0 | 0 | 0 |
| | S | 21.4 | 0.9 | 0 | 0 | 0 | 0 | 0 | 0 | 0 | 0 | 0 | 0 | 0 | 0 |
| TAVISTOCK | J | 45.8 | 4.2 | 1.4 | 2.8 | 0 | 0 | 0 | 1.4 | 0 | 0 | 0 | 0 | 0 | 1.4 |
| | S | 53.6 | 6.3 | 0.9 | 0.9 | 0 | 0 | 0 | 2.8 | 1.4 | 0 | 0 | 0.9 | 0 | 0 |
| TOTALS | J | 81.9 | 7.0 | 2.8 | 2.8 | 0 | 0 | 0 | 0 | 0.9 | 0 | 0 | 0 | 0 | 0 |
| | S | 83.9 | 9.9 | 0.9 | 0.9 | 0.9 | 0.9 | 0.9 | 0 | 0.9 | 0 | 0 | 0.9 | 0 | 0 |

*Table 7 continued*

**1629** weight in pounds (1,000s)

| | | Under1 | 1-2 | 2-3 | 3-4 | 4-5 | 5-6 |
|---|---|---|---|---|---|---|---|
| CHAGFORD | J | 0 | 0 | 0 | 4.8 | 0 | 0 |
| | S | 7.4 | 4.8 | 3.7 | 3.7 | 0 | 0 |
| ASHBURTON | J | 9.5 | 0 | 0 | 0 | 0 | 0 |
| | S | 3.7 | 0 | 0 | 0 | 0 | 0 |
| PLYMPTON | J | 4.8 | 0 | 0 | 4.8 | 0 | 0 |
| | S | 3.7 | 3.7 | 0 | 0 | 0 | 0 |
| TAVISTOCK | J | 52.4 | 14.3 | 0 | 0 | 0 | 4.8 |
| | S | 66.7 | 3.7 | 0 | 0 | 0 | 3.7 |
| TOTALS | J | 66.7 | 19.1 | 0 | 9.6 | 0 | 4.8 |
| | S | 81.5 | 7.4 | 3.7 | 3.7 | 0 | 3.7 |

**1642** weight in pounds (1,000s)

| | | Under1 | 1-2 | 2-3 | 3-4 |
|---|---|---|---|---|---|
| CHAGFORD | J | 0 | 0 | 0 | 0 |
| | S | 0 | 0 | 0 | 0 |
| ASHBURTON | J | 18.2 | 0 | 0 | 0 |
| | S | 20.0 | 0 | 0 | 0 |
| PLYMPTON | J | 18.2 | 0 | 0 | 0 |
| | S | 6.7 | 0 | 0 | 0 |
| TAVISTOCK | J | 54.5 | 0 | 0 | 9.1 |
| | S | 66.7 | 0 | 6.7 | 0 |
| TOTALS | J | 90.9 | 0 | 0 | 9.1 |
| | S | 93.4 | 0 | 6.7 | 0 |

J=June
S=September

**1610** weight in pounds (1,000s)

| | | Under1 | 1-2 | 2-3 | 3-4 | 4-5 | 5-6 | 6-7 |
|---|---|---|---|---|---|---|---|---|
| CHAGFORD | J | 0 | 0 | 0 | 2.3 | 2.3 | 0 | 2.3 |
| | S | 1.9 | 1.9 | 1.9 | 1.9 | 0 | 1.9 | 0 |
| ASHBURTON | J | 18.2 | 4.5 | 0 | 0 | 0 | 0 | 0 |
| | S | 18.5 | 3.7 | 0 | 0 | 0 | 0 | 0 |
| PLYMPTON | J | 4.5 | 0 | 2.3 | 0 | 0 | 0 | 0 |
| | S | 7.4 | 0 | 1.9 | 0 | 0 | 0 | 0 |
| TAVISTOCK | J | 40.9 | 18.2 | 0 | 2.3 | 0 | 0 | 0 |
| | S | 48.1 | 9.3 | 0 | 0 | 1.9 | 0 | 0 |
| TOTALS | J | 63.6 | 22.7 | 2.3 | 4.6 | 2.3 | 0 | 4.6 |
| | S | 75.9 | 14.9 | 3.8 | 1.9 | 1.9 | 1.9 | 0 |

**1625** weight in pounds (1,000s)

| | | Under1 | 1-2 | 2-3 | 3-4 | 4-5 | 5-6 | 6-7 | 7-8 | 8-9 |
|---|---|---|---|---|---|---|---|---|---|---|
| CHAGFORD | J | 5.3 | 0 | 5.3 | 2.6 | 0 | 0 | 0 | 0 | 0 |
| | S | 13.3 | 3.3 | 0 | 0 | 3.3 | 0 | 0 | 0 | 0 |
| ASHBURTON | J | 13.2 | 0 | 0 | 0 | 0 | 0 | 0 | 0 | 0 |
| | S | 6.7 | 3.3 | 3.3 | 0 | 0 | 0 | 0 | 0 | 0 |
| PLYMPTON | J | 5.3 | 0 | 0 | 0 | 0 | 0 | 0 | 0 | 0 |
| | S | 10.0 | 0 | 0 | 0 | 0 | 2.6 | 0 | 0 | 2.6 |
| TAVISTOCK | J | 47.4 | 15.8 | 0 | 0 | 0 | 0 | 0 | 0 | 0 |
| | S | 40.0 | 13.3 | 0 | 3.3 | 0 | 0 | 0 | 0 | 0 |
| TOTALS | J | 71.2 | 15.8 | 5.3 | 2.6 | 0 | 0 | 0 | 0 | 0 |
| | S | 70.0 | 19.9 | 3.3 | 3.3 | 3.3 | 2.6 | 0 | 0 | 2.6 |

## TABLE 8

*Average weight per head of tin metal presented for coinage in each Devon stannary 1456–1642, June and September.*

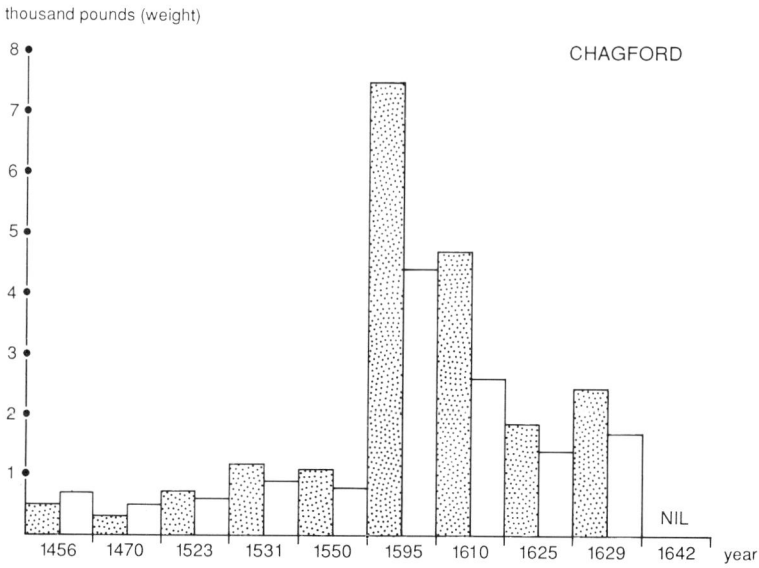

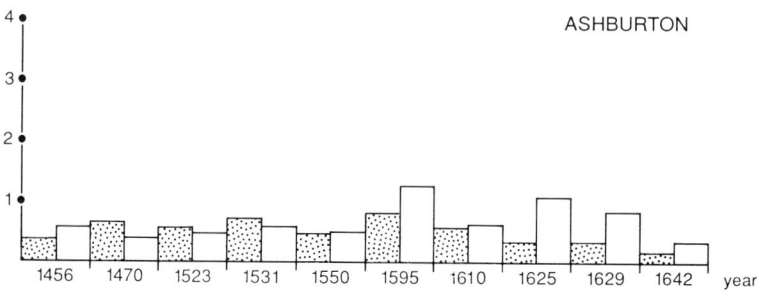

*Table 8 continued*

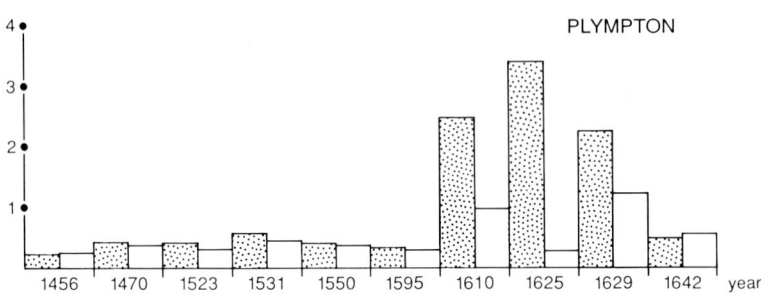

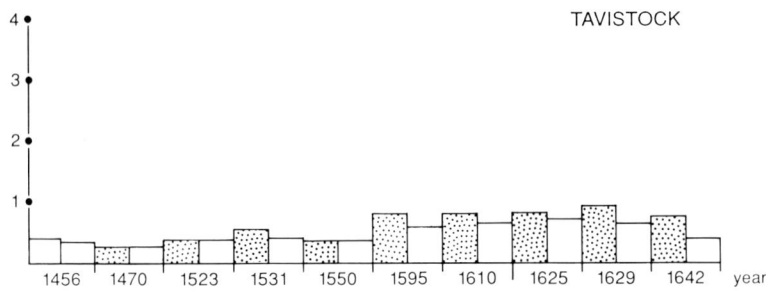

# Locality and Parliament: The Legislative Activities of Devon's MPs during the Reign of Elizabeth

## David Dean

During the parliament of 1601 the diarist Hayward Townshend noted that a bill concerning the coarse cloths known as fustians was opposed by the men of Devon who 'made a faction against it'.[1] His remark implies not only that Devon's MPs were capable of united action in face of an undesirable measure, but also that they formed a readily identifiable group in the House of Commons. Certainly some, notably Sir Walter Raleigh, Sir Francis Drake, John Hooker, Sir John Hele and Richard Martin, were among the most active members of the Elizabethan Commons. This the records of parliament itself tell us: the bills and acts, the journals and the private diaries which have survived. Yet local archives also yield much about the nature of parliamentary activity in this period, and Devon's records, particularly those of Exeter, are among the most informative. It is the purpose of this paper to chart the parliamentary record of Devon's Elizabethan MPs throughout the reign. It reveals how a specific locality made use of parliament in this period, and in so doing provides a perspective different from previous studies which have been largely confined to London and its livery companies.[2]

## The Members

Devon's parliamentary representation consisted of two knights of the shire and sixteen burgesses sitting for Barnstaple, Bere Alston, Dartmouth, Exeter, Plymouth, Plympton Erle, Tavistock and Totnes. Bere Alston was

enfranchised by Elizabeth and only returned MPs from the Parliament of
1584–5. In the early half of the reign Francis Russell, second Earl of
Bedford (1555–85), a member of the Privy Council and Lord Lieutenant
of Devon, Dorset and Cornwall, had much influence over elections in the
county.[3] All the knights of the shire elected for 1559 and 1563 had been
Bedford's deputy lieutenants. His friend Sir John Chichester of Raleigh,
senior knight in 1563 and 1566 (the second session of the 1563 parliament), had sat in Elizabeth's first parliament for Barnstaple where he was
Recorder. In 1566 he bought the borough and re-sold it to the corporation
while retaining the right to nominate one MP. Sir Peter Carew was of
sufficient local standing not to need Bedford's support as senior knight in
1559; he had been knight of the shire in both parliaments of 1553. Sir
Gawain Carew had served as knight of the shire in the later Henrician
parliaments and had also been implicated in Wyatt's rebellion of 1554; he
sat for Plympton Erle in 1559 and as junior knight in 1563. The junior
knight of 1559, Sir John St Leger, sat as senior knight in 1571 and in the
three sessions of the 1572 parliament (1572, 1576 and 1581).

Bedford's support is evident in the selection of many burgesses in the
early parliaments of the reign. All but one of Tavistock's MPs between
1559 and 1586 were Bedford nominees, as he owned the town. There, and
in other boroughs, the nature of the relationship varied. Some were
servants, followers and agents, such as Drake's friend Edmund Tremayne
(Tavistock, 1559; Plymouth, 1572–81), Edward Yarde (Dartmouth, 1559),
Cuthbert Reynolds (Dartmouth, 1581), Hugh Vaughan (Dartmouth,
1584–5) and Christopher Harris (Plymouth, 1584–5), a later servant of
Raleigh. Some were relatives: Robert Monson (Totnes, 1572), his stepson
Charles Morison (Tavistock, 1576, 1581) and, more distantly, his
daughter-in-law's brother, Richard Cooke (Tavistock, 1563, 1566). Others
were friends, such as Sir Arthur Bassett (Barnstaple 1563, 1566; knight
of the shire 1572–81; an overseer to Bedford's will), or companions-
in-arms such as Sir Arthur Champernowne (Totnes, 1563, 1566) and
Sir John More (Dartmouth, 1563, 1566); they were with Bedford at
St Quentin where the Cheshire gentleman Richard Hurleston (Totnes,
1571) had also been present (though with William Herbert, first Earl of
Pembroke).

Perhaps the most significant fact about Bedford's influence is that it
was placed at the disposal of friends and associates at the centre of
Elizabethan political life. William Cecil, Lord Burghley from 1571 and
Lord Treasurer from 1572, secured seats for his distant Yorkshire-
based kinsman John Vaughan (Dartmouth, 1571) and his secretary

Vincent Skinner (Barnstaple, 1572–81). Lord Keeper Nicholas Bacon secured seats for his sons Nathaniel and Edward (Tavistock, 1571, 1572–81, 1584–5) and possibly for Edmund Wiseman (Plympton Erle, 1566). Lord Chancellor Thomas Bromley's son found a seat at Plymouth for the 1584–5 Parliament. The courtier John Stanhope secured a place at Totnes in 1571, and another Cecilian associate, the Lord Treasurer's Remembrancer in the Exchequer, Peter Osborne, at Plympton Erle in 1572–81. Robert Beale, Clerk of the Privy Council, sat for Totnes in 1576 and 1581.

Several of Bedford's apparent nominees were on the radical side of Elizabethan protestantism and some had been Marian exiles. Sir Peter Carew had been attainted and exiled for his association with Wyatt's rebellion; he secured an act reversing the attainder in 1563. Another exile was Sir Nicholas Throckmorton (Tavistock, 1563, 1566). An associate of the Dedham 'classis', William Cardinall secured a seat at Dartmouth (1572–81). The famous puritan Peter Wentworth found his first parliamentary seat at Barnstaple in 1571.

While acknowledging Bedford's undoubted influence on some of these selections, it is important to stress that the evidence is often circumstantial.[4] Bedford died in July 1585 and was succeeded by his thirteen-year-old grandson. Since Chichester and Sir Peter Carew had pre-deceased him, and Bassett died the following year, later Elizabethan elections were relatively free from the Bedford-centred network of friends, relatives and associates so evident earlier. William Bourchier, third Earl of Bath, who became Lord Lieutenant in 1587 and whose second wife was Bedford's daughter Elizabeth, had some influence. As Recorder at Barnstaple, only a few miles from the family seat at Tawstock, he was particularly successful, nominating his unpopular land agent Thomas Hinson (in 1586–7, 1589 and 1597–8), George Chittinge, described as 'a gentleman of my Lord of Bath' (1593), and Edward Hancock, clerk of assize in the western circuit and a servant of Sir Walter Raleigh (1601). In 1597–8 Bath succeeded in getting the town to de-select Bartholomew Harris and return George Peard instead; both, however, were local men. Bath's servant Roger Papworth sat for Dartmouth in 1589. At Tavistock itself it was the young Earl of Bedford's guardian, Ambrose Dudley, Earl of Warwick, who exercised influence. His relation Valentine Knightley sat in 1584–5, 1586–7 and again in 1597–8 having lost a place at Northampton. In true Bedford style, both MPs for 1589 held central office: Michael Heneage, one of the Keepers of the Records in the Tower, was brother to the Vice-Chamberlain, and Anthony Ashley, a Clerk to the Privy Council.

Elsewhere local men benefited from the absence of a strong noble influence and several boroughs resisted Warwick's request for nominations. At the county level Sir Walter Raleigh, who succeeded Bedford as Warden of the Stannaries, was the junior knight in 1584–5 and the senior in 1586–7. In the latter parliament he was accompanied by John Chudleigh of Ashton, a member of Sir Humphrey Gilbert's last expedition; in 1584–5 the senior knight was Sir William Courtenay of Powderham. Deputy lieutenant from 1586, Courtenay sat as senior knight again in 1589 and 1601, despite his religious conservatism. The remaining knights of the shire were all local landowners of high standing, and all but the last served as Elizabethan deputy lieutenants: George Cary of Cockington (1589), who had sat for Dartmouth in 1586–7; Sir Thomas Dennis of Holcombe Burnell (1593); Sir Edward Seymour of Berry Pomeroy (1593 and 1601); Sir William Strode of Newnham, in Plympton (1597–8); and the wealthy Amias Bampfield of Poltimore and South Molton (1597–8).

Barnstaple was the only parliamentary borough in north Devon and it suffered from more electoral interference than most. Nevertheless, apart from 1601, one MP was always a townsman, often from one of the leading merchant families: John Darte (1559) and his son Lewis (1586–7), Robert Apley (1563, 1566, 1571 and 1572–81), Robert Prowse (1584–5), Sir John Doddridge (1589) and George Peard (1597–8). Apley was especially involved in Barnstaple's parliamentary businesses, having sat in the second parliament of 1554 and in 1555; the town clerk noted on his death in 1596 that 'all his time [Apley] was earnest in upholding the liberties of this town'. Another prominent member, Richard Martin, was the son of an Exeter merchant and a lawyer at the Middle Temple. Sitting for Barnstaple in 1601, he played a role in the agitation over monopolies.

Dartmouth was less successful at maintaining a presence of townsmen early in the reign: only Thomas Southcote (1559) and Thomas Gourney (1571, 1572) were local men, the latter a merchant and former mayor. After Bedford's death, however, most MPs were local: Sir Thomas Ridgeway (1584–5) had married Mary Southcote, daughter of the 1559 MP; Robert Petre (1586–7) was an auditor of receipt in the Exchequer but had local standing; Richard Drew (1589) was town clerk; the town's counsellor, William Bastard (1597–8, 1601), who also did legal work for Totnes, later became Recorder. Nicholas Hayman (1593), Thomas Holland (1593) and John Treherne (1601) were merchants. Hayman had sat for Totnes in 1586–7 and served there as mayor in 1589–90, but had then moved to Dartmouth, possibly because of an unpaid debt.

The stannary town of Plympton Erle also found it easier to secure seats for local men after Bedford's death, although Jasper Cholmley (1586–7) was a lawyer working for the Russells and the Countess of Warwick. Two families, especially prominent in tin-mining, supplied several MPs: the Strodes and the Southcotes. Richard Strode sat for Plympton in 1559, as did his brother William (1572–81) and son William (1601, and most Jacobean parliaments). Both the London lawyer Richard Grafton (1589) and Raleigh's follower Edward Hancock (1597–8) probably owed their seats to the Strodes. Thomas Southcote sat for Plympton in 1558 (and Dartmouth in 1559); his sons Richard and George sat in 1593 and 1597–8 respectively. By this time the families were related: William Strode (Richard's son) married Mary Southcote (Thomas' daughter) in 1581. It is probable that the prominent Jacobean MP Edwin Sandys owed his elections at Plympton Erle in 1589 and 1593 to the Southcotes; his second wife was Anne Southcote, another of Thomas' daughters. Other MPs were Sir John Hele of Wembury (1584–5), a wealthy lawyer and money-lender who later sat for Exeter in three parliaments; his second son, also John, who sat for Plympton in 1601; his older brother Warwick who did so in most Jacobean parliaments; and Hannibal Vivian, who purchased part of the manor of Plympton in 1582 and represented the borough in 1584–5.

Totnes also benefited from the withdrawal of Bedford's influence, but the last years of the reign were troubled times for the town as the wealthier merchants attempted to restrict authority to themselves; the dispute focused on the new charter of 1596.[5] In the early part of the reign elections were still influenced by the Edgcumbes, who had sold the borough in 1559: Peter Edgcumbe had sat for Totnes in 1555 and for Devon in 1571 before finally withdrawing to Cornwall in the late 1570s; his brother Richard sat for Totnes in 1563 and 1566, and his first son, also Richard, in 1589. Several early Elizabethan MPs were locals, such as the mayor Leonard Yeo (1559), and most later burgesses were townsmen: the pilchard merchant Nicholas Ball (1584–5) who became mayor of Totnes the following year; Christopher Savery (1584–5), one of the merchant élite who sat again in 1593 when he was mayor; his opponents in the 1590s dispute, John Giles (1586–7) and his son Edward (1597–8, and several Jacobean parliaments); Nicholas Hayman (1586–7), one of the founders of the Merchants Company who later moved to Dartmouth; Recorder Richard Sparry (1593), a neutral in the dispute who was later forced out by the élite and replaced by Sir George Cary of Cockington (MP for Dartmouth, 1586–7 and Devon, 1589); and Christopher Buggin (1597–8), son of the merchant Walter Buggin, another enemy of Savery. Both 1601

MPs, however, were supporters of the élite faction: Leonard Darr, mayor in 1593–4, and Philip Holditch, mayor in 1598–9. They wrote a letter on 30 November 1601 noting that there were 'many threats given out against us that there shall be bills preferred in the parliament house against us for many matters, but we can hear none read yet. When they come I doubt not that we shall answer them.' Both had been assiduous in their attendance 'lest that in our absence they should overtake us'.[6]

Bedford had some influence in Plymouth, but the leading family there were the Champernownes of Modbury: Sir Arthur sat in 1559, and his nephews Henry Champernowne (1563, 1566) and Sir Humphrey Gilbert (1571) also secured seats. Bedford nominees included Henry Bromley in 1584–5, who was returned again in 1586–7 after Bedford's death, accompanied by the former Bedford steward, Hugh Vaughan; the son of one of Bedford's deputy wardens of stannaries, Robert Bassett, sat in 1593. Most of Plymouth's MPs, however, were local men, as the town had legislated in 1570 and 1601:[7] John Hawkins (1571, 1572–81); Sir Francis Drake (1593), mayor in 1581–2; Nicholas Slanning (1559), town clerk and a later mayor; Sir William Periam (1563, 1566), who drew up a bill for the town's almshouses in 1566 and later became a lawyer and judge in London; Sir Warwick Hele of Wembury (1597–8), whose father John later became Recorder of Plymouth and Plympton Erle; the merchant William Stallenge (1597–8, 1601), who was much involved in the rebuilding of Plymouth haven; and the merchant and former mayor, James Bagg (1601).

As the largest city in the South West, with its own sheriff and Lord Lieutenant, Exeter was more able than any other borough to avoid outside influence during Elizabeth's reign. Bedford sought a nomination for the 1563 parliament but was refused, remarking 'I thought I had for my goodwill towards you somewhat better deserved than in so trifling a matter to have such a repulse'. Almost all the Elizabethan MPs were merchants or leading tradesmen: Richard Prestwood (1559), Simon Knight (1572–81), Thomas Brewerton (1584–5), Richard Prowse (1584–5), John Periam (1589, 1593), William Martin (1597–8) and John Howell (1601); all at one time served as sheriff and all but Prestwood as mayor. Several were connected with the Merchant Adventurers and served as governors.[8] Two MPs were also recorders: Geoffrey Tothill (1563, 1566, 1571, 1572) and John Hele (1593, 1597–8, 1601). The lawyer Edward Drewe (1586–7, 1589) was also recorder for a short time in 1592; other lawyers were Thomas Williams of Stowford (1563) and Edward Ameredith (1576, 1581). Williams, retained also by Plymouth as legal counsel, became Speaker in 1563; Ameredith's father had been a mayor of Exeter although he himself was based in London until around 1593. That notable Elizabethan, John Hooker alias Vowell, was Chamberlain when he sat in 1571, a parliament for which he kept the first private diary which has survived for the reign; he sat again in 1586–7. The two 'outsiders' chosen were the MP of 1555, Sir John Pollard (1559), and Sir Peter Carew (1566); both were made freemen of the city. One Exeter merchant secured a seat at Bere Alston, Nicholas Martin (1586–7), brother to William Martin (Exeter, 1597–8) and also a mayor, sheriff and Merchant Adventurer. Bere Alston was enfranchised in 1584 and its MPs were nominated by the joint owners, the Marquis of Winchester and Lord Mountjoy. Besides Martin, two MPs, Thomas Burgoyne (1593) and John Langford (1601), were Devon men.

It is worth noting that several Devonians sat for constituencies outside the county. Sir Walter Raleigh has the distinction of being the only Elizabethan who sat as knight of the shire for three different counties: Devon (1584–5, 1586–7), Dorset (1597–8) and Cornwall (1601). He also sat for Mitchell in Cornwall in 1593. Several of Bedford's nominees in Devon found seats elsewhere through the Earl's patronage. Other Devon men moved to Cornwall: Peter Edgcumbe (Totnes, 1555) eventually sold the borough and sat for Cornwall in eight Elizabethan sessions (and Liskeard, 1584–5), although he did sit for Devon in 1571. Lewis Darte (Barnstaple, 1586–7) sat for Tregony in 1601, having moved to Pentewan. As Richard Carew noted in his *Survey of Cornwall*: 'Master Darte, who, as divers other gentlemen well descended and accommodated in Devon, do yet rather make choice of a pleasing and retired equality in the little Cornish angle.'[9] Other examples of Devon men sitting elsewhere are: Sir John Acland (Saltash, 1586–7), William Courtenay the younger (Fowey, 1601), Richard Champernowne (West Looe, 1586–7), George Chudleigh (Mitchell, 1601), Sir Humphrey Gilbert (Queenborough, 1581), Adrian Gilbert (Bridport, 1597–8), Sir John St Leger (Arundel, 1563, 1566, Tregony, 1584–5) and Edward Seymour the younger (Penryn, 1601).

Perhaps such men were united by a notion of being distinctively 'Westcountry men', and they certainly shared experiences on the commissions of the peace or in the service of the Admiralty. Many had gone to Ireland with Sir Peter Carew, had invested in the expeditions of Raleigh, Hawkins, Drake and Gilbert, or in the speculation of goods from captured Spanish carracks. Another important link between MPs was marriage, as already noted with the Strodes and the Southcotes at Plympton Erle. The kinship networks of the South West were complex, as a few examples will illustrate. Sir Arthur Bassett married Eleanor, daughter of Sir John Chichester. Eleanor was the mother of Robert Bassett; he married the daughter of William Periam whose brother John sat for Exeter in the 1593 parliament along with Bassett sitting for Plymouth. Chichester, like Warwick Hele, married a daughter of Sir William Courtenay, and the Courtenays were related to other MPs. The famous half-brothers, Humphrey and Adrian Gilbert and Walter and Carew Raleigh, were linked by their mother Katherine Champernowne, the daughter of a Carew and sister to Sir Arthur Champernowne. His nephew Henry married into the Edgcumbes and his daughter Elizabeth married Edward Seymour. Richard Sparry was also related to the Champernownes, as well as becoming stepfather to Christopher Buggin of Totnes. Edmund Tremayne married Eulalia St Leger, daughter of Sir John, and Hannibal Vivian married Philippa Tremayne ten years before he sat for Plympton Erle in 1584–5. Edward Hancock married Dorothy, daughter of Amias Bampfield, and so both son-in-law and father-in-law sat in the 1597–8 parliament.

These examples suggest that Devon's MPs had many interests and experiences in common. Of course, familial relationships were not necessarily cohesive, any more than shared experiences in mercantile expeditions, land speculation, privateering or royal business could be. However, it certainly appears that the Devon men in parliament presented a common front on the major issues which affected their community.

## Legislative Activities

The first significant account of the work of Devon's MPs in Elizabeth's parliaments comes from the private archives of Exeter. On 3 January 1563, ten days before the parliament began, 'a remembrance of certain articles' was compiled for the two MPs Thomas Williams and Geoffrey Tothill. Firstly, they were to obtain an act confirming the 1561 charter 'for the godly order of orphans' which 'hath not his force'. Secondly, because the custom of gavelkind, in which all children were equal heirs, 'is most noyful to this commonwealth', causing great envy 'as when twenty, thirty or forty persons shall be joint heirs to a very small piece of land', the MPs were to obtain legislation replacing it with inheritance of primogeniture, just as Kent had done during the reign of Henry VIII. Thirdly, the benefits enjoyed by London and Norwich concerning apprentices were to be extended to include Exeter and other cities. The final three items concerned the statutes merchant and staple: the continuance of the highways act but with an additional proviso that 'every man according to his livelihood in every parish may be a contributor to the same, and that the poor be not as heretofore charged as far forth as the rich'; and an amendment to the poor relief act so that jurisdiction would be given to temporal officers 'to use cohersion against such as shall obstinately refuse to be contributories' because the 'laws ecclesiastical are not sufficient for the same'.[10]

On 31 January, 20 days after the parliament had opened, Tothill wrote to the Chamberlain, John Hooker, reporting on the action he had taken. He included copies of two bills which had been initiated 'wherein I pray God send us good success as I hope'.[11] The first, for uniting churches, had been initiated in the Lords. The second bill concerned orphans and had begun in the Commons. Tothill explained why such action was taken:

> by that time we have thoroughly considered that bill for orphans and ready to be sent off to the Lords, the Lords bill will be ready to come down. I suppose the bills be indifferently handled. If we should have put both in at one place then peradventure the house would not be best contented with two bills for our private city.

However, things did not work out the way Tothill intended. The churches bill took much longer in the Lords than he had anticipated, with a first reading only on 9 March. By this time the Lords had already seen the orphans bill initiated in the Commons. In the end the latter passed smoothly and became law. The churches bill failed in the Commons.[12]

Perhaps Tothill's confidence that both bills would be 'indifferently handled' was misplaced. His task must have been made easier when Williams was chosen as Speaker of the Commons, since he decided the order in which bills should be read. After the parliament Williams received £20 as a 'gift' from the city to cover his considerable expenses and also because he 'used himself in all friendship in preferring the suit and business of the city'.[13]

In the Lords the churches bill seems to have got caught up in more general, official solutions to the problem of inadequate church livings.[14] Exeter (and Winchester) wanted action, and the Lords committed the matter to Judge John Southcott (whose family came from Chudleigh) who prepared two legislative solutions. The first gave the bishops authority to create livings worth up to £24 per annum by uniting smaller ones; this passed the Lords but failed in the Commons where MPs lowered the upper level to 20 marks (£13 6s. 8d.). Lack of time was the evident reason for its failure.[15] The second approach gave the Lord Chancellor authority to issue letters of commission to the bishops as a way of forcing them to act; it too seems to have failed in the Commons. The whole matter became a pet project of Sir William Cecil, who initiated other proposals in 1566, 1576 and 1581.[16] As Elton suggests, although the impetus may have come from the townsmen of Exeter, the bishops probably had the leading role in trying to find a general solution. As will be seen below, later approaches to the problem of Exeter's churches suggest that Bishop William Alley might have preferred a general solution which placed control firmly in his hands rather than a single act of parliament obtained by the city's MPs. There had been a long-standing dispute between the city and the ecclesiastical authorities over jurisdiction.[17]

Tothill's concern not to overload either house with two bills for Exeter is also reflected in the remaining contents of his letter to Hooker. Referring to the instructions the MPs had received, he notes that

> for apprentices there is a bill in the parliament house for servants which is committed to the Master of the Rolls and others. I hope if the bill pass to get a proviso for all cities in England to take apprentices and so Exeter not named. There your [sic] will or should have been this afternoon, if my leisure had served, a bill drawn for the Londoners that shall be in the name of all the cities in the west parts and elsewhere and is not privately for us.

As in his later work for the city, Tothill was clearly concerned to save as much money as possible; to obtain a solution by general bill was to avoid the considerable fees that private bills attracted.[18] Nevertheless, any lobbying was costly and Tothill asked that £10 be sent via his brother to enable him to cover his expenses 'as I have retained divers in these causes and must give money about the same'. Anxious to ensure that his hard work was noticed, Tothill ended 'I pray you make the masters of the city partakers of this my letter and truth of the two bills . . .'. His work was noticed: on 11 May 'in consideration of his great pains and charges at and about the parliament' he received £22 from the city.[19]

Whatever action Tothill took concerning apprentices, Exeter, unlike London and Norwich, did not secure an exemption from the statute of artificers.[20] With regard to poor relief, a successful Lords' bill, much amended in the Commons, created a parish fund to be administered by the churchwardens. It went some way to meet Exeter's demands: those refusing to contribute were to be bound by the ecclesiastical authorities for the sum of £10 and to appear before the justices at the next general sessions where they would be rated and could be imprisoned if they continued to refuse. It is possible, as Elton suggests, that there was a considerable clerical input into the making of the act, but it seems likely too that secular authorities such as those at Exeter were involved.[21] With regards to highways, an act continuing a Marian statute was successful and carried many additional clauses; none directly reflect Exeter's wishes but supervisors and justices were given greater powers to deal with defaulters.[22] There is no surviving evidence that anything was done in parliament concerning the statutes merchant and staple or gavelkind land.

Before the second session of the 1563 parliament met on the last day of September 1566, Williams had died and was replaced by Sir Peter Carew who was sworn in beforehand.[23] No specific instructions survive for this session (although a general bill would have set up commissions to enquire into landing facilities), but a bill for Hartland quay was promoted, as was one for Plymouth and Dartmouth in 1571.[24] This was the parliament for which Chamberlain Hooker (who accompanied Tothill) compiled his diary, perhaps to justify his claims for expenses or simply to satisfy his own substantial interest in the institutions of his country. He was a member of the committee dealing with a bill 'for the havens in Devon and Cornwall' which failed in the Lords; the committee seems to have merged it with a bill 'for cognizances of pleas in the Stannery'.[25]

Exeter's MPs were very active in the three sessions of the 1572 parliament. Tothill sat with Simon Knight in 1572 but died in 1574 and was replaced by Edward Ameredith for the 1576 and 1581 sessions. Tothill, at least, would have been interested in the 1572 poor relief act because it fulfilled Exeter's earlier desire for a compulsory poor rate. Both MPs received expenses and repayments for money spent in 1572, including a sum to the Speaker.[26] They were unsuccessful in their attempt to secure an act for gavelkind; desired in 1563, this time it only got as far as the Lords. It did become law in 1581 and a grateful city rewarded Knight with £20.[27] In 1572 the city also desired the MPs to secure bills 'that all merchants and adventurers beyond the seas shall dwell in cities and towns corporate' and 'that the statute staple shall be reduced to this city again'.[28] Although there is no parliamentary reference to the latter in 1572, failed bills concerning the entering of defeazances on the statutes of the staple were read in 1576 and 1581 and may have offered some chance of lobbying.[29] In 1563 a bill had attempted to limit overseas trading to 19 designated port towns (including Dartmouth, Plymouth, Exeter and Barnstaple); in 1572 a measure restricted the right to export to those serving a seven-year apprenticeship or trading for 12 years.[30] Perhaps Barnstaple's Robert Apley was active in this; he certainly spoke against a pro-London imports bill on 6 June.[31] In 1576 a bill 'that the Queen might limit by commission at what wharf in every county men might load and unload' started in the Lords but was rejected after amendments in the Commons; it was revived again in later parliaments.[32]

Totnes merchants also played a vital role in promoting this sort of legislation. On 6 February 1581, a few weeks after the session had begun, they wrote to Exeter hoping to have 'advice in joining with other cities for the exhibiting of a bill' restricting merchants to towns and cities 'if it may be had'. They proposed that both towns send a reliable person 'to solicit the same unto your and our burgesses' and also suggested that a bill be initiated for the better regulation of making and selling Devonshire kerseys, 'the principalest commodity of our country'. Undoubtedly of interest to the MPs were the bills for the Merchant Adventurers initiated in 1581, one of which especially pertained to those 'not being free of the City of London'.[33]

The coarse, narrow cloths known as kerseys had been the subject of legislation in 1572 when a law was passed limiting them to 18 yards; Apley had been a delegate to the conference held with the Lords.[34] The Devon men now sought further limitations to those kerseys known as dozens (15lb. weight and 15 yd. length), as well as stopping London's searchers from examining cloth brought to fairs and markets and restricting producers to those serving a seven-year apprenticeship. Sir John St Leger and Sir Arthur Bassett were members of the committee appointed on its second reading. New bills for Devon kerseys and those made in Surrey, Sussex and Hampshire were drafted but did not pass the Commons.[35]

In 1581 Exeter's MPs also seem to have revived the bill uniting the town's 19 churches and chapels into five or six larger parish churches. On this occasion there is no doubt that Bishop John Woolton had strong misgivings about the measure which he had copied into the Bishop's Act Book or Register.[36] His instructions—'to my procurators in the parliament house'—reflected official moves in 1563: if such changes were deemed necessary, then a commission (to include himself, Bedford and some of the incumbents) should carry them out. Steps had to be taken to protect the cathedral churchyard, the goods of the churches, and the stipends, as well as providing for the wages and lodgings of ministers and their families. 'To persuade this', he noted,

> you may not stick or fear to notify the cold charity of these people towards their pastors where lately by the instigation of some good

men entertaining a preacher to catechize their youth and instruct themselves could not be induced to entertain him with a simple stipend sure and certain but only for one year and no more . . .[37]

There is, however, no parliamentary record of the bill.

In 1584–5, shortly before reassembly following the Christmas break, Exeter's MPs Thomas Brewerton and Richard Prowse received specific instructions to deal with four matters: salmon fishing in the haven, imposts of wine, mustering of horses and the lease of the fee-farm of Ottery St Mary.[38] It is not at all clear that these were instructions for legislative solutions; some may have been additional matters to pursue with government officials while they were in London. Certainly the MPs were told only to 'take advice' on them, and there is no explicit reference to bills as had been the case in 1563. None seem to have come up in this parliament.[39]

However, Brewerton and Prowse, the one a leading moneylender and the other an important draper, revived the quest for legislation pertaining to Devon kerseys. In this they were undoubtedly joined by the MPs for Totnes, Christopher Savery and Nicholas Ball, two of the signatories to the Totnes letter of 1581. Shortly before the session Exeter's Merchant Adventurers decided to promote a bill restricting merchants to towns and cities; others were to cease trading unless they had been so engaged for 18 years or apprenticed for at least seven. The company agreed to cover the MPs' expenses by levying a rate on freemen.[40] They also decided to suport the kerseys bill (again, these were to be 15lb. in weight and 15yd in length), covering costs up to £10.[41]

These provisions are also similar to the measure relating to the Devonshire and Cornish cloth known as plain white and pinned white straights which became law in this parliament and in which Richard Carew of Antony in east Cornwall played a part.[42] The bill relating to Devonshire kerseys failed to reach a third reading in the lower house. Providing, as in 1581, that penalties were to be imposed on the weaver, it was committed on its second reading and the bill was entrusted to Richard Prowse. However, since the diarist Thomas Cromwell reported its proceedings, it seems that Exeter's interests lost out in the deliberations; the amended measure had no further proceedings although 13 days remained in the session.[43]

Soon after the Merchant Adventurers were dealing with a new problem, the patent granted to Sir Edward Stafford for reformation of kerseys, and early in 1586 the Privy Council ordered the justices of assize in Devon and

Cornwall to restrain farmers who were making kerseys on the side.[44] Although no work was requested of the MPs for 1586–7 (Edward Drew and John Hooker) or 1589 (Drew and John Periam), they received payment.[45] In 1592 Devon's JPs 'and other expert and grave men of that county' succeeded in lobbying the Privy Council for a proclamation effecting their earlier legislative desires. The Merchant Adventurers resolved to obtain statutory confirmation of the proclamation in 1593, and so instructed the MPs, Periam and Recorder John Hele. Official support (the Privy Council had also received complaints about faulty cloth from the Dutch) probably explains why they succeeded. The knights and burgesses of Devon were appointed to both the large first committee (with those of six other counties) and the smaller one that did the work; Sir Thomas Dennis reported back to the house.[46] They were probably active also in the attempt to exempt Devon from earlier legislation confining yarn-making to corporate towns on the grounds that it was a very populous county and its inhabitants had very small tenements. The preamble also asserted that livelihoods had been threatened, clothworkers made destitute and clothiers had lost the ability to pay subsidy money and contribute to arms.[47] One of Devon's knights in 1586–7, John Chudleigh, had moved for a similar bill but it got only as far as a first reading; in 1593 the bill arrived in the Lords with insufficient time to proceed.[48]

In May 1593 the appointment of three searchers and markers of kerseys was noted in Exeter's Act Book, and the city had paid Periam his wages for 73 days—as well as 9s. 'ordinary charges'—in April.[49] One of the searchers appointed, George Howell, might have been a relative of the 1601 MP John Howell who was one of the ten men appointed on 15 October, 12 days before the session began, to meet at John Periam's house and confer over 'what things be most necessary to be preferred to the parliament house for the causes of the commonwealth of this country and city' and to set the same down in writing. Five days before the session began, articles were prepared and were to be presented as bills according to the discretion of the MPs. Two days into the session, they received a letter from the chamber, asking them to prevent any attempt at incorporation by the brewers 'with all their force'.[50] Howell and his fellow MP John Hele were probably concerned with the unsuccessful attempt to repeal the 1572 kerseys act and among those Devon men making a 'faction' against the 1601 fustians bill. Committed in the Commons and returning apparently unchanged, only some six MPs were in favour of it going further.[51]

Exeter's later Elizabethan MPs were concerned with matters other than cloth. In 1584–5 Prowse and Brewerton might have kept a watchful eye on a successful Lords' bill concerning the bishop, dean and chapter of Exeter which tried to clear up confusion over conveyances caused by the deprivation and restitution of the Marian dean, Cardinal Pole. Bishop John Woolton was on the Lords' committee appointed to consider the bill.[52] All of Devon's MPs must have been interested when Humphrey Coningsby (sitting for St Albans) offered a proviso to a 1586–7 bill 'for breeding of horses in the waste grounds of Devon and Cornwall', and perhaps they secured the rejection of both bill and proviso.[53] John Hele and William Martin were certainly involved in the failed 1597–8 bill confirming the Merchant Adventurers charter. Although Hele was put in charge of the bill when it was committed, it was Bristol's Recorder and MP, George Snigge, who reported their decision that it was 'not fit to pass in this House'.[54] Perhaps the committee had discovered that the charter had been secured in the face of considerable opposition from the guild of tailors and other artisans of the town.[55] Bristol had its own difficulties over the Merchant Adventurers and the charter, and Snigge was one of the feoffees for the Bristol company's property.[56]

In the last Elizabethan parliament Exeter tried again to secure a measure 'for uniting and consolidation of certain small churches in the city of Exeter', having resolved the previous year to agree to the uniting of St Petrock and St Pancras if the bishop, Ordinary, incumbents, patron and parishioners agreed.[57] In parliament the bill stimulated a lively debate with one member (noted by Hayward Townshend as a servant of William Cotton, bishop of Exeter) arguing that its promoters wanted land only to build a privy, earning Richard Martin's retort that he had spoken more 'for his master's benefit than he did for God's honour'. Martin also noted the absence of John Hele, who had the previous day during the subsidy debate 'so much flattered his Prince' but was now not present to do 'his country good service'. Martin successfully urged a committal of the churches bill to a large number of members, including the knights of Devon, the burgesses of Exeter and a good many Cornish MPs, Raleigh among them.[58]

The measure, which has survived, stressed the poor quality of services caused by the large number of small churches in the city, and empowered the town's authorities to build a large parish church capable of supporting two thousand people. Six churches (St Petrock, St George, St Pancras, St Kerrian, St Mary Arches and St Clare) were to be destroyed, with all proceeds to go towards building the new church and a new living. All but one of these churches were located in the area between the north gate and just beyond Fore Street and High Street; the chapel of St Clare lay beyond the town's south gate in the parish of Heavitree. The bill did not emerge from the committee.[59]

Nine days later the mayor and several aldermen wrote to Secretary Sir Robert Cecil, informing him that this matter, and others presently before Parliament and the Privy Council, had been entrusted to Howell; it seems that the town's authorities were dissatisfied with Hele's performance, and his absence from the house during the crucial debate must have been reported home: one of the signatories was Richard Martin's father who had been an MP with Hele in 1597–8.[60] Hele's general character may not have been helpful to the town's causes: three years later, when Lord Keeper Egerton came to assess Hele's qualities in connection with the Mastership of the Rolls, he concluded that Hele was 'a most greedy and insatiable taker of fees' and a drunkard known not only for 'brawling words, but sometimes blows also'. Although Hele retained the town's recordership until 1605, he was not selected as MP again in 1604.[61]

Many of Exeter's legislative initiatives failed, and in the early part of the reign Plymouth was no more successful. In 1572 their MPs, John Hawkins and Edmund Tremayne, promoted a bill confirming grants for an almshouse 'therefore moved by reason that their evidence is burnt'.[62] William Periam, MP in 1563 and 1566, had received 10s. for drafting such a bill in 1566. An identical sum had been paid 'To Mr Fleetwood for his counsell in penning the same bill and to speak in favour of the bill in the parliament house'; another 5s. to the sergeant, 'for putting the Speaker in mind to read the bill'; and 12d. to the Clerk of the Crown, for 'searching the books for the burgesses' names'. This too, then, seems to be a measure revived in a later parliament.[63] Such intense lobbying was unsuccessful, and in the next parliament (1584–5) Plymouth chose two 'outsiders' to represent them: Henry Bromley and Christopher Harris. The fact that it was in this parliament that Plymouth secured an act for its harbour proves that townsmen were not necessarily needed to lobby parliament successfully. Harris was especially active, receiving £17 6s. 'for his help', and the town wrote to Sir Francis Drake (one of the committee members, sitting for Bossiney) and John Hele (sitting for Plympton Erle) 'touching our burgesses'. Hele was paid £9 1s. 6d. for 'his help at London for furthering of our suit for bringing in of the water'. The act allowed Plymouth to increase its supply of fresh water by cutting a trench from the river Meavy and carried provisos protecting the owners of gardens and orchards and mill owners.[64]

In 1593 Plymouth's MPs Sir Francis Drake and Robert Bassett were involved in a measure which an anonymous diarist described as providing 'that all mills that hereafter shall be erected upon Plymouth River were to be plucked down except the parties having mills there already be compounded with'. It was handed over to the committee appointed to consider a measure for East Stonehouse, near Plymouth, but did not reappear. Drake, Richard Edgcumbe and Sir Thomas Dennis were members of the committee, and Drake was put in charge of the bill. He seems to have had some direct interest in the matter.[65]

The measure for East Stonehouse was successful. It authorised the cutting of a trench between the town and a local stream in order to increase water supply, and had been moved by Peter Edgcumbe whose father had settled nearby. However, the committee shelved a third bill which conveyed the right to reclaim Plympton marsh to Thomas Payton.[66]

Devon's MPs, perhaps especially those of Barnstaple, were involved in the 1601 bill pertaining to a harbour and quay on the Severn, 'for the safeguard of men and shipping and to the public good of the commonwealth'. It was a measure in the form of a petition from 'Sir Robert Bassett knight, the manors of Barnstaple and Biddeford with other the inhabitants and parts near thereunto adjoining', and allowed Richard Cole to build a harbour on the north coast. However, the bill was vetoed by the Queen, perhaps because it affected the Lord Admiral's interests, as had been asserted in the Commons.[67]

Several of Devon's MPs used parliament to pursue private interests. Sir John St Leger saw that a bill concerning his sons' restitution (they had been attainted and outlawed for murder) reached the statute book in 1581.[68] In 1601 a bill concerning the Seymour estates was of obvious concern to the Devon knight of the shire who sat on the committee, but it was vetoed by the Queen.[69] Another failed bill sought to confirm Raleigh's grant 'touching the discovery and inhabiting of certain foreign lands and countries'. It passed the Commons—after amendment by a committee which included 'many that were to go in the journey [to] Waingandacow'—but failed in the Lords. Members of the Commons' committee included William Courtenay and Sir Francis Drake.[70]

## Conclusion

The legislation pursued by Devon's MPs in Elizabeth's reign concerned a wide range of issues. Many of these were of particular local concern, but it is clear that these MPs, and those they represented, did not only see parliament as an opportunity to clear up local problems. In light of their experiences as collectors of funds for highway repair and poor relief, they had suggestions to make to the 1563 parliament. As members of mercantile and seafaring communities, they proposed legislation on cloth production, trade and harbours. Many were involved in the subsidy committees of the period. Others participated in the biggest parliamentary issues of the day: Peter Carew, Sir Arthur Champernowne, Sir John Chichester and Sir John More were appointed to the succession committee in 1566, while Raleigh, Seymour, Strode, Courtenay and Richard Martin were among those involved in the monopolies agitation in 1597–8 and 1601. Raleigh informed the House of Commons during the 1593 subsidy debate that 'the West Country since the Parliament begun, had taken from them the worth of four hundred and forty thousand pound', while Martin, the London lawyer with Devon roots, claimed in 1601 to speak for Barnstaple, 'a town that grieves and pines', and 'for a country that groaneth and languisheth . . .' under the burden of monopolies.[71] Robert Apley of Barnstaple and the Devon knight Sir Arthur Bassett were appointed to consider weights and measures in 1572; George Cary was involved in 1589 legislation on Dover and Hartlepool havens; and Raleigh was especially named to the 1601 piracy committee, a matter of concern to Exeter and Totnes before and after the parliament.[72]

Such activities reveal them to be men engaged in both local and national affairs whose legislative proposals show an awareness of other communities. They formed an active lobby in Elizabeth's parliaments, readily identified, as by Hayward Townshend, as a distinct group of colleagues and friends. It comes as no surprise to read the intimate postscript Sir William Strode added to the letter he sent to Edward Seymour in October 1601: 'I hope we shall meet at the parliament very shortly.'[73]

## Notes

1. Sir Simon D'Ewes, *The Journals of All the Parliaments During the Reign of Queen Elizabeth, Both of the House of Lords and House of Commons* (1682, repr. Shannon, Ireland, 1973), 668; BL, Stowe MS 362 (Hayward Townshend's Diary), fols 210v.–11.

2. Two general studies of localities and parliament are Robert Tittler, 'Elizabethan Towns and the "Points of Contact": Parliament', *Parliamentary History* 8 (1989), 275–88 and D.M. Dean, Parliament and Locality', in D.M. Dean and N.L. Jones (eds), *The Parliaments of Elizabethan England* (Oxford, 1990), pp. 139–62. For references to articles on the parliamentary activities of London and its companies,

and Great Yarmouth, see D.M. Dean, 'Parliament, Privy Council and Local Politics in Elizabethan England: The Yarmouth–Lowestoft Fishing Dispute', *Albion* 22 (1990), 39–40 (n. 3, 4 and 6).

3. What follows is drawn heavily from the constituency reports and the biographies in P.W. Hasler, *The History of Parliament: The House of Commons 1558–1603* (3 vols, 1981).

4. See J.D. Alsop, 'Exchequer Office-Holders in the House of Commons, 1559–1601', *Parl. Hist.* viii (1989), 245–53.

5. DRO, Totnes Borough Records, 1579A/10/1–15.

6. DRO, Totnes Borough Records, 1579A/10/13.

7. WDRO, Plymouth Municipal Records, W48 (White Book), fols. 27v., 64v.

8. See William Cotton, *An Elizabethan Guild of the City of Exeter: An Account of the Proceedings of the Society of Merchant Adventurers During the Latter Half of the 16th Century* (Exeter, 1873), 39–40.

9. Hasler, ii. 20.

10. DRO, ECA, Exeter City Act Book, B 1/4 (1581–8), 206. The first part of this manuscript is a commonplace book covering the years 1559–76.

11. DRO, Exeter City Letterbook 60A (1524–99), fols 118–19v., fully calendared in HMC, *Report on the Records of the City of Exeter* (1916), 51–2 and discussed briefly by G.R. Elton, *The Parliament of England, 1559–1581* (Cambridge, 1986), 76.

12. *Lords Journals* (hearafter *LJ*), i. 593, 594, 600, 602, 603, 604, 606; *Commons Journals* (hereafter *CJ*), i. 64, 65, 66, 69, 70; HLRO, Original Acts, 5 Eliz., OA 34; DRO, Exeter Charter xxxix.

13. DRO, Exeter City Act Book B 1/3 (1560–81), 98.

14. Elton, *Parliament*, 69–70.

15. *LJ* i. 597, 598, 600, 602, 603, 604; *CJ* i. 69, 70, 72.

16. *LJ* i. 610; *CJ*, i. 71; Elton, *Parliament*, 217–19.

17. See Wallace T. MacCaffrey, *Exeter, 1540–1650: The Growth of an English County Town* (Cambridge, Mass., 1958), 196–7 and Muriel E. Curtis, *Some Disputes between the City and the Cathedral Authorities of Exeter* (History of Exeter Research Group, Monograph No. 5, Manchester, 1932), 44–54; DRO, Exeter City Act Book B 1/3, 128, 186, 241; Book 51 (Hooker's Commonplace Book), fols 109–111, 129v.–31v., 361; Exeter Misc. Rolls, 102 and 103.

18. See DRO, Exeter City Letterbook 60A, fol. 135v. (printed in HMC, *Exeter*, 52–3).

19. DRO, Exeter City Act Book B 1/3, 101.

20. *Statutes of the Realm* (hereafter *SR*), iv. 421. York also sought exemption: Elton, *Parliament*, 263–7.

21. HLRO, 5 Eliz., c. 3, OA 18; *SR*, iv. 411–14; Elton, *Parliament*, 268.

22. *SR*, iv. 441–3 (esp. clauses 7 and 8).

23. DRO, Exeter City Act Book B 1/3, 181.

24. *CJ* i. 76, 79, 80, 81, 89, 90, 91, 92; *LJ* i. 659, 660, 661, 698–9. Elton, *Parliament*, 257–8 errs in attributing all these bills to 1566.

25. T.E. Hartley (ed.), *Proceedings in the Parliaments of Elizabeth I, Volume i: 1558–1581* (Leicester, 1981), 252, 253, 254, 255; *LJ* i. 698–9; Elton, *Parliament*, 110; DRO, Exeter City Receivers Account rolls, 12–13 Eliz.

26. DRO, Exeter City Receivers Account Rolls, 13–14 Eliz. and Act Book, B 1/3, 267.
27. Elton, *Parliament*, 298; *CJ* i. 102, 103; *LJ* i. 723; Hartley, *Proceedings*, 403, 406, 409; HLRO, 23 Eliz. OA 24; *SR* iv. 702; DRO, Exeter City Act Book B 1/3, 15, 18; Receivers Account Rolls, 22–3 Eliz.
28. DRO, Exeter City Act Book B 1/3, 279.
29. *CJ* i. 113, 120.
30. Hartley, *Proceedings*, 384; Elton, *Parliament*, 254–5.
31. Hartley, *Proceedings*, 390.
32. *LJ* i. 744; *CJ* i. 113, 114, 115; Hartley, *Proceedings*, 491, 493; *LJ* ii. 27, 28, 66, 67; BL Egerton MS 2222 (Hayward Townshend's diary), fol. 87.
33. DRO, Exeter Merchant Adventurers Minute Book, 58/7/11, fols 95–5v., repr. Cotton, 129–30; *CJ* i. 128, 130, 132.
34. *CJ* i. 101, 103; *LJ* i. 723, 726; Hartley, *Proceedings*, 385, 401, 409; HLRO, 14 Eliz. OA 10; *SR* iv. 601.
35. *CJ* i. 121, 123, 130, 131, 132; Hartley, *Proceedings*, 531–2, 533, 540, 542, 543.
36. DRO, Chanter 41, 155–63.
37. DRO, Chanter 41, 164–6.
38. DRO, Exeter City Act Book B 1/4, 458.
39. Cf. Hasler, i. 146, 507–8, who also states that Brewerton 'corresponded with the city' about these matters, but his evidence has eluded me.
40. DRO, Exeter Merchant Adventurers Minute Book, 58/7/11, fols 121v.–2, repr. Cotton, 159–60.
41. DRO, Exeter Merchant Adventurers Minute Book, 58/7/11, fol. 122, not printed by Cotton.
42. Trinity College Dublin (hereafter TCD) MS 1045 (Thomas Cromwell's Diary), fols 81v., 86v., 89; D'Ewes, 364; Hasler, i. 542–3; *LJ* ii. 99, 101, 104, 105; *SR* iv. 725–6. Although D'Ewes records the MP as Richard Carey this must be Richard Carew as the former sat for Whitchurch, Hampshire only in 1597–8.
43. D'Ewes, 368; TCD MS 1045, fols 89v., 90v.; DRO, Exeter Merchant Adventurers Minute Book, 58/7/11, fol. 124v.
44. DRO, Exeter Merchant Adventurers Minute Book, 58/7/11, fols 130–1; Cotton, 131–2; J.R. Dasent (ed.), *Acts of the Privy Council of England 1586–87* (New Series, 1897), xiv. 21–2.
45. DRO, Exeter City Act Book B 1/5, 88, 123.
46. DRO, Exeter Merchant Adventurers Minute Book, 58/7/11, fol. 170v.; Cotton, 132; D'Ewes, 507, 513, 514, 519; BL Cotton MS Titus Fii, fols 62, 78, 90v.; *LJ* ii. 188, 189; HLRO, Main Papers 1593, fols 97–100; *SR* iv. 858–60; Paul L. Hughes and James F. Larkin, *Tudor Royal Proclamations, Volume iii: The Later Tudors (1588–1603)* (New Haven and London, 1969), 102–4.
47. BL Cotton MS, Titus Fii, fol. 53; Harleian MS 1888, 141; HLRO, MP 1592–3, fols 32–4.
48. D'Ewes, 394; BL Cotton MS, Titus Fii, fols 71, 76v., 90v.; HLRO, MP 1592–3, fols 29–31.
49. DRO, Exeter City Act Book B 1/5, 250, 251.
50. DRO, Exeter City Act Book B 1/6, 6, 8, 9.

51. BL Egerton MS 2222, fol. 153v.; D'Ewes, 684–5. Fustians: D'Ewes, 668; BL Stowe MS 362, fols 210v.–11.

52. *LJ* ii. 82, 85, 87, 89, 98; D'Ewes, 362, 368; TCD MS 1045, fols 88, 89, 90; HLRO, 27 Eliz. OA 33.

53. D'Ewes, 417

54. D'Ewes, 571, 572; Hasler, iii. 413; DRO, Exeter Merchant Adventurers Minute Book, 58/7/11, fols 212, 212v.

55. DRO, Exeter Merchant Adventurers, Book 185, and Merchant Adventurers Minute Book, 58/7/11; Cotton, *Elizabethan Guild*; MacCaffrey, *Exeter*, 136–48; DRO, Exeter Guild of Tailors Act Book, 1478–1600, fols 88, 88v.

56. Patrick McGrath, *The Merchant Venturers of Bristol* (Bristol, 1975), 10–23 and David Sacks, *Trade, Society and Politics in Bristol, 1500–1640* (New York and London, 1985), 596–605.

57. DRO, Exeter City Act Book B 1/5, 487.

58. BL Egerton MS 2222, fol. 29v.; Stowe MS 362, fol. 94v.; D'Ewes, 633; PRO, SP 12/282/50.

59. PRO, SP 12/282/49; MacCaffrey, *Exeter*, endmap; Beatrix F. Cresswell, *Exeter Churches* (Exeter, 1908), 47–9.

60. HMC, *Calendar of the Manuscripts of the Most Honourable The Marquis of Salisbury* xi (Dublin, 1906), 499; Hatfield MS 89/117 (BL microfilm 485/17).

61. Hasler, ii. 288.

62. Hartley, *Proceedings*, 342, 343.

63. WDRO, Plymouth Municipal Records, W359/7 (volume of correspondence), note of disbursements of Nicholas Slanning for 1566; WDRO, Plymouth Municipal Records, W131 (Receivers Book 1560–69), fol. 35 (1567); *CJ* i. 78, 80, 81; *LJ* i. 663.

64. WDRO, Plymouth Municipal Records, W132 (Widey Court Book 1569–1658), fols 60, 61; D'Ewes, 337, 345, 352–3, 353, 355, 361; *LJ* ii. 89, 95, 100, 101; TCD MS 1045, fols 75v., 80, 86v.; HLRO, 27 Eliz. OA 21; *SR* iv. 728–9.

65. BL Harl. MS 1888, 162; Cotton MS Titus Fii, fol. 65; D'Ewes, 510, 512; HLRO, MP 1592–3, fols 117–21; WDRO, Plymouth Municipal Records, W132, fols 93v.–4, 96v.

66. BL Cotton MS Titus Fii, fols 48, 65, 80v.; D'Ewes, 509, 510, 511; HLRO, MP 1593, fols 54–7; *LJ* ii. 185, 186, 189; HLRO, 35 Eliz. OA 24.

67. BL Egerton MS 2222, fol. 49v.; Stowe MS 362, fol. 134; D'Ewes, 647, 658, 674, 685; *LJ* ii. 248, 249, 251, 252, 254; Maurice F. Bond (ed.), (HMC) *The Manuscripts of the House of Lords* xi (New Series), *Addenda, 1514–1714* (1962), 63–5.

68. Elton, *Parliament*, 305.

69. D'Ewes, 641, 647, 661; *LJ* ii. 238, 240, 243; HLRO, Parchment Collection Box 1E, No. 3257, noted by Bond, *Manuscripts of the House of Lords*, 62–3.

70. D'Ewes, 339, 340, 341; *LJ* ii. 76; TCD MS 1045, fols 77, 78v., 79, 94; BL Lansdowne MS 43/72, fol. 172v.; HLRO, MP 1582–5, fols 34–44.

71. D'Ewes, 492, 645–6.

72. DRO, Totnes Borough Records, 1579A/16/36; HMC, *Salisbury MSS* xii. 71; Hatfield MS 85/73 (BL micro. 485/16).

73. DRO, Seymour of Berry Pomeroy Papers, 1392 M/L16/01/14.

# Landed Society and the Emergence of the Country House in Tudor and Early Stuart Devon

STEVEN PUGSLEY

In 1669 Cosmo III, Grand Duke of Tuscany, journeyed through Devonshire on his way from Plymouth to London.[1] It was characteristic of this county of predominantly small proprietors that the men who descended upon his Highness to pay their respects were of the landed gentry rather than the peerage: Edgcumbe, Prideaux, Sparke, Acland, Rolle, Ford, Kirkham, Bampfylde and Strode. Similarly, whilst it was recorded that the Grand Duke passed 'gentlemens' seats' between Okehampton and Exeter,[2] nowhere in the chronicle of his trip through Devon is there mention of the mansions of the greater aristocracy.

This impression of the Devonshire élite and their houses is substantially confirmed by the evidence of the Hearth Tax returns for Lady Day 1674.[3] As the earliest substantial body of data surviving to permit a systematic survey, the 1674 levy provides the most convenient point of departure for a review of seats in the county in the sixteenth and early seventeenth centuries. The Hearth Tax, which operated nationally between 1662 and 1689, involved the levying of a charge upon each hearth in nearly every dwelling, with certain exemptions. As a rule the occupier was liable for payment.[4] Although its interpretation can be fraught with difficulty,[5] the tax nevertheless provides a useful guide to the number of heated rooms which a building contained, and thus an indication of absolute and relative house size. The 1674 Lady Day returns are the most complete surviving for Devon. They reveal that several hundred houses had five or more hearths (roughly speaking, the minimum necessary for genteel existence). Of these at least 90 houses possessed 15 or more hearths, the great majority occupied by members of the county gentry: Arscott, Courtenay, Chichester, Fortescue, Walrond and so forth.[6] It is ironic that the list should also contain the name of Sir Courtenay Pole, who had promoted the tax in Parliament and had earned himself the sobriquet 'Sir Chimney Pole' for his pains.[7] His house at Shute was assessed at 29 hearths.

The house with the greatest number of hearths, to some considerable extent, was Wembury (returned in the name of a peer, the Duke of Albermarle) with 42. This would tend to support Polwhele's claim that 'Here the famous Sir John Hele, Serjeant-at-law in the reign of Queen Elizabeth, built a noble mansion-house exceeding in magnificence all other structures of the kind in Devonshire.'[8] Its size was shown to be somewhat less exceptional, however, in the lists made out by the Wembury Parish Constables for the 1662 Hearth Tax; then it had been returned at 30 hearths, with a separate entry for the gatehouse and outhouses of 13 hearths.[9] Even at 42 hearths, Wembury is significantly smaller than the vast piles recorded for purposes of the tax elsewhere in England. In 1663, for example, Combe Abbey was returned at 51 hearths and Stoneleigh Abbey at 70,[10] both in Warwickshire, a county which had 14 houses with more than 30 hearths in 1663[11] compared with Devon's one in 1674, despite the latter's greater extent. On the other hand, only 41 houses in Warwickshire had between 15 and 30 hearths, whereas the comparable figure for Devon was more than double. Amongst other counties in the South West, Dorset had at least four houses with over 30 hearths in 1662 (Sherborne Castle had 60),[12] whilst Cornwall had three in 1664.[13]

No single reason seems to account for the dearth of very large houses in Devon. Mineral wealth of the magnitude that helped to finance two of the largest Cornish houses, Godolphin and Lanhydrock, was largely absent. Generally speaking, the smaller the landholding, the smaller the house the landowner could afford to build upon it. Devon, as a county of old enclosure, had a preponderance of small to middling estates, and perhaps offered few opportunities for building up an extended estate from unenclosed tractable land. One can compare this with Warwickshire, where fortunes were made from stock farming on newly-enclosed land in the fifteenth and sixteenth centuries. By 1650 as many as 350 gentle families held the majority of Devon manors.[14] Even by the end of the following century, the situation had hardly changed: in 1794 Robert Fraser noted that 'the freehold property of the county of Devon is also very much divided . . . a few families excepted there are no very great proprietors . . .'.[15]

Of the greater landowners in Tudor and early Stuart Devon, two did not have a seat in the county at all. Henry VIII had granted John Russell, first Earl of Bedford, nearly 23,000 acres in south-west Devon alone, to support his position as President of the Council in the West.[16] Neither the first Earl nor any of his immediate successors chose to live in the county, probably because they were more than adequately seated elsewhere.[17] The Duke of Cornwall's absence was more predictable. As the patrimony of the monarch's eldest son, the Duchy of Cornwall was to all intents and purposes a part of the Crown lands, and as such it was no more likely to attract royal residence than other far-flung parts of the vast Crown estate.

As the Tudor state became increasingly centralized, so the movement of the monarch was ever more restricted to London and its environs. Elizabeth I was much given to progresses through the country, but she could not afford to abandon the capital for more than a month or two, and this perforce limited the extent of her travels. Bristol was the furthest point west the Queen reached.[18] The Devonshire élite in Tudor days did not, therefore, have the incentive—given to the likes of Bacon and Burghley—to build in anticipation of a royal visit. The early Stuarts were scarcely more venturesome. The visit of Charles I to Plymouth in 1625 was the only monarchical foray into the county between the accession of James I and the Civil War. It was on this trip that the lawyer Sir Richard Reynell was given the rare opportunity to entertain the King, at his newly remodelled seat of Ford House, Newton Abbot.

If the Court would not come to Devonshire, then Devonshire would go to the Court. Throughout the sixteenth century and on into the seventeenth, Devon men were increasingly attracted to the capital to attend upon the monarch, as well as to transact commercial or legal affairs, to be educated at the Inns of Court, or to sit in Parliament.[19] The greatest courtiers of the age to hail from Devon, Sir William Petre (*c.* 1505–72), sometime Secretary of State, and Sir Walter Raleigh (*c.* 1552–1618), failed, however, to furnish themselves with a seat in their natal county. Petre built up a considerable estate in Devon, but Essex became his adopted county—partly because Essex was the home of both his first and second wives, partly because he was fortunate enough to acquire a considerable amount of property there (including a portion of the estate of the nunnery of Our Lady and Ethelberga of Barking), and, perhaps most importantly, because Essex lay at a conveniently short distance from London for so prominent a government official.[20] Raleigh, despite holding high office in the far west (he was variously Lord Warden of the Stannaries, Vice-Admiral for Devon and Cornwall, Lord Lieutenant of Cornwall and

*Plate 10*

Ford House, drawn by J.P. Neale and engraved by E. Roberts, published 1818.

Member of Parliament for Devon, Cornwall, Dorset and the borough of
Mitchell) built himself a house at Sherborne in Dorset close to the London
road.[21] Both men were clearly motivated by considerations similar to
those of the nobility in Cornwall who, according to Carew, 'little affecting
so remote a corner liked better to transplant their possessions nearer to the
heart of the realm'.[22] More typical than either was Sir Arthur Champernowne, a member of the ancient Modbury family, who was well known at
Court, sat in four Parliaments for Devon seats and collected a small
number of plum offices (including the Vice-Admiralty of Monmouth,
presumably to help safeguard his shipping interests). Nevertheless, as a
man of relatively modest estate (assessed at £30 in 1576), he concentrated
his interests on the shire of his birth, becoming a JP for Devon in 1555
and Sheriff in 1559–60. Dabbling in former monastic property he purchased the site, barton and manor of Polsloe Priory in 1550, sold a portion
in 1554, and exchanged the remainder in 1559 for the manor of
Dartington, which place he made his principal seat thereafter.[23]

The house which Champernowne had chosen as his home possessed a
wider significance than merely as a residence of a country gentleman,
however distinguished. Dartington Hall, built by John Holand, Earl of
Huntingdon and later Duke of Exeter, between 1388 and 1400, was one of
the very first courtyard houses, the late medieval alternative to the castle
and an augury of the castle's eventual decline.[24] Dartington was also
marked out by its tremendous size, its vast north court being the largest
in a private house prior to the sixteenth century. Its scale befitted the
semi-royal status of Holand, who was half-brother to Richard II, and
reflected the extent of his retained household. Why Holand should have
determined upon his Devon estates as the location of his major seat is
unclear, although it has been suggested that the proximity of three of his
castles and anchorage for ships on the nearby Dart estuary persuaded him
of the merits of the place.[25] As to its lack of defensive features, it has been
postulated that they were felt to be unnecessary at a moment when
peaceful conditions attendant on Richard II's personal rule looked set to
continue.[26] That Holand, who owned castles and certainly had the means
to erect others, constructed a purely domestic building was a strong indication that the age of the true country house, built for comfort and show,
not defence, was tentatively dawning.

Hope of peace was not, however, realized, and without it the immediate
promise of an architectural renaissance was to be unfulfilled. Instead the
fifteenth century witnessed periodic bursts of disorder associated with the
Wars of the Roses and more localized expressions of personal and family

*Plate 11*

Dartington Hall, engraved by T. Bonnor, published by R. Polwhele, 1790.

*Plate 12*
Compton Castle, painted by John Swete, 1793.

animosities. Under these circumstances, whilst some manor houses like Bradley at Highweek retained a wholly pacific face throughout spells of rebuilding and addition in the 1400s, a number of fortified houses were constructed, too small and domestic in character to be thoroughgoing castles, but nevertheless having the trappings of defence. Affeton Castle at West Worlington was just such a fortified house, with a gatehouse built at some time between 1472 and 1488.[27] Bickleigh Castle near Tiverton was similarly a fortified house with a gatehouse of the fifteenth century. Bickleigh was held by a branch of the Courtenays, a clan involved in a long-running feud with another great Devon family, the Bonvilles, and the defensive treatment of the place was perhaps a response to the violent nature of the dispute. Undoubtedly, crenellation (whether or not sanctioned by an official licence) could be inspired by a desire to impress. But, equally, it could be entirely serious in purpose, and, thus strengthened, buildings could be perfectly capable of resisting concerted attack. Powderham, for instance, home of a junior Courtenay line allied to the Bonvilles, was a fortified manor house that withstood a siege of nearly two months' duration by Courtenay forces in 1455.[28]

The threat from local marauders did not provide the only motive for fortification. In coastal regions, particularly in south Devon, the risk of foreign incursion (particularly by the French) was keenly felt. The Pomeroy's house at Berry was turned into a properly defensible castle in the 1480s at the same time that much work was being undertaken on the defences of nearby Dartmouth. Compton, Marldon, is a good (and extremely late) example of an existing manor house given added protection. In 1520, during a period of French raiding activity on the south coast of Devon and Cornwall, Compton (which lies close to Torbay) was given a north curtain wall, dry moat walls on the other three sides, and five towers, to leave it with the appearance if not the actuality of defensibility.[29]

Even at the time it was enlarged, however, Compton was something of an anachronism, and it proved to be more or less the final outing of private fortification in the county. The declining incidence of foreign attack, coupled with the growth of internal security after about 1500, rendered such building work increasingly redundant. That is not to say, though, that something of the 'castle air' was entirely removed from later Tudor and Jacobean houses: witness the early sixteenth-century entrance tower at Holcombe Court, the late sixteenth-century gatehouse at Shute, and the possibly late sixteenth-century five-storey porch at Boringdon Hall, Plympton.[30] Even Mount Edgcumbe, begun in 1546 and in many respects a forward-looking house of revolutionary design, had the mass of a keep with prominent corner towers.

The gradual onset of political stability did not result in a swift efflorescence of seat building in Devon. Rather, there was a faltering crescendo leading to a sustained climax of activity from the 1560s. An examination of a provisional list of datable building work (both major and minor) in Devon in the sixteenth and early seventeenth centuries reveals a pattern strikingly similar to that observed elsewhere in the country. Between 1501 and 1560 some ten pieces of work are recorded, six of them in the period from 1546 to 1553. Between 1561 and 1620 the figure is nearer 48, declining to seven from 1621 to 1640 and six between 1641 and 1660. To take one example in comparison: in Warwickshire, whilst seven major country houses were built between 1500 and 1560, 20 arose between 1560 and 1630, but few thence forward in the reign of Charles I.[31] Furthermore, from a survey of four disparate counties, including Devon's neighbour Somerset, Lawrence Stone has concluded that the level of country house building in the 50 years from 1570 to 1620 was extremely high and far exceeded that of any subsequent half century.[32]

It is a commonplace that the Dissolution of the Monasteries from the 1530s produced a radical restructuring of landed society and led to the creation of new lay estates requiring new country seats. In Devon, at any rate, this generalization obscures a more complex situation.[33] In the first place, a considerable amount of the property the Crown had at its disposal was not monastic at all, but was secular and had fallen into its hands through confiscation and attainder. In the second place, Crown sales supplemented and stimulated, but formed less than half of, a wider land market. Moreover, it has been calculated that between 1536 and 1558 200 Devon manors may have changed hands through heiresses, as many as were granted by the Crown in the same period.[34] In the third place, very few men actually seem to have built up a sizeable estate in the county consisting wholly or predominantly of former monastic property—perhaps no more than seven in the first 20 years following the Dissolution.

Devon monastic lands neither went in large amounts to the local nobility (Russell's grant was entirely exceptional and in any case he was an absentee), nor were they widely dispersed among yeoman farmers. Of the monastic land alienated before 1558, 17 per cent went to Russell, 7 per cent to the dean and canons of Windsor, and 4 per cent to Sir William Petre, none of whom felt the need for a seat in Devon. Of the remainder, eleven per cent went to four owners (including two out-of-county peers) and a full 46 per cent passed to 75 grantees in small to medium sized

*Plate 13*

Boringdon Hall in Plympton, engraved by William Woolnoth, drawn by J.R. Thompson after a sketch by S. Prout, published 1800.

parcels worth between £1 and £100 a year—hardly of a magnitude to dislocate the established pattern of land ownership.[35] Many in this last group were middle-ranking men, often younger sons of well-established local families or scions of junior lines who acquired other land by purchase or already possessed a small estate of their own. Some, like John Arscott, a younger son of a minor north-west Devon gentleman, had made money in government service (he had been Surveyor of Woods Beyond Trent for the Court of Augmentations). Arscott bought three former monastic manors at second-hand in 1552, but chose to live on the non-monastic manor of Tetcott which he bought in the same year. Others, like John Drake of Musbury, sprang from the more stay-at-home local gentry: Drake nevertheless managed to build up an estate of once monastic land around his patrimony at Ashe, which his family had gained through marriage with an heiress in the fifteenth century.

Neither Arscott nor Drake appear to have indulged in constructing or reconstructing their seats, and on the whole other grantees of monastic holdings were equally disinclined to build, at least in the short term and on former conventual property. There were, of course, a few adventurous souls among the new owners. Richard Duke adapted part of the monastic buildings of Otterton priory into a house, and William Abbot, Henry VIII's Sergeant of the Cellar, turned a portion of Hartland abbey into a dwelling. Generally speaking, however, their example of conversion was not quickly followed. The Grenvilles do not seem to have modified Buckland abbey for domestic use until the 1570s when (highly unusually) they inserted a dwelling into the abbey church itself. Similarly, Torre abbey was not turned into a country house until the Ridgeways took it in hand after 1598, and Forde abbey had to wait until the 1650s before Sir Edmund Prideaux remodelled the remains into a seat.

It could be conjectured that a residual reverence for these once spiritual places inhibited the use of conventual buildings for secular habitation, or—more prosaically—that purchasers were unwilling to invest further on such property until the Protestant religious settlement was secure. In many instances the re-use of a monastic site did not take place until the manor on which it stood was sold off from the estate of the original grantee a generation or two after the redistribution: from being an appendage to an old estate it could thus become the focus of a new one. By that time, though, such a process had more to do with the workings of the ordinary, if expanded, land market than any enriching effects flowing directly from the Dissolution. The manors of Wembury and Broadhembury, for example, were granted to Thomas Wriothesley, Earl of South-

*Plate 14*

Ashe in Musbury, painted by John Swete, 1793.

*Plate 15*

Hartland Abbey in 1767, a view from the east.

ampton, in 1547. The former, late of Plympton Priory, was sold by the second Earl in 1579 to one Robert Chamberleyne, who in turn parted with it to the lawyer John Hele in 1592: Hele created his magnificent mansion from the remnants of a cell of the Priory.[36] The latter, late of Dunkeswell Abbey, was sold by the first Earl's grandson to Sir Edward Drewe, Serjeant-at-law to Queen Elizabeth: Drewe's son Thomas built a new house at the location of the abbey grange about 1610.[37]

The sites of erstwhile monastic buildings attracted later development, partly because having been quasi-domestic they usually possessed qualities desirable in a lay dwelling—easy access to a water supply, tolerably sheltered position, and so forth—and partly because they provided a ready source of cut building stone. Some individuals, indeed, regarded dissolved religious foundations as little more than quarries for construction materials. Vincent Calmady obtained permission from Queen Elizabeth in 1578 to collect stone and timber from the ruinous houses of Plympton Priory, and it is quite probable that this was destined for use in his fast-arising new seat at Langdon Court, Wembury parish.[38] Similarly, John Haydon, legal adviser to the city of Exeter and bencher of Lincoln's Inn, rebuilt his wife's family's home at Cadhay, Ottery St Mary, between 1546 and 1550. Having been appointed a governor of the church of St Mary in Ottery, following the surrender of the Warden of the College of Priests in 1545, Haydon apparently made liberal use of stone from the demolished college buildings for his new house. Certainly, in 1539 he had obtained the fabric of the church and other buildings of Dunkeswell abbey for £28 from John, Lord Russell, and it is quite conceivable that materials from there were 'plundered' for the same purpose.[39]

John Haydon chose to direct his building efforts upon an existing family estate—his monastic acquisitions were principally, after all, in the form of structures not land. But even amongst original grantees of quite sizeable holdings, electing to rebuild an ancestral seat was not unusual: both Sir Roger Bluett at Holcombe Rogus and Sir Thomas Dennis at Holcombe Burnell were notable in this respect.[40]

In sum, therefore, the Dissolution of the Monasteries had considerable impact, but—in terms of country houses, at any rate—produced no consistent effect in Devon. Moreover, it would be dangerous to assume that monastic pickings provided the sole spur to house construction, especially as several seats were built in the mid and later Tudor period by men who did not benefit directly from the Dissolution at all. The overall state of the economy—and its dominant component, agriculture, above all—is likely to have had a far more profound influence and, indeed, there is a

*Plate 16*

View of Cadhay House in Ottery St Mary, published 1820.

reasonably close correlation between periods of prosperity and heightened seat-building activity.

Broadly speaking, it was in the 1520s that the inflation of prices above fifteenth-century levels first became a significant phenomenon, and especially from the 1540s that landowners benefited from increased agricultural prices, entry fines and rents in relation to comparatively fixed expenses. Depression in the 1550s gave way to renewed economic vigour from the 1560s, and this persisted—albeit with a lengthy spell of stagnation in the last decade and a half of the sixteenth century—until the early 1620s. The 1620s and 1630s, on the other hand, were years of considerable economic difficulty.[41]

It is striking that country house building in Devon increased in momentum from the 1520s, was notably zestful in the late 1540s and early 1550s, but then became moribund until the later 1560s; the last third of the sixteenth century and the first fifth of the seventeenth were characterized by an upsurge of seat construction, thrown into higher relief by the slackening of activity from the 1620s that died away to virtually nothing in the 1640s and 1650s. A slight recovery is detectable towards the end of the Interregnum but, given a relatively prosperous agricultural sector c. 1640–63,[42] this might have been expected sooner had it not been for the accumulated indebtedness of many landowners, made worse by the dislocating effects of the Civil War and its aftermath.

It has been noted of the Caroline gentry in Devon that before the war began 'most of their estates were deeply mortgaged or encumbered in some way; few were care-free in this respect'.[43] This situation would not have been improved if they were numbered among the more than 200 royalist delinquents in the county whe were forced by parliament to pay for the recovery of their sequestered estates, fines levied varying between two and five years of the estates' annual value. Many also suffered severely from damage to property during the war. In 1642 and 1643 Edmund Parker of Boringdon lost corn and stock to the King's army:

> Besides the burning of his house with much wearing apparel of plush, velvet, and beaver hats, beads [?*sic*], bed clothes, curtains, vallances, hangings of rooms, table boards, chairs, stools, wainscot and all other household implements, with loss of much pewter and brass, in all to the value of £4,000. No man knowing how the unhappy accident befell.[44]

Colcombe Castle was so badly treated by the royalists in 1644 that the Poles never lived in it again, whilst their other seat at Shute sustained

£5,000-worth of damage in a parliamentary raid. Affeton Castle, the
Stucley residence, was destroyed, and the Carews' Bickleigh Castle was
thoroughly slighted.

Some, needless to say, did passing well out of the Commonwealth and
Protectorate. That a substantial refurbishment and an extremely important
remodelling scheme were both undertaken during this otherwise fallow
period by men with strong parliamentary links is surely not unconnected.
Edward Wise, son-in-law of the roundhead Lord St John of Bletsho, made
alterations and additions to Sydenham House at Marystow between 1654
and 1656.[45] Through his wife, Wise was distantly related to Oliver
St John, who became Lord Chief Justice of the Common Pleas in 1648
and who in 1653 began to build the outstanding Thorpe Hall, Northamptonshire to a design by Peter Mills. At the opposite end of Devon, Sir
Edmund Prideaux, Cromwell's Attorney General, set his major recon-
struction of Forde Abbey in train after 1649, classicizing the Gothic buildings of Abbot Chard.[46] To this task he brought to bear the profits of a
most successful legal career coupled with a fortune made from organizing
a weekly inland postal service.

Prideaux exemplifies, not only in the seventeenth century but
throughout the whole period under review, the two principal routes to
élite status and country house ownership, aside from birth and marriage:
the law and the fruits of office. Although not negligible, for reasons
already discussed, office holding was a less important source of wealth in
Devon than in counties nearer London. Devonshire, however, had a
remarkable propensity for breeding men to the law, many of whom were
the younger sons of county gentry and thus founded new county dynas-
ties themselves. Prideaux, indeed, was a second son: his father, Edmund,
a second son of Roger Prideaux of Soldon, Holsworthy, was likewise a
lawyer who became Double Reader of the Inner Temple and was prosperous enough to purchase and rebuild the seat of Netherton in Farway
parish and to acquire a baronetcy.[47]

Eminent Devon lawyers of the Tudor and early Stuart period are legion.
John Dodderidge (1555–1628), Solicitor General 1604–7, and a judge of
the King's Bench 1612–28, was born at Barnstaple and—although he
maintained houses in London and Exeter and a country residence at
Egham—his chief seat was Bremridge, in the parish of South Molton,
which he rebuilt in 1622.[48] Sir John Hele (c. 1542–1608), Serjeant-at-law,
amassed an estate worth more than £100,000: 'the vast wealth and riches
he acquired (with God's blessing) by his own industry', says Prince. As to
his new house at Wembury, 'the charges whereof could not be so little as

£20,000'.[49] Serjeant Drewe (*c.* 1534–98), likewise 'on the getting side', purchased extensive lands in Broadhembury, Combe Raleigh and Broad Clyst, and built himself a seat at Killerton in the latter parish.[50] Sir William Periam (1534–1604), Chief Baron of the Exchequer from 1593, retired to the estate he had bought near Crediton known as Little Fulford, 'where he built himself a fair house', according to Risdon.[51] Of an earlier generation, Sir Lewis Pollard (*c.* 1465–1540), ascended to be Justice of the Common Pleas: Prince remarks that 'he had very great practise in his time, whereby he was enabled to purchase a fair estate in this county, to himself and his family, at King's Nympton not far from Chulmleigh where he raised a handsome dwelling with a large park adjoining'.[52]

Other Devonians, no less worthy or learned in the law, could be included in the list. Occasionally the county attracted such figures to settle from elsewhere. George Rolle (1486–1552), for example, the Dorset-born Keeper of the Records of the Court of Common Pleas, accumulated considerable property in north Devon, and upon his freehold estate of Stevenstone he erected 'a right fair house of brick', probably between 1524 and 1539.[53]

At this date brick was an uncommon building material in the West Country. Apart from the gatehouse at Tawstock it was barely used again in Devon until the later seventeenth century. Rolle is likely to have become familiar with its use in the houses of Court connections and friends. In the same manner, many contemporary trends and fashions in architecture would have been introduced to the county by men who moved in cosmopolitan London circles. Perhaps the most adventurous of all Tudor residences in Devon, exhibiting a comprehension of Renaissance forms then rare in England, was added as a north wing to Berry Pomeroy Castle between 1547 and 1552 by Edward, Duke of Somerset and Lord Protector, the supreme architectural patron of his age. Prince describes the plainly classical loggia at the castle thus:

> Before the doors of the great hall was a noble walk, whose length was the breadth of the court, arch'd over with curiously carved freestone, supported, in the fore-part, by several stately pillars of the same stone of great dimensions after the Corinthian order, standing on pedestals, having cornices or friezes finely wrought; behind which were placed in the wall several seals of frieze-stone also, cut into the form of an escallop shell, in which the company, when aweary, might repose themselves.[54]

Ideas associated with the Tudor architectural renaissance were seemingly slow to be put into practice in Devon. In part this may be ascribed to the county's lack of easily-worked building stone which made the carving of classical detail far from easy. More fundamentally, the limited financial resources available to the owners of Devon's characteristically small-to-medium-sized estates tended to result in piecemeal alteration rather than in more thoroughgoing building schemes which would admit symmetrical exteriors of the type to be found elsewhere in England. Bradfield, Cadhay, Canonteign, Ford (Newton Abbot), Heanton Satchville, Sydenham and Warleigh are prominent among the very few pre-Restoration houses in the county to have possessed symmetrical façades.

At Collacombe, Lamerton, Edward Tremayne modernized his family seat around 1574. Tremayne, a Clerk to the Privy Council who had spent two years in Italy, was somewhat out of the run of ordinary Devonshire squires. Nevertheless, although the forecourt gateway, with Doric columns carrying an entablature, and the porch entrance, flanked by Doric columns supporting a pediment, suggest a degree of classical sophistication, there is little outside to conjure up the spirit of the Renaissance. The interior, however, features an elaborately-decorated hall, still of the conventional two storeys, but with an up-to-date plaster ceiling of the intersecting single rib and pendant variety which had become popular in England in the 1560s, a classical overmantel, the royal arms executed in plaster and five modelled satyrs concealing the brackets supporting an internal jetty.[55] Collacombe thus typifies the Devonshire inclination to adapt country houses to the prevailing taste by refurbishing the interior rather than by refashioning (usually at much greater expense) the exterior.

This applied as much to fittings as fixtures. Despite the grievous loss of the Exeter Probate Registry in 1942, sufficient household inventories survive in various forms to indicate that furnishings increased in quantity and luxury during this period. At Shute in 1559, for instance, the majority of the furniture had consisted of long boards, trestles, square tables, standing cupboards, joined forms, chairs of wainscot, bedsteads of wainscot and little in the way of hangings or upholstery.[56] This seems particularly spartan when compared with the contents of Columbjohn listed in 1646. These included cushions, two pairs of virginals, an organ, cloth-covered chairs and stools, a looking-glass, bed-hangings and a carpet. In the Red Chamber alone could be found one feather bed, a bedstead with curtains, one livery table, one couch, two chairs and three stools. In addition, there were a pair of bellows, a pair of andirons and a pair of tongs.[57]

*Plate 17*
Entrance to Collacombe in Lamerton.

The absence of such fireplace equipment from the Shute inventory should not necessarily be taken to mean that the rooms were unheated. Their frequent appearance in the Columbjohn list, however, underscores the progress of comfort and material culture that had taken place in Tudor and early Stuart Devon as much as in the rest of England, and helps to make understandable Sir Courtenay Pole's later enthusiasm for tax based on hearth numbers as an index of wealth.

The advance of luxury should not, however, obscure the central reality that throughout the period under review Devon country houses tended to be relatively modest in scale. Distance from London discouraged courtier mansions; non-residence of the county's two greatest landowners deprived it of houses commensurate with their status; and, above all, the characteristically limited extent of estates in Devon restricted the wealth from which funds could be drawn for building.

Such seat-enhancing activity as there was, was undertaken predominantly by country squires dependent upon agriculture for their finance, or by men whose incomes were derived from careers in the law. Although building work could be substantial (and, occasionally, remarkably ambitious), expenditure was typically upon remodelling rather than grand rebuilding and was often concentrated on interior refurbishment.

Modernization resourced from limited incomes continued to be the keynote of country house development in Devon in the later Stuart and early Georgian period. The newly-built country house on a compact plan made a tentative appearance in the late seventeenth century. However, architectural conservatism and financial restraint, which had distinguished landed society in Devonshire in the days of the Tudors, were by then well-established traits and were not easily overturned.[58]

## Notes

1. 'The Travels of Cosmo III, Grand Duke of Tuscany, through England', in R.P. Chope (ed.), *Early Tours in Devon and Cornwall* (Exeter, 1918, repr. Newton Abbot, 1967), 92–111.
2. Chope, *Early Tours*, 104.
3. T.L. Stoate (ed.), *Devon Hearth Tax Returns 1674* (Bristol, 1984), 3.
4. G.D. Chandaman, *The English Public Revenue, 1660–1688* (Oxford, 1975).
5. E.g., although the name of the occupier is listed in the return, the name of the house, generally speaking, is not. Some doubt occasionally arises as to whether the right occupier has been matched to the right house. Moreover, a house sometimes was divided for occupation by more than one family. In such a case the house could have more than one return relating to it, none of them truly reflecting its size.
6. Stoate, *Hearth Tax*.
7. Chandaman, *Public Revenue*, 76–7.
8. R. Polwhele, *The History of Devonshire* (Exeter, 1793–1806), iii, 454.
9. DRO, DQS, 79/1/33, Wembury Parish Constables list, 1662.
10. G. Tyack, *The Making of the Warwickshire Country House, 1500–1650* (Warwickshire Local History Soc., Occasional Paper 4, 1982), 39.

11. G. Tyack, *Warwickshire Country Houses in the Age of Classicism, 1650–1800* (Warwickshire Local History Soc., Occasional Paper 3, 1980), esp. 3–4 and 72, n. 3.

12. C.F. Meekings (ed.), *Dorset Hearth Tax, 1662–1664* (Dorchester, 1951), xxviii–xxix.

13. T.L. Stoate (ed.), *Cornwall Hearth and Poll Taxes* (Bristol, 1981), xxi.

14. W.G. Hoskins, 'The Ownership and Occupation of the Land in Devonshire 1650–1800' (unpublished PhD thesis, University of London, 1938), 23.

15. R. Fraser, *General View of the County of Devon* (1794), 17.

16. Hoskins, 'The Ownership and Occupation of the Land in Devonshire', 25.

17. Notably at Chenies in Buckinghamshire and later at Woburn in Bedfordshire; see D. Willen, *John Russell, 1st Earl of Bedford* (1981).

18. J.E. Neale, *Queen Elizabeth* (1934), 212.

19. E.g., see P.W. Hasler, *The History of Parliament: The House of Commons, 1558–1603* (1981), 3 vols; W.K. Willcocks, 'Devonshire Men at the Inner Temple', *DAT* xvii (1885), 246–65; J.C. Roberts, 'The Parliamentary Representation of Devon and Dorset, 1559–1601' (unpublished MA thesis, University of London, 1958).

20. F.G. Emmison, *Tudor Secretary: Sir William Petre* (1961), esp. 22–4 and Ch. 14.

21. See J.A. Youings, 'The Elizabethan Militia in the South West', 61–2, in R.A. Higham (ed.), *Security and Defence in South Western England before 1800* (Exeter, 1987).

22. F.E. Halliday (ed.), *Richard Carew of Antony: The Survey of Cornwall* (1953), 135.

23. Hasler, *House of Commons, 1558–1603*, i. 592–3; J.A. Youings (ed.), *Devon Monastic Lands: Particulars for Grants, 1536–58*, DCRS (New Series 1, 1955), 102.

24. See M.W. Thompson, *The Decline of the Castle* (Cambridge, 1987), Ch. 4; for Dartington, see esp. A. Emery, 'Dartington Hall, Devonshire', *Archaeological Journal* cxv (1958), 184–202.

25. C. Hussey, 'Dartington Hall Revisited', *Country Life* cxlv (1969), 179.

26. Emery, 'Dartington Hall', 188–90.

27. W.G. Hoskins, *Devon* (1954), 275; Sir Dennis Stucley, 'A Devon Parish Lost, A New Home Discovered', *DAT* 108 (1976), 1–13.

28. For Powderham and Berry Pomeroy, see R.A. Higham, 'Public and Private Defence in the Medieval South West' in Higham (ed.), *Security and Defence*, 40–6, and R.A. Higham, 'The Castles of Medieval Devon' (unpublished PhD thesis, University of Exeter, 1979).

29. For Compton, see A.W. Everett, 'Compton Castle,' *DAT* lxxi (1939), 343–5; *Compton Castle* (National Trust, 1985) and R. Haslam, 'Compton Castle', *Country Life* clxx (1981), 1546–50.

30. Hoskins, *Devon*, 276; Bridget Cherry and Nikolaus Pevsner, *The Buildings of England: Devon* (1989), 487–90, 729–30, 189–90.

31. M. Airs, *The Making of the English Country House, 1500–1640* (1975), 1; Tyack, *Warwickshire Country House, 1500–1650*.

32. Lawrence Stone, *The Crisis of the Aristocracy, 1558–1641* (Oxford, 1965), 551.

33. On the matter of the Dissolution of the Monasteries, as discussed here, see John Kew, 'The Disposal of Crown Lands and the Devon Land Market, 1536–58', *Agricultural History Review* xviii (1970), 93–105; John Kew, 'Mortgages in Mid-

Tudor Devonshire', *DAT* xcix (1967), 165–79; John Kew, 'Regional Variations in the Devon Land Market, 1536–58', in Michael Havinden and C. King (eds), *The South West and the Land* (Exeter, 1969), 27–42; Youings, *Devon Monastic Lands*; J.A. Youings, 'Landlords in England: The Church', in J. Thirsk (ed.), *The Agrarian History of England and Wales* (Cambridge, 1967), iv. 306–56.

34. Kew, 'The Disposal of Crown Lands and the Devon Land Market', 97.

35. Youings, *Devon Monastic Lands*, xx–xxix.

36. D. and S. Lysons, *Magna Britannia: Devonshire*, Pt 2 (1822), 49–50.

37. Lysons, *Devonshire*, 266.

38. WDRO, Introduction to Calmady Papers, Accession 372.

39. Youings, *Devon Monastic Lands*, 7.

40. For Holcombe Burnell and Holcombe Rogus, see Hoskins, *Devon*, 410.

41. Peter Bowden, 'Agricultural Prices, Farm Profits and Rents', in Thirsk, *Agrarian History*, iv.

42. Peter Bowden, 'Agricultural Prices, Wages, Farm Profits and Rents', in Joan Thirsk (ed.), *The Agrarian History of England and Wales* v (Cambridge, 1985).

43. W.G. Hoskins, 'The Estates of the Caroline Gentry', in W.G. Hoskins and H.P.R. Finberg (eds), *Devonshire Studies* (1952), 353. On the question of the financial state of the elite before the Civil War, see H.J. Habakkuk, 'Landowners and the Civil War', *Economic History Rev.* (2nd Series, viii 1965), 130–51; J.T. Cliffe, *The Yorkshire Gentry from the Reformation to the Civil War* (1969), Ch. 15.

44. HMC, Duke of Somerset MSS, 15th Report, Appendix, Pt. 7 (1898), 64.

45. A. Oswald, 'Sydenham House, Devon', *Country Life* cxix (1956), 1420–3 and cxx (1956), 16–19.

46. O. Hill and J. Cornforth, *English Country Houses: Caroline, 1625–1685* (1966), 111–18.

47. J. Prince, *The Worthies of Devon* (1810 edn), 650–3.

48. C. Stebbings, *A Man of Great Knowledge* (Exeter, 1989), 18.

49. Prince, *Worthies*, 485; *DNB*; Hasler, *House of Commons, 1558–1603*, ii. 287–8.

50. Prince, *Worthies*, 337; *DNB*; Hasler, *House of Commons, 1558–1603*, ii. 55–6.

51. Hasler, *House of Commons, 1558–1603*, iii. 209; T. Risdon, *Survey of Devon* (1811 edn), 95.

52. *DNB*; Prince, *Worthies*, 641.

53. 'The Itinerary of John Leland the Antiquary', in Chope, *Early Tours*, 7; Hoskins, *Devon*, 469.

54. Prince, *Worthies*, 649; Cherry and Pevsner, *Devon*, 168.

55. C. Hussey, 'Collacombe Manor in Devon', *Country Life* cxxxi (1962), 970–3.

56. DRO, Petre 123 M/E/98.

57. DRO, Acland 1148 M add/24/2–10.

58. Bridget Cherry, 'The Devon Country House in the Late Seventeenth and Early Eighteenth Centuries', *Devon Archaeological Society Proceedings* 46 (1988), 91–135.

# Breaking the Mould:
# North Devon Maritime Enterprise
# 1560–1640

ALISON GRANT

## *Introduction: North Devon on the Eve of Expansion*

In the sixteenth and early seventeenth centuries, westcountry merchants and seamen began to look beyond traditional European markets and open up trade and settlement further afield. Some built up contacts with Atlantic islands off the west coast of Africa, and a few sailed to the mainland of Guinea. Wartime voyages in search of Spanish and Portuguese prizes brought increasing familiarity with these southern waters where ships could pick up the trade winds and sail to the Caribbean in search of more plunder. Further north the Newfoundland fishery drew increasing numbers of ships across the Atlantic, and expeditions were sent out to explore and plant settlements on the American mainland. The part played in this expansion by South Devon ports like Plymouth and Dartmouth is well known, but the purpose of this study is to examine the contribution of the lesser-known ports on Devon's north coast to ventures beyond Europe in later Tudor and early Stuart times.

Barnstaple, a borough and market centre since Saxon times, was the largest north Devon town. Its corporation, after shaking off some ancient restrictions during the Reformation and securing virtually all manorial rights in 1565, ruled the town in the interests of its merchant members, whose main wealth came from seaborne trade, both coastal and foreign. In spite of silting in the river Taw, it was, in terms of trade, the leading north Devon port at this time. Its near neighbours, Bideford on the straighter, deeper river Torridge, and Appledore with a deep-water anchorage near the confluence of the two rivers, had greater natural advantages, but the former was said to be 'impoverished' in 1574, and the latter 'meanly inhabited' at about the same time.¹ Although beginning to expand their trading potential, they were not, at this time, in competition with Barnstaple.

Details of dutiable goods sent or received from overseas are to be found in some of the Exchequer Port Books, which were first kept in 1565. The Barnstaple books included records for Bideford and Appledore, the latter under the name of Northam, the parish of which it formed part. They also show that small trading ships were owned at other places with a shore or creek on the Taw–Torridge estuary, Heanton Punchardon, Instow, and Fremington, for instance. Ilfracombe, a harbour of refuge on the north coast, also had some trading vessels, but those owned up-river at Torrington, or westward along the coast at Hartland, where there was as yet no quay, would have traded from Bideford or Appledore.

Barnstaple port books for the 12 months from Easter 1565 to Easter 1566 show that almost all exporters were from corporate towns long established as centres for the cloth trade. Twenty-five Barnstaple merchants exported cloth to Spain and Portugal, and only one, a pewterer, sent anything else. Most of the trade was in kerseys, fairly coarse, lightweight, local cloths, usually about 12 yards long, hence the name Devon dozens. Few Barnstaple merchants traded on such a large scale as the six from Great Torrington, who, with another from the nearby village of Huntshaw shipped out 355 kerseys from a total of 1,489 exported during those 12 months. These records indicate that at this time Torrington was more prosperous than Bideford, where, in spite of a more favourable downstream position, only three merchants were exporting cloth.

North Devon attracted trade from more distant cloth centres. In 1565–6 three merchants from Tiverton, and one each from Exeter and Cullompton shipped 407 kerseys to 'Biscay'—27 per cent of the kerseys, and about 25 per cent of the total export of cloth. At a time when markets were uncertain, due to civil wars in France as well as depression and political unrest in the Low Countries, they may have been attracted to north Devon by its established trade with northern Spain. One merchant from Bristol also shipped cloth there, and last, but by no means least, a South Molton merchant, Richard Dodderidge, exported 100 kerseys, all to Biscay.²

The pattern of north Devon's trade in 1565–6 was already long-established, with exports of cloth, and imports of wine, dried fruits, oil, and salt from Portugal and southern Spain, and iron and a little wool from the Biscay ports. From the west of France came more wine and salt, vinegar, prunes, pitch and rosin. As in many provincial ports in the sixteenth century, each merchant's ventures were small enough to minimize over-heads and risks, and voyages were short enough to bring frequent returns. While this kind of trading brought even moderate prosperity there was no need to venture further afield, but the unsettled political and economic climate of the following years affected traditional markets, and helped to bring changes of direction. Places with little or no part in the cloth trade were already branching out; Northam, with the town of Bideford on one side and water on the other three, had no surrounding villages to produce cloth for export, and therefore specialized in building, owning and manning ships.

The north Devon port books of 1565 show Northam ships acting as carriers for merchants from Barnstaple and elsewhere. The majority of these vessels were probably built at Appledore, where there was a shel-tered creek with easy access to the Torridge. Bideford, where at East-the-Water 20 years earlier Leland had noted a 'pretty quick Street of Smiths and other Occupiers for Ship craft', was also a shipbuilding centre, and there is a record that a vessel of 250 tons was built there for an Exeter merchant in 1565. Vessels employed locally were much smaller, however, for in that year the six or seven Bideford ships trading overseas, together represented approximately 143 tons, and only three ships totalling 76 tons were recorded for Barnstaple, although it seems that a number of Barnstaple ships were hired by Bristol merchants at this time. Eight vessels owned in Northam accounted for 50 per cent of the total recorded tonnage of 594 tons in overseas trade in 1565–6. The largest was the *Jesus* of Northam, 80 tons, which sailed under a Northam master, as did a number of Barnstaple and Bideford ships. It is likely that many crewmen came from the same maritime parish.[3]

Northam, including Appledore as it did, was a large parish, with a growing population. Although numbers were also increasing in Barnstaple and other local parishes, Northam outpaced the rest. A recent demog-raphic study shows growth rates of 0.7 there in the mid-1540s, 0.4 in the 1550s, then 0.6 from 1560 to *c.* 1620.[4] The Northam register shows 112 boys baptized in the years 1540–9, 107 in the 1550s, and 140 in the 1560s.[5] Even after infant mortality and other ills had taken their toll, increasing numbers of young men became available in the period under discussion to join their elders as shipwrights, seamen and fishermen. The hope of employment at sea is also likely to have attracted immigrants from other parts of north Devon where there was population pressure, so Northam had every cause to seek and support maritime expansion.

## First Transatlantic Ventures: Newfoundland

Fishing voyages to Newfoundland are difficult to trace, because non-dutiable goods, which included provisions out and fish home, did not have to be recorded in overseas port books. Vessels which had made a fishing trip to the Banks, then sold their catch in European ports before returning home, were usually listed in from the last port visited, with no mention of Newfoundland. All coastal cargoes, however, had to be recorded, and in 1577–8 23 tons and 2 hogsheads of train oil processed from cod were shipped coastwise out of north Devon. Another 23 tons were shipped the next year, when some coastal cargoes also included Newfoundland fish.[6] Overseas records are not available to show whether the train oil, which was dutiable, came direct from Newfoundland, but the quantities seem too large to represent chance imports from other English ports or abroad, so north Devon ships were now probably among the westcountry vessels on the Banks, where English ships were said to have increased from 30 to 50 at about this time.[7]

The Newfoundland trade attracted not only small traders and enterprising master mariners investing spare capital, but also some of the richer merchants. Richard Dodderidge of South Molton, who had now moved to Barnstaple and become one of its leading traders, could afford to tie up ships and money in longer voyages, and, through contacts with Plymouth and other westcountry ports already in the Newfoundland trade, would have been well aware of the profits to be made. An indication that Dodderidge was among the first Barnstaple merchants in the trade is provided by the coastal port book of 1578–9, which shows that he sent four tons of train oil to Bristol and six to Chester, together with spices and dried fruit from Spain or Portugal, where, making use of his established trading connections, he could already have been selling cargoes of fish. If Dodderidge had not himself imported the train oil, other Barnstaple merchants may have ventured into the trade by this time. Before the end of the century, several of them had made enough money to have sizeable new ships built for voyages to Newfoundland; meanwhile there were ships and seamen to be hired at Appledore.[8]

The coastal port books of 1578–9 indicate that the growing Northam/ Appledore community played a part in establishing the Newfoundland trade, for William Leigh and John Edwards of Northam between them shipped the same quantity of train oil as Richard Dodderidge; four and six tons respectively to Bristol. The few surviving overseas records show that they and other Northam merchants and master mariners were also shipping home very large quantities of salt. Edwards was master of the 40-ton *Mary Edwards*, probably his own ship, which was one of three Northam vessels which returned from La Rochelle in June 1580. They brought in 37 'weys' of salt—probably about 37 tons—customs officers sometimes used the words interchangeably. Northam men predominated in the salt trade as early as 1565–6, when they shipped 144 weys out of a total of 197 into north Devon. Then, as later, William Leigh was the chief importer, bringing in salt with other goods from both France and Spain. He could have been supplying local fishermen, for he shipped 64 barrels of white herrings to London in 1577. Once involved in the Newfoundland trade, he and his fellow Northam merchants would have had little difficulty in finding ships, seamen, fishermen and supplies of salt.[9]

Records of north Devon's Newfoundland trade in this period are far from complete, but those that do survive provide interesting information. Vessels which brought train oil direct from Newfoundland to north Devon were listed in the port books—seven for instance in 1588–9. The trade was considered important as 'a nursery of seamen', and in 1594 six Northam ships and three from Barnstaple were freed from embargo to sail to Newfoundland. After the peace of 1604 there was steady growth: north Devon vessels which carried train oil home numbered 12 in 1612 and 16 in 1620. Although Barnstaple ships tended to be larger, Northam's were more numerous in the trade. In 1617 two Barnstaple vessels were listed as 60 and 100 tons, while six Northam vessels ranged from 30 to 60 tons. The fleet returning from Newfoundland that year also included a Braunton vessel of 40 tons, and the *Lyon* of Bideford, 20 tons. Family enterprise and merchant capital were both involved in this trade. A Northam vessel of 36 tons brought back 12 hogsheads of train oil and 16,000 fish for John Cock, who was also her master, the son of Philip Cock, a Northam ship-builder. His brother, William, was master of the larger of the two Barnstaple ships, the *Pelican*, which brought in 20 hogsheads of train oil and 8,000 fish for a leading merchant there.[10]

War with Spain and France between 1625 and 1630 seriously affected the fishing fleet. Eleven north Devon Newfoundlanders came under an embargo in 1625, although the mayor of Barnstaple wrote to say that several had already sailed. In 1628 John Delbridge, MP for Barnstaple, spoke for the whole of Devon when he complained in the House of Commons that the war had killed 'trade into France and Spain, then their fishing with Newfoundland. £100,000 a year came in thither by fishing.' Where he obtained this figure is impossible to say, but he was a merchant himself, and even if he exaggerated the sum, there was no doubt a severe loss, of which north Devon bore its share. Recovery followed peace in 1630, and three years later 14 vessels entered the port of Barnstaple with Newfoundland train oil. Anxious to keep the profits of a trade they had pioneered, westcountry ports opposed attempts by London merchants to establish a colony through which to control the fishery. The 'Western Charter' of 1634 not only prevented this, but also empowered the mayors of Barnstaple, Plymouth, Dartmouth, and other westcountry ports to regulate the seasonal fishery, which, in spite of all setbacks, continued as a mainstay of north Devon's trade into the eighteenth century, and did not entirely die out until the nineteenth.[11]

## Trade and Reprisal Voyages to Guinea: Richard Dodderidge

Professor K.R. Andrews has written of the emergence during this period of 'a substantial body of Londoners and outport men with a primary interest in extra-European trade . . . a gradual and cumulative movement of trading capital'. The pioneers of new, rich trades were 'remarkably often Anglo–Iberian traders' who combined shipowning and importing, in a period when there was a growing demand for luxuries from an increasingly affluent upper class. In north Devon, in the 1570s, imports of Portuguese colonial produce through Lisbon included such things as sugar from Brazil, 'calico-cloth' and spices from the east, and cochineal and pepper from Guinea. From Spain came dried fruits and sherry-sack, from the Azores green woad, a valuable dyestuff, and from Madeira and the Canary Islands wine. Such cargoes now drew a few north Devon ships regularly to the Atlantic islands, accustoming merchants to invest in longer voyages in the hope of better profits from direct trade. Mariners, venturing farther south and west than before, incidentally learnt much about Spanish and Portuguese settlements and shipping.[12]

The valuable Iberian trade of north Devon and other westcountry merchants was threatened by an unstable political climate made worse by English attempts to break into Spanish and Portuguese colonial trade, and the harsh retribution inflicted on those caught. In July 1561, for example, two Barnstaple and three Bristol ships laden with woad were impounded in the Azores by the Spaniards. By October some of the men were lame, 'destroyed with the torment they had given them'. In 1570 some of the crew of the 70-ton *Falcon* of Barnstaple, taken in a similar incident, were sent to the galleys. First reactions were cautious; in 1571 it was resolved that 'considering the Inquisition is so cruelly executed in Spain, the

*Plate 18*
Dodderidge's house, Barnstaple, drawn by Bruce Oliver.

merchants [of Bristol and Barnstaple] shall find it commodious for them to convert the most part of their trade into Portugal.'[13] This, however, had little effect, and in any case, Portugal was soon annexed by Spain. By that time many English shipowners and mariners had gone on the offensive, and armed their ships to seek reprisal for losses incurred.

'Reprising' provided unscrupulous owners and captains with a pretext for attacking and plundering foreign shipping. England was not at war with France in 1587 when Roger Norwood of Torrington, claiming injuries sustained by his ship *Zeraphyn* at the hands of a French warship, petitioned the Privy Council for 'letters to make stay of some Frenchmen's goods, or letters of license to be revenged as I may'. The *Zeraphyn*, a vessel of 180 or 200 tons, very large by north Devon standards, had probably been bought or built for privateering, so on this occasion may well have been 'the biter bit'. She had been accused of piratical intent when 'stayed' in Cadiz in 1585, but her officers later denied this on oath, blaming the Spaniards, whose king, Philip II, had ordered the arrest of all English ships in Spanish ports at that time. This action provoked many reprisal voyages, 'legalised' by the increased number of letters of marque now issued by the Crown.[14]

War with Spain after 1585 widened the horizons of merchants, shipowners and mariners, as ships sought and pursued the enemy westward into the Caribbean, or lay in wait for returning fleets off the Atlantic islands or the coast of Guinea. Although English cloth could be traded for Spanish and Portuguese products through French ports like La Rochelle, Bayonne and St Jean de Luz, such new arrangements were indirect, slow, costly and unreliable, and merchants anxious for a continued flow of imports and profits needed to look elsewhere. Some turned to privateering which was now both patriotic and profitable, while others sought new trading opportunities outside Europe. In north Devon, one merchant, Richard Dodderidge, did both.

Dodderidge, finding himself cut off from easy access to goods previously obtained in Lisbon, soon joined in a bid to import some goods direct. He was one of eight merchants named in 'A Patent granted to certaine Merchants of Exeter, and other of the West parts, and of London, for a trade to the river of Senega and Gambia in Guinea, 1588'. The man born and brought up in moderate circumstances in the small town of South Molton, was now among Devon's leading merchants, and the next year became mayor of Barnstaple. Family connections helped to cement trading partnerships, and John Darracott, another member of this Guinea Company, married Dodderidge's daughter in 1596. The partners in the new company were granted the monopoly of English trade with the Senegambia region free of customs duties for ten years. Thus motivated, Richard Dodderidge developed his interest in the Guinea trade.[15]

In Andrews' view 'the combination of shipowning and importing was the hallmark of the rich trades'.[16] Dodderidge may well have previously owned one or more of Barnstaple's relatively small vessels, or at least some shares in them, but for long voyages in wartime large armed ships were needed. Dodderidge therefore invested in the *Prudence*, a 100-ton vessel which sailed out over the bar with 80 men in 1590, ready for privateering as well as trade. Early the next year her return was recorded by Barnstaple's town clerk, Philip Wyot, in his diary:

> Arrived the Prudence, with a prize taken on the coast of Guinea, having in her 4 chests of gold to the value of £16,000 and divers chains of gold with civet and other things of great value. Such a prize as this was never before brought into this port.[17]

The port book shows that this vessel, brought 'from the seas by reprisal', was the 70-ton *Spiritu Sancto* of Lisbon, and that as well as the gold and civet she carried 72 hundredweight of 'elephants' tooths' and 183 hundredweight of grains (cochineal), typical imports from Guinea. The next year more gold, said to have been found in an old chest on board, was also declared. Dodderidge's partners in the venture, a merchant from Bristol, and the Barnstaple merchants James Downe and his younger brother Nicholas (Dodderidge's brother-in-law and son-in-law respectively), must have made appreciable gains on their investment, while Dodderidge, shipowner, trader and entrepreneur, was enhancing his status as well as his wealth. Before the end of the year one of his sons had married into the local gentry, and the *Prudence* had sent home two more prizes. In 1592 she captured yet another, which, according to Philip Wyot, was worth £10,000.[18]

Richard Dodderidge had 'struck it rich', but he also appears to have organized his privateering expeditions well; how long he remained in the Guinea trade is uncertain, but the patent went elsewhere at the end of the ten-year period. Possible evidence of a voyage or voyages after 1591 is to be found in the record in Barnstaple parish register of three black Africans baptized in 1596, 1598 and 1605. In 1596 there was also one burial, of a man who had been the servant of John Norris, a Barnstaple merchant also involved in privateering at this time; a few weeks earlier, the parish clerk had entered the first baptism of a black: 'Grace, a neiger servante of Mr Richard Doddridge'.[19]

## *Colonization and Privateering: Sir Richard Grenville*

Privateering attracted gentry as well as merchants, and in north Devon one of the most aggressive in the quest for plunder was Sir Richard Grenville, whose maritime interests incidentally helped to refound the fortunes of Bideford, where he was lord of the manor. He first used the port for expeditions to Ireland in 1568–9, although his attempts at planting settlements in Munster failed. In 1574, perhaps with an eye to the future, he made an alliance with Bideford merchants to secure the town a royal charter, which, while safeguarding his own rights, helped them establish a strong corporation as a sound basis for progress. Trade appears to have picked up, and 12 years later Grenville was able to use the port for a major expedition. According to a contemporary account,

> he returned to the river at Bideford, which is at the mouth of Barnstaple, and there he fitted out six ships, one of 150 tons and the rest from 100 down to 60 tons. With them and with 400 soldiers and sailors and provisions for a year he put to sea on 2 May 1586.[20]

In his diary for 1586, Philip Wyot noted both the departure of this expedition of Grenville's and its return to north Devon at the end of the year with a prize 'laden with sugar, ginger, and hides.'[21] Although Grenville went to great lengths to secure prizes, he had officially set out to supply the colony he had set up the previous year for Sir Walter Raleigh on Roanoke Island, part of the area newly named Virginia. The first expedition had set out from Plymouth, but for this second one Grenville must have recruited many north Devon seamen, some of whom were perhaps among the fifteen men he inadvisedly left on Roanoke Island when he found it deserted, the settlers he had left the previous year having, unknown to him, returned with Drake. The men Grenville left this time, however, were attacked by American natives, and never came home.

Grenville did not go back to Virginia, for although he had an expedition ready in Bideford in 1588, his larger ships were diverted to Plymouth to await the Armada. Two small Bideford ships, the *Brave* and the *Roe*, were allowed to set out under John White, who had set up a new Virginia colony the previous year. The masters and crews of these vessels set off in reckless pursuit of prizes, but met more opposition than they had bargained for. After a grim struggle and some loss of life, they abandoned the voyage, so no settlers or supplies reached Virginia that year. With this unfortunate episode, north Devon's connection with the earliest settlements in Virginia came to an end. Privateering, however, continued, and Grenville's ships brought a number of prizes back to Bideford before the last fight of the *Revenge* 'at Flores in the Azores' brought about his death in 1591.[22]

It is often forgotten that Grenville, who led expeditions to Virginia for Raleigh, had himself put forward the idea of planting English colonists in the new world ten years before Raleigh's Virginia project was conceived. At the last moment, however, Elizabeth I, fearing trouble with Spain, revoked the permission she had given Grenville to plant English settlements in South America as part of a project which would have taken him through the Straits of Magellan into the Pacific. Three years later, in 1577, Drake was allowed to carry out what was in effect Grenville's voyage without the settlements, thus gaining the glory and profit of the first English circumnavigation. Grenville had sought the support of a number of local gentry and merchants, 'the West Country lying the aptest of all parts of England for navigation southward'. In his argument for the voyage he also mentioned 'mariners and sailors to whom the passage almost thither [South America] is known', 'ships of our own, well prepared', the need to export cloth, and the chance of discovering treasure.[23] None of these ideas was new or original in 1574, but they had not before been gathered together and put forward by an influential man. They probably helped to convince others, as well as Drake, that the time had come to exploit at least some of the opportunities of the new world.

The extent of Grenville's influence on north Devon's expansion by sea cannot be documented, but it was he who had an American native christened 'Raleigh' in Bideford church in 1588, literally bringing home evidence of new lands to be explored, settled or opened up for trade. His privateering voyages and expeditions provided experience for many local seamen, and encouraged them to take risks in search of profit. It was dangerous employment, but if casualties were high so were rewards, and it was largely through Grenville that Bideford began to develop her potential, as north Devon men 'picked the lock of the New World'.[24]

## Colonization and Trade: John Delbridge

Towards the end of Elizabeth's reign English voyages of trade and exploration became widely known through the publication of Richard Hakluyt's *Principal Navigations*, so there was no lack of information for those interested in pioneering new trades. In Barnstaple, as in other westcountry ports, fine new houses bore witness to rewards gained by venturing outside traditional markets, yet for a time there was no sign of further oceanic enterprise. The Guinea patent had fallen into other hands, Dodderidge was ageing, Grenville dead, Virginia a lost colony, and in 1604 when peace with Spain put an end to the privateering free-for-all, merchants quickly resumed the cloth trade with their pre-war markets. Only the Newfoundland fishery drew north Devon ships across the Atlantic, until another Barnstaple merchant, John Delbridge, began to exploit some of the opportunities of the new century.

Delbridge, a successful cloth merchant and a leading member of Barnstaple Corporation, became one of the town's MPs in 1610. This gave him useful contacts, and he joined the Virginia Company of London in 1612, at a time when the Jamestown settlement had overcome some of its early problems. By 1616 tobacco was transforming the colony's economy, and the company promised land grants to anyone who could provide labour. Delbridge applied for a plantation, and in 1619/20 sent out 71 settlers on the 100-ton *Swan* of Barnstaple. Pleased with these 'choice men . . . out of Devonshire . . . brought up to husbandry', the Company resolved that 'some other ships might be sent out of Barnstaple by the help of Mr. Delbridge'. His importance in the early development of the colony was acknowledged when he was made a member of His Majesty's Council for Virginia in 1621.[25]

Delbridge also became involved with the settlement of Bermuda, having joined the Somers Islands Company, which had been set up in 1615 as an offshoot of the Virginia Company. In 1619 he volunteered to send out 30 or 40 'poor hard-working boys or girls which may do good service' for two of the promoters of the company, Sir Edwin Sandys and the Earl of Warwick. Although he was probably anxious to provide good settlers for the new colony, Delbridge also needed to cover the expenses of the voyage. Pointing out the 'extraordinary' cost of sending a ship to Bermuda, as 'our owners and mariners are fearful of that place, being ever reported a place very dangerous', he said he would need to charge £5 per passenger, or be 'in hazard to lose'. He also proposed to send some settlers of his own, four heifers and a bull, provisions for the voyage, and 'some quantity of meal and bread' for the emigrants to land with them, all aboard a vessel scarcely 100 feet on the waterline! The *Pelican* of Barnstaple had previously been in the Newfoundland trade, but Delbridge described her as 'a ship most fit for passage of people', so she perhaps had two decks, between which passengers could be accommodated with about 4' 6" headroom. Emigrants' passage money increased the profits of such voyages, but Delbridge provisioned his ships well, and was upset when, eight years later, three passengers died through circumstances beyond his control. At that time he wrote, '. . . having sent divers times small ships both to Virginia and Bermuda, and that full of people, I never lost man woman or child going or coming before this last voyage.' In spite of the three deaths, his record was probably unequalled in the period.[26]

John Delbridge did much to establish and maintain settlement in Bermuda. The vessel he sent in 1620 carried 'well-chosen labouring boys for apprentices', while the 'ladies and gentlemen of fashion' brought by the company's London ships, were as out of place in pioneer settlements as the poor, diseased wretches from Newgate who were sent to increase the profits of those who procured and shipped them. These London traders grudged Delbridge's small ship her return cargo of 10,000 pounds of tobacco, although the company's vessel took a full lading of 60,000 pounds.[27] Delbridge, however, steadfastly maintained his right to 'free trade' over the next ten years, and without his north Devon emigrants and the supplies he sent out each year the colony would have had far less chance of success. So, at least, the settlers themselves thought, as shown by a letter sent to the company by the island council in 1629:

> First, the least Barque that ever came from him [Delbridge] hath furnished the country with most needful commodities, as shoes, shirts, canvas, clothing, butter, cheese, meal, soap, nails etc., more than any London ship ever did and at far cheaper rates. Beside, if the poorest man among us send home to him an adventure of 20 or 30 or 40 pounds of Tobacco, he is sure of a return for what he writes for packed up for him, which under God hath given such encouragement to the poor inhabitants that they may subsist thereby with great comfort, and praise God for him.[28]

This unsolicited testimonial came at the end of a sustained effort by the Somers Islands Company to restrict trade to London ships. Having earlier imposed a levy of £2 on each of Delbridge's passengers and 2*d.* on every pound of tobacco he shipped, they refused, in 1626, to allow his ship to leave for home until the captain entered into a bond to pay off the accumulated charges. Delbridge then paid £200 to settle the quarrel, and in 1627 agreed not to send ships to Bermuda without the company's consent. When the company refused exemption for a ship already at sea, however, Delbridge wrote a long protest, declaring that even if he was not allowed to bring home tobacco he would continue to ship provisions for the settlers, who, he said, included 'at least a hundred poor souls' he had himself sent out.[29]

Delbridge appears to have had no trouble finding settlers; he wrote in 1619 that a number were 'willing to go' for him. Following the usual practice of apprenticeship in Barnstaple and elsewhere, they were indentured to him, probably for seven years, at the end of which they received a sum of money and one or two suits of clothing. Delbridge's factors in Bermuda, including his sister's son, Godheard Asser, who became a permanent resident, probably hired the men out, for most of Delbridge's own land was disappointingly barren. Many labourers worked 'at halves', sharing the tobacco crop they produced with their landlords. At least one of Delbridge's settlers did well enough to buy himself out early from his indentures, and in the end many may have been better off than labourers at home, where rising population was causing pressure on rural land and employment, and a consequent migration to towns and ports.[30] Tristram Risdon, a contemporary of Delbridge, thought Barnstaple so populous as to be 'little inferior to some cities', while Appledore might 'for multitude compare with some towns', so much had it grown in a generation. Successful propaganda had also led to a rising interest in emigration; the Virginia Company's lottery had been promoted in Devon in 1619, and although intended to stimulate investment, it also aroused great excitement among ordinary people. This 'circus' is known to have visited Torrington, and as the organisers would scarcely have failed to 'take in' Barnstaple, the largest town in the area, it is likely that a good many people in north Devon had heard Virginia described as a new Garden of Eden.[31]

In the event Virginia was no paradise for early settlers, and in 1622, 347 of them, probably including a number from north Devon, were killed in a native uprising. Delbridge, again at odds with London traders, had virtually left the Virginia Company, but continued to send north Devon ships to the colony. The range of his trading interests can be seen from the voyage of the 30-ton *Success* of Barnstaple at this time. After a fishing expedition to northern waters, she sailed to Virginia, where her catch helped to relieve settlers 'destitute of food', the Virginia Company having been too preoccupied by its own internal quarrels to send supplies to the survivors of the massacre. The vessel then went on to Bermuda, and finally arrived back in Barnstaple in 1624 with '7,566lb. weight of Bermudas tobacco value £1,491 10s., for John Delbridge, merchant'. Intercolonial trade made long voyages more profitable, and although New England ships later took over a good deal of it, a few north Devon ships were still to be found trading along the North American coast in the later seventeenth century.[32]

Delbridge had probably had such coastal fishing and trading voyages in mind in 1619, when he applied to the London Virginia Company for permission to fish at Cape Cod to offset the expenses of his Virginia plantation. Two Virginia Companies, however, had been founded in 1606, and the area north of 38°N. was controlled by the Plymouth Company under Sir Ferdinando Gorges. Delbridge therefore had to negotiate with this company, and its successor, the Council for New England, for fishing licences for north Devon vessels. He seems to have had to agree to police the system in return, for in 1622 the Council enquired 'what course Mr Delbridge of Barnstaple taketh against any touching abuses done in New England', and was told that he had taken out a warrant against five master mariners from north Devon. Five others, whose names were crossed out, may have paid up, for some were granted fishing licences a few months later. They probably owed this concession to Delbridge, who had actively pursued it.[33]

In 1623 a group of Barnstaple merchants was negotiating the purchase of a plantation from the Council for New England at a cost of £250, but there is no record that it was ever set up. Eight years later, however, Delbridge was granted a plantation of his own, probably to use as a fishing base, but no details of its whereabouts survive. In the 1630s, according to letters sent home from a plantation owned by a Plymouth merchant, north Devon ships were more numerous than any others off the coast of Maine. They were also good at their trade: one 'made a singular industrious voyage, far beyond ours, and no man can find the cause of the difference'; at another time 'a small bark of Barnstaple that came in here first, sold his goods at great rates . . .'. The correspondence shows that there was a good market for provisions, salt, fishing gear and ships' supplies, and mentions 'a ship of Barnstaple built here in the Country', the earliest reference to the colonial shipbuilding that was to remain an important feature of north Devon transatlantic trade for over 200 years.[34]

Many north Devon fishing vessels returned by way of Bilbao or San Sebastian to market their fish, while others traded south to the growing settlements of Massachusetts Bay and Plymouth Colony, which were attracting a number of emigrants from north Devon. Names are not always easy to trace, but the New England settler Richard Collicut was probably the Richard Collacott married in Barnstaple in 1627. The last record of his name in the Barnstaple registers was in 1633, when an infant son was buried. The tract of land Richard Collicut secured on Cape Cod had, by 1639, become Barnstable, Massachusetts. Appledore Island in the Isles of Shoals, in easy reach of good fishing off the coast of New Hampshire, may have been named at about the same time. It was, however, many years before a fishing harbour further north became Biddeford, Maine, although Bideford ships and settlers were in New England in the 1630s.[35]

One of the earliest Bideford emigrants was Abraham Shurt, who, as agent of two Bristol merchants, founded a fishing station and settlement at Pemaquid, Maine, probably in 1628 or 1629. The discovery by archaeologists of considerable amounts of north Devon pottery on the site shows that this settlement increased trade for north Devon as well as Bristol. In the 12 months from Christmas 1630 nine vessels left north Devon with cargoes for North America, three specifically listed for New England, and the rest for Virginia. At that time, however, the latter name often included New England, to which the majority of these vessels probably went, for few returned with tobacco from the south. As with Newfoundland, fishing vessels were not listed out unless they carried other goods, but some 'extra' ships returned from La Rochelle, not only with salt purchased there for the next fishing trip, but beaver and otter skins bought from New England settlers. The merchants in this trade included George Shurt of Bideford, who sent out blankets, perhaps for his brother's northern settlement. There was also a market for cattle, tools, clothing, household goods, firearms and woollen cloth, so even the more conservative Barnstaple merchants, Pentecost Dodderidge for one, now joined in transatlantic ventures. Like his late father Richard, he could recognize a good trading opportunity when it appeared; unlike him, he had not led the way.[36]

## Trade into the Caribbean

Voyages to Virginia probably initiated north Devon's trading contacts with the Caribbean, for in this period vessels sailed south to pick up the south-east trades, thus reaching West Indian outposts before turning north for Virginia. In the mid-1620s some 'merchants of Bastable in the west country' employed Anthony Hilton, a Durham man, as a factor on a voyage to Virginia. The mariners, 'passing by St Christopher [St Kitts] as they knew no other way, came a Shore and waited on the Governor Captain Thomas Warner . . .'. This inspired Hilton to return to set up a tobacco plantation. He moved to the neighbouring island of Nevis in 1628, where he founded a settlement. Thus the Barnstaple merchants, of whom John Delbridge, with his interests in Virginia, was probably one, played an indirect part in establishing an English colony in the West Indies.[37]

In the 1620s Delbridge imported most of his tobacco from Bermuda, but over-cultivation there ruined the land, as the governor pointed out in 1629:

> And as for this Island . . . in a short time it will be a very small value or profit, especially so much tobacco now being planted and brought home of better quality and from richer climates and plantations . . .[38]

The 'richer plantations' of the West Indies may have attracted John Delbridge as early as 1631, when the Privy Council called him to account for unloading tobacco in Barnstaple in defiance of a royal proclamation that it had to be landed in London. One source gives the origin of the disputed cargo as St Christopher, another Bermuda. His vessel may, of course, have called at both places. In 1632 restrictions on the import of tobacco were lifted, and the first certain indication that north Devon ships were now trading with the West Indies is found in the port book entry for the last day of that year, showing that the *Charles* of Barnstaple returned 'from St Christophers and Ireland'. She had left her home port on 10 April, arriving at Boston in early June with one or two emigrants. She may have set out for a fishing voyage, which would have given her a cargo to sell in Virginia or St Christopher. On her return she discharged not only Irish goods but salt taken on board at St Martin's (Isle of Rhé), where she had also called on the homeward voyage. This again suggests fishing interests on the part of her owners or charterers. They probably secured a fair return on each leg of the voyage, but the most valuable cargo was about 1,700 pounds of St Christopher tobacco, although this was not a great deal to show for a long voyage. It is possible that some had been sold in France or Ireland, in defiance of the regulation that it should be declared in an English port first.[39]

Tobacco was a perishable commodity, and small amounts were enough for many provincial merchants to risk. Some of the gentry took an interest in colonial ventures at this time, and Arthur Bassett and Humphry Cary, who respectively paid duty on 500 pounds and 80 pounds of the tobacco carried by the *Charles*, may also have had shares in her voyage. John Witheridge, the master, is also likely to have had a share in the venture, if not the vessel. His 400 pounds of tobacco valued at £100 probably represented a good return on his investment. The rest of the tobacco was shared out between several merchants, who imported between 100 and 300 pounds each. One name missing from the list was that of John Delbridge, whose trade was on a larger scale.[40]

In March 1633 the 80-ton *Friendship* of Bideford, and the 40-ton *John* of Barnstaple, arrived together from Virginia. The *John*, owned or part-owned by Delbridge himself, had sailed the previous summer with Barnstaple bayes and other cloth for Madeira, where she was in a favour-able position to go on to the Caribbean. She returned with 1,250 pounds of tobacco from Dulcina (Barbuda) and 4,164 pounds from Virginia. Like that brought by the *Charles* from nearby St Christopher, the *John*'s Dulcina tobacco was valued by the customs officer at 5s. per pound, compared with 3s. 4d. for her Virginia tobacco and 2s. 1d. for the 1,070 pounds Delbridge imported from Virginia in the *Friendship*. These figures reveal the reason for the sudden burgeoning of north Devon's Caribbean trade.[41]

Tobacco was not the only commodity brought to north Devon from the West Indies at this time, for in June 1633 the *Guift* of Barnstaple came home with dyewood and cotton. Adam Horden, her master, was one of those who sailed regularly to the New England fisheries, then, after catching his next cargo, took his ship 'tramping' wherever trade led him—in this case to Barbados. The *Guift* was the last vessel home from the Caribbean in 1633; and, with most subsequent Barnstaple port books lost, there is no evidence of any further connection until 1640. The arrival of the 80-ton *Greyhound* of Bideford from St Christopher in November that year marked both a beginning and an end. She carried over 20,000 pounds of tobacco, presaging the large-scale trade which would make fortunes for Bideford merchants after 1660. She was also the last recorded vessel to return to north Devon from the Carribbean before the Civil War.[42]

## Conclusion: Continuity and Context

In the 25 years before 1640 voyages from north Devon to the new world had become commonplace, and, in spite of periodic reverses caused by depression and war, there had been considerable economic expansion. It is not easy to say, however, whether earlier efforts to trade outside Europe had contributed to this, or were merely disconnected incidents. North Devon's first ventures outside European waters had occurred in the sixteenth century. One of them, Richard Dodderidge's pioneering venture into trade with Guinea, was not followed up after 1600. Without the incentive of privateering with which it was associated, this trade promised little, and would have needed greater capital than most north Devon merchants were either willing or able to invest. On the other hand, privateering, although brought to an end by the peace of 1604, had played a significant part in expansion by helping merchants and shipowners accumulate capital. It had also given seamen knowledge of oceanic voyages, which could be passed on to succeeding generations.

Grenville's Roanoke voyages, although they appear to have had no immediate results in north Devon, increased local awareness of Virginia, if only through tales told by returning crewmen, and the sight of an American native in Bideford. These voyages from home waters to the new world must also have given Barnstaple's leading merchants plenty to discuss. In 1584 Delbridge had joined their ranks by his marriage to the daughter of Henry Downe, whose family was associated with Dodderidge's privateering ventures.[43] With such connections a young man could hardly fail to take a keen interest in potential opportunities in the new world. Although the expansion of his own trade began only after he met the promoters of the Virginia Company founded in the next century, the interest of the man who sent out the *Swan* of Barnstaple with settlers for Virginia in 1619/20, could well have been kindled when Grenville set out for the new world from north Devon some 35 years earlier.

John Delbridge was the key to most of north Devon's seventeenth-century expansion into transatlantic trade. With his knowledge of ships and voyages, of the kind of people who would make good settlers and of the supplies needed to sustain them, he played a greater practical part in planting and maintaining settlements than most of the London entrepreneurs who sought to exclude him. Known even in his lifetime as 'the free trader', he tried to open up a place for his fellow townsmen and other outport merchants in new world trade. In Bermuda, the Somers Islands Company prevented this, and by the 1630s with the tobacco crop failing, there was little to pursue there in any case. The Virginia Company having destroyed itself through internal quarrels, Virginia came under the Crown in 1625, after which it was harder for London merchants to keep others out, although restrictions were placed on the import of tobacco for a time. By the 1630s, however, others besides Delbridge were sending north Devon ships to Virginia, and the way was prepared for a trade which, after the Restoration, would expand to make fortunes for large-scale importers of tobacco into Bideford.

Transatlantic fishing voyages provided continuity throughout the period, stimulating seamanship, shipping and trade. Thanks to Delbridge's negotiations for licences, north Devon ships were among the earliest to exploit the rich New England fisheries, and take their catches to Virginia and further south to the Caribbean. In the 1630s they were also busy supplying settlements in New England, a profitable trade while it lasted, especially when combined with good fishing voyages. Ironically, the settlers they helped to take out and establish in New England shortly afterwards took over both the fisheries there, and the coastal and inter-colonial trade. The Newfoundland trade, however, continued, free to all prepared to face the rigours of northern voyages and risk attacks from foreign ships from time to time. Over the years north Devon shipowners, merchants and masters took such risks, and many of them reaped profits.

North Devon's expansion should perhaps be viewed in the context of other Devon ports and towns. The seafaring and fishing community of Appledore, within the parish of Northam, was to Barnstaple as Dartmouth to Totnes—a useful deep-water anchorage and source of ships and seamen for an old-established town poorly situated some miles upstream, but with commercial contacts, goods to trade, and capital for voyages. This was a good partnership for expansion in this period, and although Northam's growth did not match Dartmouth's in degree, it was much the same in kind. Topsham played the same role *vis-à-vis* Exeter, sending a considerable number of vessels to Newfoundland. Most city merchants were more interested in the export of cloth than expansion outside Europe, but some did become involved in distant voyages.[44] Plymouth, with a smaller stake in the cloth trade, the best harbour in the South West, an enviable position for Atlantic trade, and men like the Hawkinses and Drake, was able to lead the way to the new world.

Barnstaple therefore had some examples to follow, and also some negative incentives to branch into distant trades, being smaller and less well-placed for European trade than the ports or cloth centres of the south. Apart from the common western interest in fishing voyages, the greatest enterprise was shown by two individuals, Richard Dodderidge and John Delbridge, whose remarkable contributions arose from the context of their times and the opportunities they discovered and exploited from north Devon.

## Notes

1. John Watkins, *An Essay towards a History of Bideford* (Exeter, 1792, repr. Bideford, 1883), 20; T. Risdon, *Survey of the County of Devon* (1811, repr. Barnstaple, 1970), 287.

2. PRO, E190, Exchequer, King's Remembrancer Port Books, 925/1, 925/10; J.A. Youings, *Tuckers Hall Exeter* (Exeter, 1968), 2.

3. Lucy Toulmin Smith (ed.), *The Itinerary of John Leland* (1907), ii. 171; HMC *Report on the Records of the City of Exeter* (1916), 376; J. Vanes (ed.), 'Documents Illustrating the Overseas Trade of Bristol in the Sixteenth Century', *Bristol Record Society* xxxi (1979), 156–7, 145; PRO, E190,925/1, 925/10; NB There are some probable errors in the records of Bideford vessels in these port books, which makes it impossible to give their exact number and tonnage.

4. A.L. Wilson, 'Contributions to the Historical Demography of the Taw–Torridge Region of North Devon' (Paper presented to British Association, 1977), 7. Growth rates may be a little inflated, as mariners who died at sea or abroad were not buried in their home parishes.

5. NDRO, Northam Parish Registers for the years shown. Numbers quoted may not be quite exact as the Northam clerk did not always write in 'son' or 'daughter', and some names could be used for either boys or girls.

6. PRO, E190/930/34, 931/6, 931/12.

7. Richard Hakluyt, *The Principal Navigations, Voyages, Traffiques and Discoveries of the English Nation* (Everyman 1907, repr. 1926), v. 344.

8. PRO, E190/931/12.

9. PRO, E190/925/1, 925/10.

10. PRO, E190/935/9; M.M. Oppenheim, *The Maritime History of Devon* (Exeter, 1968), 36; PRO, E190/941/5, 944/8, 943/9; WCS, Moger Wills, P. Cocke.

11. M.F. Keeler, M.J. Cole and W.B. Bidwell (eds), *Proceedings in Parliament 1628* (New Haven and London, 1977–83), II. 314; PRO, E190/948/10; C.B. Judah 'The North American Fisheries and British Policy to 1713', *Illinois Studies in the Social Sciences* xviii, nos. 3–4, (Urban, Ill., 1933), 78–82.

12. K.R. Andrews, *Trade, Plunder and Settlement* (Cambridge, 1984), 18–21.

13. Vanes, *Overseas Trade of Bristol*, 154–7.

14. *CSPD 1581–90*, 449; DRO, Z16/1/3/14, Depositions *re Zeraphin* of Torrington. Alison Grant, 'Matters of Controversy: The *Zeraphyn* of Torrington', *DH* 43 (October 1991), 4–8.

15. Hakluyt, *Principal Navigations*, 285–91; Andrews, *Trade, Plunder and Settlement*, 112.

16. Andrews, *Trade, Plunder and Settlement*, 20.

17. 'The Diary of Philip Wyot, Town Clerk of Barnstaple from 1586–1606', in J.R. Chanter, *Some Striking Incidents in the History of Barnstaple* (Barnstaple, 1866), 96–8.

18. PRO, E190, 935/14, 939/3; T. Wainwright (transcriber), *Barnstaple Parish Register 1538 AD–1812 AD* (Exeter, 1903). The marriages entries for 1591 show Robert Dodderidge married Margaret Ackland, from a leading local family.

19. Wainwright, *Barnstaple Parish Register*, baptisms and burial for years quoted.

20. 'The relation of Pedro Diaz', in D.B. Quinn (ed.), *New American World* (1979), iii. 327.

21. Wyot, 'Diary', 92.

22. Quinn, *New American World* iii. 323–5; A. Grant, *Grenville* (Appledore, 1991), 36–8.

23. R. Pearse Chope, 'New Light on Sir Richard Grenville', *DAT* xlix (1917), 237–8.

24. NDRO, Bideford parish registers—Baptism of 'Raleigh a Wynganditoian' 1588, and his burial 1589; Charles Kingsley, *Westward Ho!*, Ch. 1.

25. A. Grant, 'John Delbridge, Barnstaple Merchant, 1564–1639', in S. Fisher (ed.), *Innovation in Shipping and Trade* (Exeter Maritime Studies 6, University of Exeter 1989), 93, 96; S.M. Kingsbury (ed.), *The Records of the Virginia Company of London* (Washington DC, 1906–35), i. 259, 351, 409–10, 473; iii. 309.

26. Vernon A. Ives (ed.), *The Rich Papers* (Bermuda, 1984), 127–9, letter from Delbridge to Sandys, 1619.

27. J.H. Lefroy (ed.), *History of the Bermudas* (Hakluyt Society Publications, 1882), 188; A. Grant, 'Bermuda Adventurer: John Delbridge of Barnstaple, 1564–1639', *Bermuda Journal of Archaeology and Maritime History* 3 (1991), 1–17 *passim*.

28. Ives, *Rich Papers*, 305.

29. J.H. Lefroy, *Memorials of the Bermudas or Somers Islands, 1615–1685* (1882), i. 444–8.

30. Ives, *Rich Papers*, 127–9, Letter of 1619; Bermuda Archives, Colonial Records, I/3 Assize Courts Record, 11 Apr. 1626, Discharge of John Davies.

31. Risdon, *Survey of Devon*, 287, 327; C. Andrews, *The Colonial Period of American History* (New Haven, 1934), i. 137–8.

32. Kingsbury, *Virginia Company Records*, i. 373; 945/7.

33. Kingsbury, *Virginia Company Records*, i. 277; *CSPC 1574–1669*, 33–4, 37, 45.

34. *CSPC 1574–1669*, 46, 157; James Phinney Baxter (ed.), *The Trelawny Papers* (Portland, Me., 1884), *passim* and 143.

35. A. Grant, 'The Name's (Almost) the Same', *North Devon Heritage* 3 (1991), 30; D.G. Trayser (ed.), *Three Centuries of a Cape Cod Town* (Hyannis, Mass., 1939), 29.

36. A. Grant, *North Devon Pottery: The Seventeenth Century* (Exeter, 1983), 123; E.A. Churchill, 'Colonial Pemaquid', in H.B. Camp, *Archaeological Excavations at Pemaquid, Maine, 1965–1974* (Augusta, Me., 1975), ix–x; PRO, E190/947/9.

37. V.T. Harlow (ed.), *Colonising Expeditions to the West Indies and Guiana, 1623–7* (Hakluyt Soc. 2nd Series lvi, 1924), 4.

38. Ives, *Rich Papers*, 321.

39. *CSPD 1631–33*, 141, 252; *APC Colonial* I, nos. 209, 269, 271; PRO, E190/948/10; A.M. Burge, 'Emigration from Devon and Cornwall 1623–38', *DCNQ* xvii. (1932–3) 67.

40. PRO, E190/948/10.

41. PRO, E190/948/10.

42. PRO, E190/948/9; 951/5.

43. Grant, 'John Delbridge', 91.

44. W.B. Stephens, 'Roger Mallock, Merchant and Royalist', *DAT* 92 (1960), 288.

# English Wine Imports
## c. 1603–40, with Special Reference to the Devon Ports

W.B. Stephens

Wine was one of the four chief commodities imported into England in the early modern period (the others being textiles, timber and groceries),[1] yet historians have devoted relatively little attention to analysis of the extent and nature of the trade either in Elizabeth I's reign or in the period covered in this essay. Simon's standard work[2] certainly devotes a whole volume to the seventeenth century, but he is more interested in the retail trade than in imports, and though providing much useful data often fails to give precise and identifiable citations for his sources, and, moreover, presents statistics of wine imports of doubtful validity. Francis' recent monograph[3] discusses the early seventeenth century only briefly and tends to accept Simon's import figures. This essay seeks to provide fuller information, and to suggest that the early seventeenth century was a period when the volume of wine imports was particularly large compared with preceding and succeeding periods, and for certain ports extremely significant.

### National Import Statistics

For Henry VIII's reign Schanz has published annual statistics of English wine imports based on the enrolled customs accounts (PRO, E356),[4] and these are summarized in Table 1A. They suggest an annual average import into the country of some 10,000 tuns. On the grounds that Simon 'estimated [that] the total imports of wines may at times have reached 30,000 tuns' in Henry's reign, Francis suggests that Schanz's figures are 'perhaps on the modest side', but this seems unlikely. Although Schanz's totals are based on the recorded imports for London and fifteen of the provincial ports, these last include all ports likely to have been of significance in the trade. His figures must embrace the bulk of the trade. Simon provides no reference for his statements that for the years 1509–18 imports 'must have reached an average of 50,000 tuns a year', that those for 1529–34 'probably averaged 20,000 tuns a year', and that for 1535–57 imports amounted 'to about 30,000 tuns yearly'.[5] These seem improbably large when compared with Schanz's well-documented figures, even if Simon's totals perhaps included privileged wine exempt from duty.

Again, the suggestion by Simon that wine imports for 1558–9 'were about 25,000 tuns', for 1559–60 'very nearly 100,000', for 1560–1 'about

TABLE 1

*Wine Imports, 1509–1546 (tuns)*[a]

| A   Annual national averages[b] | |
| --- | --- |
| 1509 | 9,820 |
| 1519–29 | 9,810 |
| 1529–39 | 10,947 |
| 1539–46 | 9,403 |

| B   Annual averages at main wine-importing ports, 1541–2 to 1545–6[c] | |
| --- | --- |
| London | 5,303 |
| Bristol | 1,358 |
| Southampton | 450 |
| Exeter and Dartmouth | 378 |
| Plymouth and Fowey | 189 |
| Poole | 117 |
| Hull | 96 |

(a) Deduced from G. Schanz, *Englische Handelspolitik gegen Ende des Mittelalters* (Leipzig, 1881), ii. 128–50.

(b) These are for regnal years 1–2 Henry VIII through 37–8 Henry VIII (22 April 1509–21 April 1510 through 22 April 1545–21 April 1546). Figures for 38 Henry VIII (22 April 1546–28 January 1547), provided by Schanz, are not included in these calculations.

(c) These cover the five regnal years 33–4 to 37–8 Henry VIII (22 April 1541–21 April 1546), except for Hull where the average is of the four regnal years 1541–2 to 1544–5.

70,000', for 1561–2 'about 60,000', for 1562–3 'only 25,000 or 30,000', and for 1563–4 'nearly 60,000 tuns, and perhaps more'—an annual average of 'about 58,000' for those years, and one which he claims 'remained practically unaltered or only slightly lower until the last years of the century when [there was] a sharp decline' to 'approximately 35,000 or 40,000 tuns per annum' for 1595–1600,[6] are, to say the least, puzzling. Not only does Simon give no reference whatever as to his sources, but his later figures conflict markedly with the evidence of the Exchequer customs records. Those for London show the wine imports of the capital (which must have accounted for some 60 per cent of the trade)[7] to have amounted to a mere 4,319 tuns in 1579 and to have averaged only some 5,000 tuns annually for the years 1561, 1562, 1567 and 1568, and about 7,000 tuns annually for the years 1597, 1599, 1600, 1601 and 1602.[8] Moreover, the annual aggregate of the imports of three of the four most important provincial wine ports at the turn of the century was probably smaller than London's import: in 1600, less than 500 tuns were imported into Southampton and into Exeter (with member ports), and records indicate that less than 2,000 tuns were unloaded in Bristol in 1601 (see below, page 168). Again, a French source put the annual average import of French wine into London over the years 1591–1604 at about 5,000 tuns, and about 8,000 for London together with the provincial ports.[9] Since the amounts of Spanish wine imported in those years of war with Spain were much smaller than those of French wine,[10] annual totals certainly fell far short of Simon's figures. This problem could no doubt be resolved without great difficulty: overall annual import figures for all the ports for the latter half of the sixteenth century are available in the enrolled customs accounts, which the Exchequer continued to maintain after the period for which Schanz used them until just into James I's reign.[11]

Such a course is not, however, possible for the period covered by this paper. The enrolled accounts were no longer kept from soon after the accession of James I and the later Inspector General's ledgers had not yet begun. It is not surprising, then, that there are—so far as I am aware—no published national statistics of wine imports for the early decades of the seventeenth century, for the means of easily compiling them are lacking.[12] To fill the gap (in so far as that may be possible), historians will need to analyse, among other records, all the surviving port books for each port. These documents provide details of individual import consignments of wine, with some indication as to type, quantity, names of importers, and details of whence importing ships came. A comprehensive analysis of the port books would, however, be a colossal undertaking. No such daunting task is attempted here. Instead a more modest exercise has been undertaken. This has involved first-hand analysis of a limited number of port books, with an emphasis on those of the more important outports and of some Devon ports, to which has been added data from similar investigations by others already in print and from the unpublished tables of London wine imports compiled by the late Dr A.M. Millard.[13] All this has been augmented by information culled from other customs accounts: those of the receipts of the duties known as 'new impositions on foreign wine' (for years in the 1620s) and 'increased duties on wine' (for the later 1630s), which are found in two Exchequer record classes: E122 (King's Remembrancer, particulars of customs accounts) and E351 (Lord Treasurer's Remembrancer, declared customs accounts).[14]

## The Distribution of the Import Trade

Table 2 presents figures compiled from the records of these extra duties collected on wine for the years for which they are available. The records provide data also for some months in 1622 and 1635–6, but since these were not for full years they have not been included in the table. Similarly, for the years 1637–41 small amounts of imported wine which are not broken down in the accounts by port of entry have also been omitted.

TABLE 2

*Imports of French and Spanish/sweet wine, 1623–4, 1637–41 (tuns)*[a]

| Headport | 1623 | 1624 | 1637 | 1638 | 1639 | 1640 | 1641 |
|---|---|---|---|---|---|---|---|
| Berwick | 10 | 0 | 53 | 72 | 19 | 136 | 78 |
| Boston[b] | 183 | 126 | 187 | 268 | 203 | 113 | 93 |
| Bridgwater | 61 | 47 | 68 | 105 | 70 | 59 | 23 |
| Bristol | 1,498 | 1,760 | 2,550 | 3,220 | 3,150 | 2,229 | 1,979 |
| Cardiff[c] | 0 | 40 | 65 | 99 | 5 | 0 | 4 |
| Carlisle | 0 | 0 | 0 | 0 | 0 | 0 | 0 |
| Chester[d] | 386 | 325 | 806[e] | 1,053 | 772 | 456 | 334 |
| Chichester | 68 | 50 | 32 | 57 | 69 | 42 | 30 |
| Exeter | 532 | 465[f] | 857 | 872 | 995 | 584 | 579 |
| Gloucester | 0 | 0 | 0 | 0 | 0 | 0 | 0 |
| Hull | 1,047 | 1,144 | 2,267 | 2,411 | 2,679 | 1,360 | 1,722 |

| Headport | 1623 | 1624 | 1637 | 1638 | 1639 | 1640 | 1641 |
|---|---|---|---|---|---|---|---|
| Ipswich | 424 | 599 | 750 | 861 | 885 | 606 | 486 |
| King's Lynn[g] | 283 | 400 | 395 | 605 | 507 | 80 | 326 |
| Milford[h] | 11 | 71 | 2 | 2 | 2 | 1 | 0 |
| Newcastle | 232 | 255 | 327 | 611 | 669 | 378 | 149 |
| Plymouth | 288 | 347 | 431 | 608 | 616 | 339 | 324 |
| Poole | 168 | 174 | 272 | 438 | 312 | 680 | 251 |
| Sandwich[i] | 420 | 301 | 1,020 | 987 | 775 | 745 | 469 |
| Southampton | 800 | 901 | 1,358 | 1,467 | 1,517 | 870 | 708 |
| Yarmouth, Gt[j] | 176 | 576 | 990 | 1,085 | 169 | 529 | 351 |
| Dover[i] | — | — | 3,899 | 4,205 | 5,981 | 3,874 | 2,642 |
| London | 14,121 | 13,232 | 15,896 | 30,420 | 28,668 | 16,398 | 18,815 |
| Totals | 20,708 | 20,813 | 32,225 | 49,446 | 48,063 | 29,479 | 29,363 |

(a) PRO, E351/900–01, 903–4 (for 1623, 1624); E122/198/7 (1637, 1638); E351/906–10 (1637–41). Years are for twelve months ending at Michaelmas of the year stated. The sources distinguish French and Spanish wines (except for 1641), but these figures have not been reproduced here, though those for London, Bristol, Hull, Southampton and the Devon and Cornish ports are given in the Appendix. For averages across these, see Table 3 below.

(b) R.W.K. Hinton, *The Port Books of Boston, 1601–1640* (Lincoln Record Soc. l, 1956), App. B, pp. lii–liii, provides figures for wine imports (derived from the Exchequer port books) for various years 1601–2 through 1634, none of which coincide with the years in this Table, but which suggest that the figures above for Boston were typical.

(c) Cardiff imported 37 tuns in 1598–9 and 40 in 1602–3 (Michaelmas to Michaelmas); Swansea (with Neath)—a member of Cardiff—imported 31 tuns in 1600–1 (Michaelmas to Michaelmas): Lewis, *Welsh Port Books* (as text n. 20), 23, 37–40, 48.

(d) See W.B. Stephens, 'The Overseas Trade of Chester in the Early Seventeenth Century', *Trans. Historical Soc. of Lancashire and Cheshire* cxx (1968), 33, for breakdown into French and Spanish. In 1602–3 (Michaelmas to Michaelmas) Chester imported 219 tuns: D.M Woodward, *The Trade of Elizabethan Chester* (Hull, 1970), 136, based on E190/1328/20.

(e) E122/212/19 gives 771 tuns of French wine imported in the year ended 25 March 1637. The source cited in this table gives 710 tuns for the year ended Michaelmas 1637.

(f) Approx.

(g) King's Lynn imported 369 tuns in the year ended Christmas 1621: E122/101/46. For imports in the later sixteenth century, to 1598–9, see N.J. Williams, *The Maritime Trade of the East Anglian Ports, 1550–1590* (Oxford, 1988), 296–7.

(h) Lewis, *Welsh Port Books*, 177–9, 182, 190, 193, 195, 206, 232, shows Milford in the years 1598–9 to 1602–3 importing very little wine direct from Europe—most came via Ireland.

(i) Some wine imported at Dover, 1637–41, is included under Sandwich. Cf., for 1636, E122/198/7.

(j) For imports in the later sixteenth century, to 1597–8, see Williams, *Maritime Trade*, 297–8.

They were in aggregate so insignificant[15] that their omission is unlikely to affect any conclusions drawn from the data in the table.

Table 3 more clearly illustrates the comparative distribution of the trade. While many ports were importing some wine, certain of them stand out as particularly significant. The pre-eminence of London (with 68 and 64 per cent in 1623 and 1624, and about 50 to 65 per cent of the trade in the later 1630s)[16] is not surprising. Of the outports in the years in the 1620s and 1630s for which we have comprehensive totals, Bristol, Hull and Southampton were the most consistently important, with wine imports far exceeding those of the other provincial ports (except Dover in the 1630s, a special case discussed below). As for those other provincial ports, they appear to fall roughly into three groups. A group of five ports

TABLE 3

*Rank order of wine-importing ports, 1620s and 1630s*[a]

| Headport | Average annual import (tuns) |
|---|---|
| 1. London | 19,650 |
| 2. Bristol | 2,341 |
| 3. Hull | 1,804 |
| 4. Southampton | 1,089 |
| 5. Exeter | 698 |
| 6. Sandwich | 674 |
| 7. Ipswich | 659 |
| 8. Chester | 590 |
| 9. Yarmouth, Gt | 554 |
| 10. Plymouth | 422 |
| 11. Newcastle | 374 |
| 12. King's Lynn | 371 |
| 13. Poole | 328 |
| 14. Boston | 168 |
| 15. Bridgwater | 62 |
| 16. Berwick | 53 |
| 17. Chichester | 50 |
| 18. Cardiff | 30 |
| 19. Milford | 13 |

(a) Based on data in Table 2 above. As indicated in the text, Dover, as a special case, is excluded here: its average annual import, 1637–41, was 2,943 tuns.

whose annual wine imports averaged between about 550 and 800 tuns was headed by Exeter in the west, with substantial average imports of over one-third of those of Hull and some 70 per cent of Southampton's. Other ports in this group, and therefore reasonably significant in the trade, were geographically well distributed: Chester in the north-west, Sandwich on the south coast, and Ipswich and Great Yarmouth in East Anglia. A second group, with average imports of between about 170 and 420 tuns, embraced Plymouth and Poole in the West Country, Newcastle in the north-east, the East Anglian port of King's Lynn and Boston in Lincoln-shire. The third group, with average annual imports of 60 tuns or less, comprised five ports of comparatively little significance in the trade.

The provincial ports named in Tables 2 and 3, however, represent head-ports together with member ports. Thus the wine imports against 'Plymouth' include those of all the Cornish ports; those against 'Exeter' embrace the imports of Dartmouth and the north Devon ports; the data for 'Poole' are for Poole, Weymouth and Lyme Regis. That some of these member ports were importing more wine than those headports listed at the lower end of Table 3 is illustrated for the westcountry ports in Table 4. That table also illustrates that, at least for 1635–6 for which we have evidence, while the wine trade of Dartmouth was quite important, Exeter dominated its members in that trade. In the headport of Poole, however, it would appear that the shares of Lyme Regis and Weymouth were greater than that of Poole itself.[17] As for Plymouth, it was usually the case that the headport's trade accounted for the bulk of the import. Cranfield's records of Spanish wine imported for parts of the years 1613–14, 1616–17 and 1617–18 (but covering the months when most wine was imported) show totals of, respectively, 91, 71 and 41 tuns for Plymouth and 22, 15 and 46 tuns for the combined Cornish ports.[18] Other examples of significance include Colchester, which in 1635–6 accounted for one-third of the wine imported into the port of Ipswich, and Liverpool, which in the same year imported half of the intake of the headport and members of Chester.[19] In 1636–7, too, of French wine imported into 'Chester', Chester itself accounted for 526 tuns, Beaumaris 3 tuns, Liver-pool 232 tuns and Poulton 11 tuns.[20] The totals against Bristol, Hull and Southampton in Tables 2 and 3, however, represented almost entirely wine imported into those ports, for none of them had members with any trade in wine to speak of.[21] The considerable difference between the scale of the wine trade at these three ports compared with all other provincial ports, is, therefore, enhanced when this is taken into consideration.

TABLE 4

*Distribution of imports of wine within westcountry ports,*
*1 November 1635–29 September 1636 (tuns)*[a]

|  | *French* | *Spanish* | *Total* |
|---|---|---|---|
| *Headport of Exeter* | | | |
| Exeter | 221 | 268 | 489 |
| Dartmouth | 48 | 86 | 134 |
| Barnstaple | 114 | 23 | 137 |
|  | 383 | 377 | 760 |
| *Headport of Plymouth* | | | |
| Plymouth | 222 | 188 | 410 |
| Padstow | 0 | 4 | 4 |
|  | 222 | 192 | 414 |
| *Headport of Poole* | | | |
| Poole | 0 | 45 | 45 |
| Lyme Regis | 105 | 25 | 130 |
| Weymouth | 115 | 32 | 147 |
|  | 220 | 102 | 322 |

(a) E122/198/7. E351/905 gives a total for Exeter of 755 tuns and for Plymouth of 416 tuns for the same period.

Comparison of the average wine imports for 1541–2 to 1545–6 (Table 1B) with those for the 1620s and 1630s (Tables 2 and 3) suggests that the relative significance of London, Bristol and Southampton, and to a lesser extent Exeter and Plymouth, was of long standing, but that the wine trade of Hull, while significant in the fourteenth and fifteenth centuries, does not seem to have been relatively so important in the early sixteenth century[22] as it became again in the seventeenth.[23]

The extent of the trade of Dover revealed in Table 2 is intriguing. In 1623 and 1624 it is not recorded in the new impositions returns as importing wine, and the Dover port books before the later 1630s show only relatively modest amounts of the commodity being imported there: in 1604–5 113 tuns, in 1616–17 247 tuns, in 1628–9 157 tuns, and in 1634–5 657 tuns.[24] The records of the increased duties on wine for the 1630s, however, indicate that whereas the tax was levied on wines entering London at 20s. a tun and on those coming into the outports at 13s. 4d., the vast bulk of wine imported into Dover attracted duty of only 3s. 4d. a tun.[25] Why this should have been so has not been discovered, but it seems likely that as a consequence Dover was taking wine in the later 1630s which would otherwise have gone through London, and that Dover was not, except in those years, one of the main wine ports.

The Appendix (on pages 167–72) draws together, from various customs records, data on the quantities of wine imported into London and the three provincial ports most significant in that trade—Bristol, Hull and Southampton, together with figures for Exeter, Dartmouth, Barnstaple and Plymouth. The Appendix confirms what is shown by Table 3—that London dominated, that Bristol stood out as the most important provincial wine port, with Hull and Southampton respectively second and third, and that Exeter's trade, while significant, fell well behind. As was also suggested by the data in Table 4, it demonstrates that within the port of Exeter, Exeter itself accounted for the bulk of the traffic, though Dartmouth had a respectable trade. The tunnage imported at Barnstaple (which embraced Bideford) appears to have been generally smaller. Plymouth, which had been the fourth most important outport for wine in the mid-sixteenth century (Table 1B), did not compare with Exeter in the early seventeenth century as a wine port, but its imports were not inconsiderable and were greater than those of otherwise more important ports, like Poole and its members (Table 2).[26]

## Chronological Fluctuations in Imports

More generally, the chronological distribution of wine imports into the ports represented in the Appendix indicates (as do the data in Table 2) substantial fluctuations in the volume of trade from year to year. As with other trades, this reflected to a considerable degree political and other events outside the control of the merchant community—in particular, English relations with foreign powers. Embargoes, customs duties used as political weapons in peace, and the impact of wars and piracy, all affected trade. The wine trade was also affected by the general state of English commerce, particularly by the fortunes of the cloth export trade. Thus, in the early years of the seventeenth century, an increase in Spanish wine imports is discernible after the peace of 1604 in the figures for London, Exeter, Bristol and Southampton, though with Dartmouth the effect is less obvious.[27] Again, the trade crisis related to the Cockayne project and the commercial troubles of the early 1620s, which had an adverse impact on English cloth exports,[28] may well have had detrimental effects on wine imports of the provincial ports—the Hull merchants in the early 1620s complained to the Privy Council: 'Our trade, is the exportation of [cloth] . . . into the Eastland; and also the same goods, with lead, into Germany, Holland, and France, for the vintage; all of which, at present, we find much to be decayed.'[29] Certainly Hull's wine imports for 1623 and 1624, when trade generally was beginning to pick up, were considerably greater than those for 1622. Southampton merchants, too, at this time indicated a connection between the level of their sale of English cloth abroad and that of their wine imports.[30]

In the later 1620s war with Spain (1625–30), prohibition of French wine imports in 1626, war with France in 1627, and continuance of political difficulties for merchants even after peace with that country in 1629,[31] affected English trade generally and the wine trade in particular.[32] Again, import and export trades were shown to be linked, and decline in the staple cloth export trade undoubtedly had an adverse impact on imports.[33] The fall in wine imports in these years is illustrated for London, Exeter and Southampton in the Appendix.[34] The Southampton port books show no French wine being imported in the last two quarters of 1627 or the last quarter of 1629.[35]

The less troubled period entered into in the 1630s is reflected in a very considerable increase in wine imports in the early and middle years of that decade over the levels of the 1620s at London and at the three most important outports (Bristol, Hull and Southampton), as well as at Exeter. Re-emergence of political difficulties in the years immediately preceding the outbreak of the Civil War, which included wrangles between the merchant community and the Crown over the King's attempt to impose extra duties on the wine trade (of which more below), must have been a cause in the decline in wine imports evident in the figures for all five ports in 1640 and 1641. Table 2 shows a similar decline in the wine imports at Chester, Dover, Ipswich, King's Lynn and Newcastle in those years, at Great Yarmouth from 1639, and at Poole and Sandwich in 1641.

However, fluctuations in amounts of wine imported, illustrated in Table 2 and the Appendix, are not explicable solely in terms of politically-inspired trade crises and influences of that kind. Trade in wine was very much affected by the nature of the supply, which in its turn reflected variations in weather conditions. Both the quantity and the quality of vintages differed from year to year,[36] and this must have affected the level of English imports in different ways. Further complications in assessing fluctuations in imports result from the relationship between the time of the vintage (at varying periods in September and October) and the dates covered by the fiscal returns on which historians rely for trade statistics.[37] Since the accounting year ran from Michaelmas to Michaelmas, for the new impositions on wine of the 1620s, the extra duty on wines of the 1630s, and for the port books before 1605 shipments of one season's vintage probably fell within a single fiscal year. But the port books from 1605 were compiled for years beginning at Christmas, so that, since wine was shipped in quantity largely from October through March or April, a single year's port book from 1605 contains imports from successive vintages—but not in any predictable ratio (as is illustrated for Exeter in Table 5). Too subtle a comparison of figures given for individual years in the Appendix is therefore inappropriate.

## Types of Wine Imported

The Appendix also provides a breakdown of total imports into French and Spanish wines, and this requires some comment. First, however, it may be noted that in this period some wines from the Rhine valley ('Rhenish' wines) were imported. Since the extra duties of the 1630s were not levied on these wines, they are not represented in the totals in Table 2, and so, for comparative purposes, have been omitted from the wine imports presented in Table 4 and in the Appendix (except for London),[38] although

TABLE 5

*Chronological pattern of wine imports at Exeter, 1634–5, 1635–6 (%)*[a]

|  | 1633–4 | | 1635–6 | |
|---|---|---|---|---|
|  | *French* | *Spanish* | *French* | *Spanish* |
| Christmas to April | 33 | 44 | 25 | 100 |
| May to September | 25 | 24 | 19 | 0 |
| October to Christmas | 42 | 32 | 56 | 0 |
|  | 100 | 100 | 100 | 100 |

(a) E190/949/3 and /9. Years run from Christmas to Christmas. Dates are those when duty was entered in port books.

the port books do in fact record them. The quantities of Rhenish wine imported were, however, very small.[39] Over the six years ended at Michaelmas 1612, for instance, the average annual import of Rhenish wine into London and the outports together was said to be about 259 tuns.[40] London itself probably accounted for most of this: it averaged an import of 198 tuns a year in the seven years 1600 to 1603, 1606, 1611 and 1615. This fell to an annual average of only 59 tuns in the seven years 1619, 1620, 1628, 1630, 1632, 1633 and 1637,[41] as the Thirty Years' War saw the destruction of German vineyards. Similarly, Bristol, King's Lynn and Hull customs records show little or no Rhenish wine being imported.[42] Exeter does not appear to have imported Rhenish wine until the post-Restoration period, and then in relatively small quantities.[43]

Turning to other wines, only at London is there evidence of other than French or Spanish (or 'sweet'—see below, page 167) being imported in quantities worth noting. Of such imports muscadel, imported from the Levant direct and via Spain and Italy, was the most important, though only in 1619 did it amount to any significant proportion of the capital's intake (Table 6). As for the kinds of French and Spanish wines which embraced the vast bulk of England's wine imports, the customs records, on which this paper is largely based, do not enable us to add materially to

TABLE 6

*Imports of muscadel and Corsican wines into London, 1606–37 (tuns)*[a]

| Year | Muscadel | Corsican | PRO reference |
|------|----------|----------|---------------|
| 1606 | 292 | o | E190/13/1,3 |
| 1611 | 148 | 139 | E351/896 |
| 1615 | 496 | 32 | E190/18/2 |
| 1619 | 2,051 | o | E190/22/4; 23/5 |
| 1620 | 179 | o | E190/24/3 |
| 1628 | 446 | o | E190/32/6,7 |
| 1630 | o | o | E190/35/1 |
| 1632 | 149 | o | E190/36/4; 37/3 |
| 1633 | 673 | o | E190/37/4 |
| 1637 | o | o | E190/35/7 |

(a) Deduced from Millard portfolio (see text n. 8). E190 references are for twelve months ending at Christmas of the year stated; E351 reference is for the twelve months ending at Michaelmas 1611.

what is already known. The new impositions returns recorded only 'Spanish or sweet' and 'French' without any further qualification, and it is these categories which have been followed in Tables 4, 5 and 9, and the Appendix. It should be noted, however, that while Spain and its Atlantic islands did not have a monopoly of sweet wines, and though all Spanish wine was not 'sweet' in the modern sense, contemporary customs officials used the terms 'Spanish' and 'sweet' interchangeably to mean any wine from Spain[44] and from the Canaries. Nevertheless, 'Spanish'/'sweet' wine imported via France or the Netherlands retained its label in the Exchequer records, as did 'French' wine imported via other than French ports, though it is likely that, at times of embargo or of other difficulties interfering with direct trade with France or Spain, French wine may have been imported as Spanish and vice versa.[45]

Throughout the period London's imports of French wine greatly exceeded those of Spanish/sweet wine. In the provincial ports as a whole, too, much more French than Spanish wine was imported—81, 82 and 81 per cent respectively in the years ending at Michaelmas 1637, 1638 and 1639, for example.[46] Spanish wine was imported in large quantities only at London, Bristol, Exeter, Southampton and Hull, with greater proportions at Bristol and Exeter than at Southampton or Hull. In 1638–9 and 1639–40 only London, Dover, Sandwich, Hull, Southampton, Exeter (with Dartmouth) and Bristol imported any Spanish wine.[47]

The port books, as opposed to the records of the special duties of the 1620s and 1630s, do at times (though not always) distinguish different types of French and Spanish/sweet wines. Moreover, they indicate the ports of origin of importing ships and so provide oblique evidence of the likely kinds of wine involved. Though foreign ports did export wine which did not originate in their own natural hinterlands (and wines of all sorts were exported from the Netherlands), there was a clear tendency for the commodity to find its way from the vineyard to England through the most convenient port. The port books, therefore, offer an opportunity for an analysis of types of wines imported at all the various English ports. Such a task would, however, be a lengthy one for the individual researcher, and here the exercise is restricted to a few provincial ports.

Thus at Exeter in the early seventeenth century (Table 7) most French wine imported was from Bordeaux, the main French outlet for gascon or bordeaux wines and other wines of the hinterland. This reflects a traditional pattern. English wine imports from France had long been dominated by gascon wine, and Bordeaux's wealth had for centuries been based on its English trade.[48] So in 1575–6, for example, Exeter imported from

TABLE 7

### Types of wine Imported into Exeter (%)[a]

|  | 1603 | 1628 | 1634 | 1636 | 1638 | 1647 |
|---|---|---|---|---|---|---|
| *French* |  |  |  |  |  |  |
| 'gascon' or from Bordeaux | 47 | 8 | 34 | 23 | 64 | 39 |
| other French | 3 | 41[b] | 28 | 11 | 6 | 12 |
| *Spanish/sweet* |  |  |  |  |  |  |
| canary[c] | 5 | 16 | 3 | 8 | 0 | 0 |
| malaga[d] | 0 | 2 | 0 | 9 | 6 | 7 |
| sack | 33 | 13 | 0 | 0 | 24 | 0 |
| 'Spanish'[e] | 0 | 20 | 35 | 49 | 0 | 42 |
| other Spanish[f] | 12 | 0 | 0 | 0 | 0 | 0 |

(a) For 1603 (twelve months ended at Michaelmas of that year): DRO, Exeter town customs roll, 1602–3; for other years: E190/947/3; 949/3; 949/9; 950/7; 952/1: these are for twelve months ending at Christmas of the year stated.

(b) Of this almost half was brought in as prize, the remainder came from La Rochelle.

(c) Wine from the Canaries has been categorized as canary.

(d) Wine from Malaga has been categorized as malaga.

(e) Much of this is likely to have been sack.

(f) For 1603 see Appendix (Exeter), n. (b).

France 31 tuns of gascon and 3 tuns of 'rochelle' wine.[49] In the 1630s Exeter's French wine imports other than those likely to have been gascon came from La Rochelle, Nantes or the Normandy ports. Wines shipped from Nantes, St Malo, Morlaix and le Croisic may well have been those of the Loire valley, while 'rochelle' wines were 'small, thin' cheaper wines.[50] As far as Spanish or 'sweet' wine is concerned, small quantities of malaga wine[51] and a more substantial amount of canary wine (from the Canaries) are recorded. The bulk of Exeter's Spanish wine import was, however, either actually designated 'sack' or came via Cadiz or San Lucar, ports which served the 'sack' region of southern Spain including Jerez de la Frontera.[52] Most of the wine referred to in Exeter's port books merely as 'Spanish' was probably sack, and canary wine was not dissimilar to sack. Again, this was traditional: in 1575–6 virtually all Exeter's import of Spanish wine had been sack.[53] No wine from Portuguese ports or called Portuguese was recorded in any of the Exeter port books examined. The port wine which in later periods became so important was not imported into England until the later decades of the century.[54] The nature of Dartmouth's wine import reflected that of Exeter, with bordeaux the most significant French wine import and sack the most important Spanish.[55] Sack dominated Spanish wine imports at Plymouth, together with madeira wine brought by ships returning from the Newfoundland fisheries.[56]

The bulk of Bristol's French wine also came from Bordeaux, and while quite large quantities of malaga and canary wines were imported, sack was the most important type of Spanish wine imported there, too.[57] And the position was similar at Southampton. There in the early 1620s the merchants declared that their 'commerce consisteth chiefly for the importing of lynnen cloth and Gascoyne wynes from France'.[58] The port books bear out that the French wine imported at Southampton was largely gascon, and also that sack generally made up the bulk of the Spanish import, particularly in the earlier years of the century. In 1600, for instance, all but 10 tuns of the 368 tuns of French wine imported was 'gascon' and Spanish wine imports totalled 97 tuns of sack, 15 of 'Spanish' and one of canary. In 1602 the import of Spanish wine consisted of 111 tuns of sack and 9 tuns of canary.[59] A significant amount of malaga wine was, however, also imported at Southampton, particularly in the later 1620s.[60]

## Validity of the Customs Records

High duties on wine, and consequent smuggling and customs fraud, have been suggested by various historians as reasons to doubt the validity of data derived from customs records in the early modern period,[61] and certainly none of the many figures cited in this essay are likely to meet the standards of exactness expected by modern statisticians.[62] Corruption in the customs service, smuggling, inefficient account-keeping, and the fact that some wine legitimately paid no duties, make it pretty certain that the wine imports presented in the various tables in these pages do not represent the total traffic. Nevertheless, they are unlikely to be purely fictitious. Legitimate trade in wine in the early modern period was still very profitable.[63] That the port books were 'drawn up in a manner calculated to give an adequate check upon customs fraud',[64] is perhaps an over-sanguine view. On the other hand, Simon's strictures on the reliability of the customs figures were particularly directed at those for 1697–1702, which reflected the situation created by long wars with France and the enormous increase in duties on wine introduced from the last two decades of the seventeenth century—though even in that later period wine was not the most smuggled of commodities.[65] In the earlier seventeenth century, duties on wine, though resented, were much lower, and so the incentive for illegal (and thus unrecorded) importing was smaller. Moreover, wine was a bulky, perishable commodity usually carried in small ships which often sailed in convoy—factors also militating against smuggling.[66]

Examination of the Exchequer records relating to smuggling and other types of customs fraud reveal for Devon in the years 1625–56 no cases involving wine before 1651 (though many cases concerning tobacco). After that, perhaps because of excise increases from 1649, wine cases begin to be recorded.[67] This limited exercise is, of course, not conclusive but does suggest that malpractice may not have affected the figures presented in this essay so greatly as to invalidate their use. This is particularly the case if we regard the wine figures not as absolute totals but to be used for comparative purposes both across ports and chronologically.[68]

## The Coastal Trade in Wine

This essay is concerned mainly with the import of wine from overseas, and coastal trade in wine has not been researched in any detail. Some observations may, however, be made here. First, the main wine-importing ports—London, Hull, Southampton, Bristol, Exeter, Sandwich, Ipswich, Chester, Great Yarmouth and Plymouth—were conveniently distributed geographically to serve many inland areas by land[69] and also by river: thus wine was shipped from Bristol, usually by non-Bristol merchants, up the Severn.[70] Secondly, many other ports, large and small, were also importing some wine direct from abroad—as noted above, provincial ports listed in Tables 2 and 3 embrace members and headports under the names of headports—thus increasing the area able to be covered by land and river distribution from ports of initial import. Large-scale coastal distribution of wine was probably unnecessary. Random examination of coastal port books and evidence from the Cranfield papers supports such a view and suggests that, while such a trade certainly existed, it was not on a large scale, usually consisted of very small shipments, and had no discernible pattern. Wine was often shipped in both directions between one port and another during a year. Thus in 1605 Dartmouth received coastwise 17 tuns of wine (from Plymouth, London and Fowey) and sent 44 tuns to Bristol, 11 to Exeter and 30 to London;[71] Barnstaple in the same year imported 19 tuns coastwise (17 from Bristol) and exported 46 tuns to Bristol and ports in the Severn estuary.[72] Also in 1605, Exeter imported 28 tuns (five from London, two from Southampton, and the rest from other Devon and Cornish ports), but exported no wine coastwise.[73] Later Exeter coastal port books also reveal only an insignificant coastal wine trade: in 1627, for instance, four import shipments totalled 25 tuns (half from Plymouth, half from London) and four outward shipments amounting to 17 tuns (half to London, and half to Plymouth and Fowey).[74] Small amounts were also exported from Exeter and the north Devon ports to Ireland.[75] In the early years of the century (and probably later, too) Milford, Beaumaris and Chester were receiving wine via Ireland.[76] Analysis of the Southampton coastal port books for 1608, 1628, 1630, 1631, 1633 and 1634 shows that only a tiny total of 12 tuns was imported coastwise and a mere 78 tuns exported to other English ports during those years.[77] From Bristol wine sometimes went to north Devon and Somerset ports and to Wales by sea, as well as occasionally to London.[78] Table 8 demonstrates, however, that the import of wine into London from the provincial ports was on an extremely small scale, especially when compared with the capital's imports from abroad. The imports of sweet wine into London from the outports in the five years, from 1613–14 through to 1617–18 totalled only 307 tuns. Of this Exeter accounted for 27 per cent, Plymouth 18, Dartmouth 6,

TABLE 8

*Imports of wine into London from the Provincial Ports (tuns)*[a]

| Year | French | Spanish | Total |
|---|---|---|---|
| 1613–14 | ? | 57 | ? |
| 1614–15 | ? | 47 | ? |
| 1615–16 | ? | 68 | ? |
| 1616–17 | ? | 81 | ? |
| 1617–18 | ? | 54 | ? |
| 1635–6 | 185 | 116 | 301 |
| 1636–7 | 375 | 86 | 461 |
| 1637–8 | 148 | 100 | 248 |
| 1638–9 | 74 | 8 | 82 |
| 1639–40 | 254 | 136 | 390 |

(a) For 1613–14 through 1617–18: Kent Archives Office, Cranfield MSS, U269/1/OEC130, 20 April 1619; for 1635–6 through 1639–40: E351/905–9—of these 1635–6 runs from 1 November 1635 to 29 September 1636; other years run from Michaelmas to Michaelmas.

Weymouth, Poole and Lyme together 26 per cent, Southampton 10, Yarmouth and Ipswich together 4 per cent, Sandwich and Dover together 4 and Jersey 3 per cent.[79]

## *The Wine Importers*

At London the vast bulk of the wine was brought in by English merchants. In 1615 only 9 per cent was imported by alien merchants (comprising 17 per cent of French wines, 5 per cent of Spanish and sweet wines and 76 per cent of the small import of Rhenish wine).[80] Perusal of random port books for the provincial ports suggests that the proportion of wine imported by aliens was probably even lower than into London.

Certainly among the London merchants there were those for whom the wine trade was very important. The 'Merchants of London trading in French and Spanish wines', for instance, petitioned the king in 1628.[81] There is some random evidence to suggest that at Hull, too, certain individuals had in this period developed a special interest in the wine import trade,[82] and at Southampton some merchants appear to have been sufficiently specialized in their interests to be known as 'the wyne merchants'.[83] At Fowey one merchant was responsible for 50 per cent of recorded imports of sweet wine in 1616–17 and 80 per cent in the next year. At Plymouth in those years one man imported 26 and 45 per cent of recorded imports of the wine, and in 1638 one merchant imported 28 per cent of the port's intake of French wines (though no other merchant was particularly significant in the trade).[84] The port books, of course, would enable the researcher to discover for all the ports the numbers and names of merchants importing wine and to investigate in a disciplined way the extent to which there were men specializing in that trade. Time-limits and the scope of this article do not, however, permit investigation of this topic for all the chief wine ports, and analysis is confined here to an examination of some records relating to Exeter.

In 1602–3 six Exeter merchants imported between them about 40 per cent of the port's total intake of wine from abroad.[85] By the 1630s the trade appears to have been even more concentrated. The Exeter port book for 1634[86] reveals that 14 merchants paid duty on French wine imports in that year. Of these, three imported less than 10 tuns each. Of the remaining eleven, four Exeter merchants shipped in about 50 per cent of the port's French wine import for the year: Gilbert Sweet, mayor of Exeter in that year, and his son, Richard, together accounted for 70 tuns (20 per cent of the port's intake), John Cooze (variously spelled) imported

49 tuns and Roger Mallock 46 tuns. A further 10 per cent (33 tuns) was imported by another Exeter man, Henry Gould. The remaining six importers accounted for 5 to 6 per cent each of the port's total French wine intake. As for the Spanish wine imported in 1634, 17 merchants paid duty, of whom eleven imported less that 10 tuns each. Of the other six, John Cooze imported 59 tuns (29 per cent of all the Spanish wine brought into Exeter in that year), Roger Mallock 37 tuns (18 per cent), Gilbert and Richard Sweet 28 tuns (14 per cent), Thomas Pitt 17 tuns (8 per cent) and Hugh Crocker 19 tuns (9 per cent). Taking the Spanish and the French wine imports together, four merchants (John Cooze, Roger Mallock and the Sweets) accounted for some 54 per cent of Exeter's total wine import in 1634.

This concentration of Exeter's wine import trade in the hands of a few merchants is confirmed by analysis of the port book for 1636.[87] By then Gilbert Sweet appears to have left the scene, but his son, Richard, emerges as a very substantial wine importer. He accounted for 39 per cent of the French wine imported into Exeter in the year (in three large shipments). John Cooze and John Martin of Exeter accounted for 16 and 15 per cent respectively, and Robert Sparrow of Tiverton 10 per cent. Thus although ten Exeter and Tiverton men paid duty on French wine, 80 per cent was brought in by four merchants. Similarly with Exeter's Spanish wine import in that year (virtually all in the hands of Exeter men), Richard Sweet and John Cooze together shipped in 39 per cent. Roger Mallock 14 per cent and Hugh Crocker 9 per cent. Thus 62 per cent of the Spanish wine imported was brought in by four merchants. Of Exeter's total wine import in 1636 (French and Spanish together) Cooze and Richard Sweet accounted for 160 tuns—some 45 per cent.

Further examination of the activities of these important Exeter wine importers reveals that, although Cooze and the Sweets also imported other goods than wine, they did so on a very modest scale. As for exports, in 1636 Cooze and Richard Sweet exported small quantities of cloth, but nothing else. Wine importing was clearly their main business. Of those merchants who imported only modest amounts of wine, some appear in the port books as significant importers of other goods and as exporters. But those three merchants who exported 48 per cent of Exeter's cloth shipments in 1636[88] were not wine importers. Only one merchant appears in the late 1630s to have dealt in wine extensively while at the same time trading in other goods in significant quantities. Roger Mallock, a former receiver (treasurer) of the city of Exeter and governor of the Company of Merchants of Exeter Trading to France in 1632–3,[89] was mayor of the city in 1636.[90] He traded extensively with both France and Spain, being counted among the thirty largest cloth exporters from Exeter in 1636, a considerable importer of French canvas and linen—as well as salt and iron—and a shipowner, as well as being engaged in the Newfoundland fisheries. He is found trading not only through Exeter but also through Dartmouth, Lyme Regis and Plymouth.

Mallock's interest in wine extended beyond importing. Not only did he sell wine to Exeter vintners, but he was a vintner himself, holding licences to sell wine retail in Exeter, where he had a tavern, and in Taunton where he owned three inns.[91] In this his activities were paralleled by some Southampton merchants in this period who kept taverns in various Dorset towns.[92] In Mallock's case his wine interests and his cloth trade were probably linked. He exported large numbers of Taunton 'cottons', and his inns are likely to have been used as collecting centres for those cloths prior to export.

Wine was of sufficient importance in Exeter's economy for its importers and vintners to be involved at the highest level in protests over various extra taxes on wine, imposed by the Crown in the 1630s, and over privileges accorded to London merchants with regard to wine. Indeed, in 1638 Roger Mallock, John Cooze and Hugh Crocker together with other merchants and vintners of Exeter, Plymouth, Dartmouth, Southampton and Bristol, were summoned personally before the Privy Council to enforce their payment of the duties.[93]

After the Civil War the picture at Exeter appears to have been somewhat different. In 1647, a year for which a port book survives,[94] the bulk of the wine import was still very concentrated: Richard Sweet imported about 20 per cent of Exeter's total wine intake in that year, and Thomas Pitt over 30 per cent. Roger Mallock (who, as a royalist, suffered greatly at the hands of Parliament) and a John Martin accounted for something less than 10 per cent each. None of these men, the main wine importers in 1647, were then, however, confining themselves largely to the wine trade: Pitt was dealing extensively in French canvas and linen, Spanish iron, fruit and wool, and was engaged in the Newfoundland fisheries; Sweet was importing grain, fruit, canvas, vinegar and sugar. And all these men were exporting cloth (Sweet and Pitt on a large scale) to France and the Netherlands. Roger Mallock was exporting and importing the same commodities in which he dealt before the war, though on a smaller scale. How far this pattern might be paralleled at other ports in this period can be determined only by further research.

## Conclusion

National statistics of wine imports for certain years in the later seventeenth century, and more or less annually from 1697 through the eighteenth century, are available in print.[95] Figures for the 1660s and for the period 1697–1702 (years of peace) suggest an annual national wine import which sometimes topped 20,000 tuns but was often well below that total and averaged for the later of those periods some 19,000 tuns.[96] In the later 1680s wine imports were briefly at a much higher level (London's imports are said to have averaged 38,700 tuns a year, 1686–9),[97] but for the years 1713–16 the average annual wine import was something below 19,000 tuns, and between 1717 and 1787 just over 18,000.[98] All this suggests that levels of wine imports for the later seventeenth century, and for the eighteenth, were well below those of the 1630s. These averaged, over the years from 1637 to 1641 (Table 2), some 37,700 tuns a year. The reasons for decline in the level of imports in the later seventeenth century probably included high prices, stemming from higher duties, as well as the availability of alternative beverages.[99] The distribution of this diminished trade among the various provincial ports in the later seventeenth century awaits detailed research. Evidence for such an analysis is available not only in the port books but, for the 1670s, 1680s and 1690s, in the records of the declared customs accounts.[100] There is thus plenty of scope, both for the period sketchily outlined in this paper and for the later seventeenth century, for further investigation.

## Notes

1. Cf. Ralph Davis, *English Overseas Trade, 1500–1700* (1973), 26–31; W.E. Minchinton (ed.), *The Growth of English Overseas Trade in the Seventeenth and Eighteenth Centuries* (1969), 21–3.
2. André L. Simon, *History of the Wine Trade in England*, 3 vols (1906–9; repr. 1964).
3. A.D. Francis, *The Wine Trade* (1972).
4. G. Schanz, *Englische Handelspolitik gegen Ende des Mittelalters* (Leipzig, 1881), ii. 128–50.
5. Simon, *Wine Trade*, ii. 160–1.
6. Simon, *Wine Trade*, ii. 161.
7. Lawrence Stone, 'Elizabethan Overseas Trade', *Economic History Rev.* ii (2nd Series, 1949), 49n.

8. 1560s: Brian Dietz (ed.), *The Port and Trade of Early Elizabethan London: Documents* (London Record Soc. v.VIII, 1972), p. xvi; 1579: Exchequer Lord Treasurer's Remembrancer, Enrolled Customs Accounts, PRO, E356/28; 1597: E/190/10/4; other years: E356/29. The figures for years from 1579 have been calculated from unpublished tables compiled (from the above sources) by the late Dr A.M. Millard (hereafter cited as 'Millard portfolio') bequeathed by her to the present author. A.M. Millard, 'The Import Trade of London, 1600–1640' (unpublished PhD thesis, University of London, 1956) does not include such full data. Hereafter all documentary references to Exchequer material at the Public Record Office are cited without the prefix PRO.

9. Theophile Malvézin, *Histoire du commerce de Bordeaux depuis les origines jusqu'à nos jours* (Bordeaux, 1892), ii. 392. These figures accord well with evidence from other sources that an average of 6,000 tuns of French wine a year was imported into London, 1593–6, and an average of 3,343 tuns a year of sweet wine was shipped into the capital in 1597–9 (when an average of 1,703 tuns of sweet wine was imported into the provincial ports): Stone, 'Elizabethan Overseas Trade', 49; *CSPD, 1598–1601*, 372. See also n. 12 below.

10. E.g., for London, E190/10/4; E356/29.

11. W.B. Stephens, *Sources for English Local History* (Cambridge, 1981), 144. These have been published for Bristol, Great Yarmouth and King's Lynn: Jean Vanes (ed.), *Documents Illustrating the Overseas Trade of Bristol in the Sixteenth Century* (Bristol Record Soc. xxxi, 1979), 167; N.J. Williams, *The Maritime Trade of the East Anglian Ports, 1550–1590* (Oxford, 1988), 296–8.

12. The average annual import of French wine for the six years ended Michaelmas 1612 was said to be 7,783 tuns into London and 4,756 tuns into the outports: A.P. Newton (ed.), *Calendar of the Manuscripts of Major-General Sackville . . . Vol. i, Cranfield Papers, 1551–1612*, HMC lxxx (1942), 302.

13. Millard portfolio.

14. Stephens, *Sources for English Local History*, 143–4.

15. 1637: 461 tuns; 1638: 248 tuns; 1639: 82 tuns; 1640: 390 tuns.

16. 1637: 49 per cent; 1638: 62; 1639: 60; 1640: 56; 1641: 64 per cent.

17. Cf. W.B. Stephens, 'The Trade Fortunes of Poole, Weymouth and Lyme Regis, 1600–1640', *Dorset Natural Hist. and Archaeological Soc. Procs.* 95 (1974), 71.

18. Kent Archives Office, Cranfield MSS, U269/1/OEC39, M205, M206. I am grateful to Dr T. Gray for drawing my attention to this source.

19. E122/198/7.

20. E122/212/19. In the year ended Michaelmas 1600 Beaumaris imported only one tun from abroad (Ireland): E.A. Lewis, *The Welsh Port Books (1550–1603)* (Cymmrodorion Record Soc. xii, 1927), 291.

21. Thus for 1635–6, for which we have wine imports broken down by headports and members, no wine is shown as coming into the members of these three ports: E122/198/7. And, e.g., in 1637 Hull's members imported only 9 tuns (Scarborough, 9; Grimsby, 0): E190/318/1C; 318/2. Gloucester (sometimes recorded as a member of Bristol, but, since it was properly a headport from the later sixteenth century, also often separately noted by the collectors of wine duties in the 1620s and 1630s) is not credited with any wine imports in 1622, 1623 or 1637–41: E122/198/7; E351/905–10.

22. Hull's average import recorded in Table 1B comprises 354 tuns for 1541–2, 30 tuns for 1544–5, but none for other years. Historians of the trade of Hull have not dealt in any detail with its wine trade: see Ralph Davis, *The Trade and Shipping of Hull, 1500–1700* (East Yorks. Local History Series xvii, 1964), 27; Bertha Hall, 'The Trade of Newcastle and the North-East Coast, 1600–1640', unpublished PhD thesis, University of London, 1933 (copy in Institute of Historical Research) (mainly about Hull); G.C.F. Forster, 'Hull in the 16th and 17th Centuries', *Victory County History, York, East Riding* i (1969), 90–173.

23. M.K. James, in Elspeth M. Veale (ed.), *Studies in the Medieval Wine Trade* (Oxford, 1971), 105–16.

24. E190/650/5; 652/3; 944/2; 656/2; 658/7.

25. For 1636 and 1640 a little wine at Dover is recorded as paying at 13s. 4d. a tun: 1636—556 tuns paid at that rate and 3,388 at 3s. 4d.; 1640—397 at 13s. 4d., 2,245 at 3s. 4d.: deduced from E122/198/7; E351/910.

26. Cf. W.B. Stephens, 'The Foreign Trade of Plymouth and the Cornish Ports in the Early 17th Century', *DAT* 101 (1969), 134–5.

27. Spanish wine, of course, need not always have been imported direct from Spain or its islands.

28. B.E. Supple, *Commercial Crisis and Change in England, 1600–1642* (Cambridge, 1959), Chs 2, 3; W.B. Stephens, 'The Cloth Exports of the Provincial Ports, 1600–1640', *Economic History Rev.* (2nd Series, xxii 1969), 228–48.

29. G. Hadley, *A New and Complete History of . . . Kingston-upon-Hull* (Kingston-upon-Hull, 1788), 113.

30. BL, Hargrave MS 321, fol. 41.

31. Wine imports were banned, July 1629–February 1630: Anne Crawford, *A History of the Vintners' Company* (1977), 112.

32. Crawford, *Vintners' Company*, 111; Supple, *Commercial Crisis*, 101–2, 104–7, 110; W.B. Stephens, *Seventeenth-Century Exeter: A Study of Industrial and Commercial Development, 1625–1688* (Exeter, 1958), 14–17; W.B. Stephens, 'Trade Trends at Bristol, 1600–1700', *Transactions Bristol and Gloucestershire Archaeological Soc.* xciii (1974), 158–9.

33. Supple, *Commercial Crisis*, 108; Stephens, 'Cloth Exports'.

34. Figures for Bristol and Hull are not available for the appropriate years.

35. E190/818/11; 822/10.

36. Cf. Malvézin, *Histoire du commerce de Bordeaux*, ii. 391.

37. Cf. Francis, *Wine Trade*, 54.

38. Except possibly for Bristol 1602, 1603: but this is unlikely.

39. Cf. Simon, *Wine Trade*, iii. 300.

40. Newton, *Cranfield Papers*, 302.

41. See PRO refs in Appendix for these years (E190/35/7 for 1637).

42. David H. Sacks, *Trade, Society and Politics in Bristol, 1500–1640* (1985), i. 378–9; E122/101/46 (King's Lynn); E122/67/31 and E190/312/6 (Hull). Cf. Hadley, *Kingston-upon-Hull*, 114.

43. Stephens, *Seventeenth-Century Exeter*, 173, 176.

44. And possibly from further east in the Mediterranean, coming via Spain—though, as noted, there appears to have been little imported from those parts in this period, except at London: Table 6.

45. Cf. Ralph Davis, 'The English Wine Trade in the Eighteenth and Nineteenth Centuries', *Annales cisalpine d'histoire sociale* iii (1972), 90.

46. Calculated from E122/198/7, E351/906–8 (Dover imports excluded).

47. E351/908–9, Michaelmas to Michaelmas.

48. Simon, *Wine Trade*, iii. 163; Francis, *Wine Trade*, 29–30, 66. Here the term 'gascon' is used. Cf. E.M. Carus-Wilson, 'Effects of the Acquisition and the Loss of Gascony on the English Wine Trade', *Bull. Institute of Historical Research* xxi (1947), 154.

49. DRO, Exeter town customs roll, 1575–6. These are minimum amounts: some of the roll is illegible. Cf. Wallace T. MacCaffrey, *Exeter, 1540–1640* (Cambridge, Mass., 1958), 168.

50. Roger Dion, *Histoire de la vigne et du vin en France des origines au xix^e siècle* (Paris, 1959), 443; Simon, *Wine Trade*, iii. 291, 293; Francis, *Wine Trade*, 30, 49.

51. See Simon, *Wine Trade*, iii. 339–42.

52. For the nature of sack, see Simon, *Wine Trade*, ii. 210; iii. 322–38; Francis, *Wine Trade*, 40, 50–1, 54–5; Sacks, *Trade, Society and Politics*, i. 336.

53. DRO, Exeter town customs roll, 1575–6: 186 tuns of sack, 12 tuns of 'sack and bastard' 683 tuns of bastard. In the same year Bristol imported 393 tuns of sack and 22 tuns of other Spanish wines: Sacks, *Trade, Society and Politics*, i. 378–9.

54. Davis, 'English Wine Trade', 89, 91, 102.

55. E190/937/8 (transcript kindly supplied by Dr Alison Grant); 941/7; Jean J. Bourhis, 'Le trafic du port de Dartmouth, 1599–1641' (unpublished thesis, University of Brittany, 1972), i. 179–81.

56. See, e.g., E190/1035/10 (1638); Kent Archives Office, Cranfield MSS, U269/1/OEC39, M205, M206.

57. Deduced from Sacks, *Trade, Society and Politics*, i. 378–9. And see Anne Crawford, *Bristol and the Wine Trade* (Bristol, 1984), 14–15.

58. BL, Hargrave MS 321, fol. 41.

59. E190/818/11; 819/1.

60. Port books (E190) cited in Appendix; Simon, *Wine Trade*, iii. 149–51.

61. Williams, *Maritime Trade*, 41–9, 118–19; N.J. Williams, 'Francis Shaxton and the Elizabethan Port Books', *English Historical Rev.* lxvi (1951), 387–95; T.S. Willan (ed.), *A Tudor Book of Rates* (Manchester, 1962), xii–xiii, xvii, xlviii; Simon, *Wine Trade*, iii. 131.

62. Cf. G.D. Ramsay, 'The Smugglers' Trade: A Neglected Aspect of English Commercial Development', *Trans. Royal Historical Soc.* (5th Series, ii 1952), 157n.

63. See, e.g., Willams, *Maritime Trade*, 213–14.

64. Stone, 'Elizabethan Overseas Trade', 33.

65. Davis, 'English Wine Trade', 88, 89–90, 93.

66. Francis, *Wine Trade*, 54.

67. Exchequer King's Remembrancer agenda books, E159/17067–70 (indexes to the memoranda rolls); Exchequer King's Remembrancer bills and answers (indexes 16824–6), E112/169–72, 295–6.

68. Cf. Stephens, *Seventeenth-Century Exeter*, xxi–xxv.

69. E.g., Simon, *Wine Trade*, iii. 143–5, 156–7, 162.

70. Sacks, *Trade, Society and Politics*, i. 427–8. Sacks does not indicate quantities involved.

71. E190/939/6,7 (transcripts supplied by Dr Alison Grant). Inwards, 7 tuns French, 10 Spanish; outwards, 9 French, 35 Spanish.

72. E190/939/8 (transcript supplied by Dr Alison Grant). Inwards, 14 tuns French, 2 Spanish, rest unspecified; outwards, 7 French, 35 Spanish, rest unspecified. Cf. W.B. Stephens, 'The Trade of Barnstaple at the end of the Civil War', *DCNQ* xxxi (1970), 170, citing E190/953/1 (1654–5).

73. E190/939/2; 939/11 (transcripts supplied by Dr Alison Grant): 12 tuns French, 16 Spanish. In 1602–3, 36 tuns were imported, 24 Spanish from Dartmouth, 6 Spanish from Lyme Regis and 6 French from Plymouth: DRO, Exeter town customs roll, 1602–3.

74. E190/946/9. Cf. E190/948/5; 950/4. Plymouth was also importing wine from Exeter and Dartmouth: E190/1024/15 (1611).

75. Recorded in 'foreign' port books: e.g., Exeter, 1617, 4 tuns; 1628 1½ tuns; 1636, 7 tuns (E190/943/10; 947/3; 949/9); Barnstaple, 1647, 21 tuns, some of which had previously been shipped from Plymouth (E190/952/4).

76. Lewis, *Welsh Port Books*, 190, 193, 206, 235, 291; D.W. Woodward, *The Trade of Elizabethan Chester* (Hull, 1970), 11. Some of this was Spanish wine avoiding the war embargo: Woodward, *Chester*, 40–1.

77. Deduced from figures collected from E190/819/7; 822/7; 822/13; 822/15; 823/5; 823/8 by D.F. Lamb in his 'The Seaborne Trade of Southampton in the First Half of the Seventeenth Century' (unpublished MPhil thesis, University of Southampton, 1972), 337–60.

78. Sacks, *Trade, Society and Politics*, i. 427–8; E190/1299/14 (Carmarthen, 1600–1).

79. Kent Archives Office, Cranfield MSS, 269/1/OEC130, 20 April 1619.

80. E190/18/2, as calculated in Millard portfolio.

81. Simon, *Wine Trade*, iii. 37.

82. Forster, 'Hull in the 16th and 17th Centuries', 142; Simon, *Wine Trade*, 32.

83. J.W. Horrocks (ed.), *The Assembly Books of Southampton, vol. II, 1609–1610* (Southampton Record Soc., 1920), 30, 32, 33, 36, 75n. At Dartmouth in 1599–1600 50 of the 72 tuns of Spanish wine imported were brought in by one Totnes merchant, but no specialization in the import of French wine is evident there in that year: E190/937/8: transcript supplied by Dr Alison Grant, who is also of the opinion that no north Devon merchants specialized in wine in the seventeenth century either.

84. Kent Archives Office, Cranfield MSS, 269/1/OEC130, 20 April 1619; E190/1035/10.

85. Calculated from DRO, Exeter town customs roll, 1602–3.

86. E190/949/3.

87. E190/949/9.

88. Stephens, *Seventeenth-Century Exeter*, 44–7.

89. See W.B. Stephens, 'Merchant Companies and Commercial Policy in Exeter, 1625–1688', *DAT* lxxxvi (1954), 279–92; W.B. Stephens, 'The Officials of the French Company of Exeter in the Early Seventeenth Century', *DCNQ* xxvii (1957), 112.

90. For his career, see W.B. Stephens, 'Roger Mallock, Merchant and Royalist', *DAT* xcii (1960), 279–92. The following information is taken from that article, q.v. for exact references to sources.

91. PRO, Committee for Compounding with Delinquents, SP23/183, p. 486.

92. Horrocks, *Assembly Books*, xxxi.

93. These matters (which include the so-called Abell project) deserve a monograph but cannot be discussed here. Some information is to be found in F.C. Dietz, *English Public Finance, 1558–1641* (1932 edn), 283; Francis, *Wine Trade*, 55–6; Simon, *Wine Trade*, iii. 43–61; Crawford, *Vintners' Company*, 116–27; Stephens, 'Merchant Companies', 144; Stephens, 'Roger Mallock', 284–5; Patrick McGrath, *The Merchant Venturers of Bristol* (Bristol, 1975), 66–7; Patrick McGrath (ed.), *Records Relating to the Society of Merchant Venturers of the City of Bristol in the Seventeenth Century* (Bristol Record Soc. xvii, 1953), 221–5; William Barrett, *The History and Antiquities of the City of Bristol* (Bristol, 1789), 690. See also PRO, Privy Council Registers, PC2/44, 277, 381; 2/47, 263–4; 2/49, 549, 582; 2/50, 113, 190, 341, 358, 359, 368, 518, 529, 547, 564; SP16/414/158, 159.

94. E190/952/1.

95. See, especially, Charles Davenant, *An Account of Trade between Great-Britain, France, Holland, Spain, Portugal . . .* (1715), Pt i. 40, 43; Elizabeth B. Schumpeter, *English Overseas Trade Statistics 1697–1808* (Oxford, 1960), Tables xvi, xvii; Francis, *Wine Trade*, App.; and Ralph Davis, 'English Foreign Trade, 1660–1700', *Economic History Rev.* (2nd Series, vi 1954), 150–66, which is essential reading for all who seek to make sense of available trade statistics for the post-Restoration period. See also G.N. Clark, *Guide to English Commercial Statistics, 1696–1782* (1938), xv–xvi.

96. Francis, *Wine Trade*, 318.

97. Francis, *Wine Trade*, 317.

98. Deduced from figures in Francis, *Wine Trade*, 320, themselves calculated from Schumpeter, *English Overseas Trade Statistics*, Tables xvi, xvii. Note that these include all wine imports, whereas those in Table 2 above are confined to French and Spanish/sweet wines.

99. Davis, 'English Wine Trade', 94–5.

100. PRO Class E351: Exchequer Lord Treasurer's Remembrancer, declared customs accounts (Pipe Office). Figures for 1689–95 are published in *Calendar of Treasury Books* ix, Pt i, Introduction. For Exeter's accounts from this source, see W.G. Hoskins, *Industry, Trade and People in Exeter, 1688–1800* (Manchester, 1935), 160.

# Appendix

## WINE IMPORTS INTO LONDON, BRISTOL, HULL, SOUTHAMPTON AND THE DEVON AND CORNISH PORTS, IN THE EARLY SEVENTEENTH CENTURY (TUNS)

E190 references for dates from 1605 are for twelve months ending at Christmas of the year stated; E122, E351 and E356 references, and E190 references before 1605, are for twelve months ending at Michaelmas of the year stated. Not all available port books have been searched.

### *Imports at London, 1600–41*[a]

| Year | French | Spanish | Total French and Spanish | Total all wines[b] | PRO reference |
|------|--------|---------|--------------------------|--------------------|---------------|
| 1600 | 4,534 | 1,524 | 6,058 | 6,273 | E356/29 |
| 1601 | 2,701 | 1,237 | 3,938 | 4,138 | E356/29 |
| 1602 | 5,955 | 1,459 | 7,414 | 7,618 | E356/29 |
| 1603 | 5,287 | 2,250 | 7,537 | 7,719 | E356/29 |
| 1606 | 6,334 | 3,865 | 10,199 | 10,730 | E190/13/1,3 |
| 1609 | ? | 5,462 | ? | ? | E351/895 |
| 1611 | ?[c] | 5,501 | 6,113 | 6,572 | E351/896 |
| 1612 | ? | 3,478 | ? | ? | E351/897 |
| 1615 | 7,451 | 9,448 | 16,899 | 17,605 | E190/18/2 |
| 1619 | 5,229 | 3,179 | 8,408 | 10,509 | E190/22/4; 23/5 |
| 1620 | 11,452 | 6,565 | 18,017 | 18,254 | E190/24/3 |
| 1623 | 9,506 | 4,515 | 14,121 | ? | E351/900 |
| 1624 | 9,153 | 4,079 | 13,232 | ? | E351/901 |
| 1628 | 4,385 | 3,398 | 7,783 | 8,250 | E190/32/6,7 |
| 1630 | 8,472 | 3,092 | 11,564 | 11,633 | E190/35/1 |
| 1632 | 12,678 | 6,780 | 19,458 | 19,680 | E190/36/4; 37/3 |
| 1633 | 9,910 | 6,142 | 16,052 | 16,778 | E190/37/4 |
| 1637 | 16,602 | 5,349 | 21,951 | 22,042 | E190/35/7 |
| 1637 | 11,083 | 4,813 | 15,896 | ? | E351/906 |
| 1638 | 20,964 | 9,456 | 30,420 | ? | E351/907 |
| 1639 | 16,375 | 12,293 | 26,668 | ? | E351/908 |
| 1640 | 8,311 | 8,087 | 16,398 | ? | E351/909 |
| 1641 | 8,245 | 10,570 | 18,815 | ? | E351/910 |

(a) E356 and E190 data calculated from Millard portfolio (see text n. 8).

(b) London was the only port to import large quantities of wine other than French and Spanish/ sweet, so overall totals have been provided here, where available, for the capital. Even so the proportion of other wine imported was usually small: see also Table 6.

(c) Millard portfolio gives 612 tuns French wine imported, but this seems suspiciously low—and the other returns in this sequence (1609, 1612) record only Spanish wine.

## Imports at Bristol, 1601–41

| Year | French | Spanish | Total | PRO reference |
|------|--------|---------|-------|---------------|
| 1601 | 1,071 | 814 | 1,885 | E190/1132/11[a] |
| 1602 | ? | ? | 1,259 | E356[b] |
| 1603 | ? | ? | 1,461 | E356[b] |
| 1613 | 823 | 917 | 1,740 | E190/1134/3[c] |
| 1623 | 765 | 733 | 1,498 | E351/903 |
| 1624 | 1,219 | 541 | 1,760 | E351/904 |
| 1625 | 987 | 822 | 1,809 | E190/1135/6[d] |
| 1637 | 1,690 | 860 | 2,550 | E351/906 |
| 1638 | 2,093 | 1,127 | 3,220 | E351/907 |
| 1638 | 1,728 | 2,067 | 3,795 | E190/1136/10[e] |
| 1639 | 1,744 | 1,406 | 3,150 | E351/908 |
| 1640 | 986 | 1,242 | 2,228 | E351/909 |
| 1641 | ? | ? | 1,978 | E351/910[f] |

(a) Patrick V. McGrath (ed.), *Merchants and Merchandise in Seventeenth-Century Bristol* (Bristol Record Soc. xix, 1955), 294, using another port book (E190/1132/12) gives a total of 1,872 tuns. Jean Vanes (ed.), *Documents Illustrating the Overseas Trade of Bristol in the Sixteenth Century* (Bristol Record Soc. xxxi, 1979), 167, using the Exchequer, Lord Treasurer's Remembrancer, enrolled customs accounts (E356), found a total of 1,884 tuns.

(b) As noted by Vanes, *Trade of Bristol in the Sixteenth Century*, 167.

(c) McGrath, *Merchants and Merchandise*, 294, gives a total of 1,942 tuns, but on p. 285 notes amounts which add to 1,734 tuns. Anne Crawford, *Bristol and the Wine Trade* (Bristol, 1984), 14, gives a total of 1,733 tuns, and David H. Sacks, *Trade, Society and Politics in Bristol, 1500–1640* (1985), i. 378–9, gives 1,782 tuns.

(d) Based on figures in McGrath, *Merchants and Merchandise*, 294 (rectifying his incorrect conversion to tuns. Presumably his reference E190/1136/6 should be E190/1135/6 (1136/6 is for 1639, and when I sought it 'unfit for production').

(e) Sacks, *Trade, Society and Politics*, i. 378–9, gives a total of 3,317 tuns.

(f) Estimated from the duty paid.

## Imports at Hull, 1606–41

| Year | French | Spanish | Total | PRO reference |
|------|--------|---------|-------|---------------|
| 1606 | 1,202 | 104 | 1,306 | E122/67/31 |
| 1609 | 124 | 338 | 462 | E190/312/6 |
| 1622 | 821 | 132 | 953 | E122/67/32 |
| 1623 | 866 | 181 | 1,047 | E351/903 |
| 1624 | 1,023 | 121 | 1,144 | E351/904 |
| 1637 | 2,011 | 256 | 2,267 | E251/906 |
| 1638 | 2,273 | 138 | 2,411 | E351/907 |
| 1639 | 2,332 | 447 | 2,679 | E351/908 |
| 1640 | 1,265 | 95 | 1,360 | E351/909 |
| 1641 | ? | ? | 1,722 | E351/910[a] |

(a) Estimate from the duty paid.

*Imports at Southampton, 1600–47*[a]

| Year | French | Spanish | Total | PRO reference |
|------|--------|---------|-------|---------------|
| 1600 | 368 | 113 | 481 | E190/818/11 |
| 1602 | 501 | 120 | 621 | E190/819/1 |
| 1604 | 658 | 222 | 880 | E190/819/3 |
| 1605 | 649 | 238 | 887 | E190/819/4 |
| 1606 | 563 | 177 | 740 | E190/819/5 |
| 1609 | 845 | 786 | 1,631 | E190/819/8 |
| 1614 | 296 | 160 | 456 | E190/820/2 |
| 1617 | 665 | 149 | 814 | E190/820/12 |
| 1620 | 700 | 290 | 990 | E190/821/4 |
| 1623 | 602 | 198 | 800 | E351/903 |
| 1624 | 678 | 222 | 900 | E351/904 |
| 1625 | 660 | 233 | 893 | E190/821/13 |
| 1626 | 450 | 105 | 565 | E190/822/5 |
| 1627 | 678 | 255 | 933 | E190/822/4 |
| 1628 | 329 | 97 | 426 | E190/822/5 |
| 1629 | 310 | 349 | 659 | E190/822/10 |
| 1631 | 867 | 487 | 1,314 | E190/822/14 |
| 1635 | 738 | 240 | 978 | E190/823/4 |
| 1637 | 1,132 | 226 | 1,358 | E351/906 |
| 1638 | 1,087 | 380 | 1,467 | E351/907 |
| 1639 | 1,076 | 441 | 1,517 | E351/908 |
| 1640 | 748 | 122 | 870 | E351/909 |
| 1641 | ? | ? | 708 | E351/910[b] |
| 1647 | 316 | 396 | 712 | E190/825/4 |

(a) Figures for 1604, 1605, 1606, 1609, 1625, 1628, 1629, 1631, 1635 and 1647 are derived from D.F. Lamb, 'The Seaborne Trade of Southampton in the First Half of the Seventeenth Century' (unpublished MPhil thesis, University of Southampton, 1972), i. 124–6, based on the E190 references indicated. Figures for 1600, 1604, 1606, 1609 and 1629 are minima, since some entries in the port books for those years are illegible.

(b) Estimated from the duty paid.

*Imports at Exeter and member ports, 1600–47*[a]

| Year | Exeter only | | Exeter and member ports | | Exeter only Total | Exeter & members Total | PRO reference |
|---|---|---|---|---|---|---|---|
| | French | Spanish | French | Spanish | | | |
| 1600 | 194 | 69 | 315 | 144 | 263 | 459 | E190/937/6–8 |
| 1603 | 119 | 118 | — | — | 237 | — | [b] |
| 1612 | 415 | 259 | — | — | 674 | — | E190/941/4 |
| 1617 | 467 | 297 | — | — | 664 | — | E190/943/10 |
| 1623 | — | — | 276 | 256 | — | 532 | E351/903 |
| 1624 | 118 | 365 | — | — | 483 | — | E190/945/8 |
| 1624 | — | — | 256 | 208 | — | 464 | E351/904 |
| 1628 | 152 | 159 | — | — | 311 | — | E190/947/3 |
| 1634 | 330 | 201 | — | — | 532 | — | E190/949/3 |
| 1636 | 122 | 236 | — | — | 358 | — | E190/949/9 |
| 1637 | — | — | 522 | 335 | — | 857 | E351/906 |
| 1638 | 395 | 166 | — | — | 561 | — | E190/950/7 |
| 1638 | — | — | 546 | 326 | — | 872 | E351/907 |
| 1639 | — | — | 655 | 340 | — | 995 | E351/908 |
| 1640 | — | — | 584 | 0 | — | 584 | E351/909 |
| 1641 | — | — | ? | ? | — | 579 | E351/910[c] |
| 1647 | 163 | 155 | 195 | 188 | 318[d] | 383[d] | E190/952/1, 3–4 |

(a) Member ports were Dartmouth and the north Devon ports. 'Exeter only' figures include a few corrections to those in W.B. Stephens, *Seventeenth-Century Exeter: A Study of Industrial and Commercial Development. 1625–1688* (Exeter, 1958), Table J. But note that Table J in that work does not include all wine imported and that wine is there categorized by country from which shipped rather than as 'French' or 'Spanish' as in this Appendix.

(b) DRO, Exeter town customs roll, Michaelmas 1602–Michaelmas 1603. These figures are minima, since a small proportion of the roll is illegible. No wine was imported directly from Spain in this war year; wine counted here as 'Spanish' includes that designated 'sack', that from the Atlantic islands, and other wine recorded in butts or pipes (as was usual for Spanish wine).

(c) Deduced from the duty paid.

(d) Plus 7 tuns of unspecified wine imported from Rotterdam.

## Imports at Dartmouth, 1600–47[a]

| Year | French | Spanish | Total | PRO reference |
|------|--------|---------|-------|---------------|
| 1600 | 106 | 72 | 178 | E190/937/8 |
| 1613 | 25 | 57 | 82 | E190/941/7 |
| 1615 | 41 | 55 | 96 | E190/942/12 |
| 1618 | 22 | 31 | 53 | E190/942/2 |
| 1624 | 19 | 25 | 44 | E190/945/10 |
| 1636[b] | 48 | 86 | 134 | E122/198/7 |
| 1634 | 109 | 86 | 195 | E190/949/1 |
| 1641 | 24 | 152 | 176 | E190/951/8[c] |
| 1647 | 3 | 7 | 10 | E190/952/3 |

(a) J.J. Bourhis, 'Le trafic du port de Dartmouth, 1599–1641' (unpublished thesis, University of Brittany, 1972—copies at Institute of Historical Research and the library of the University of Exeter), 178, gives a number of totals that differ from some of the above: 1600—169 tuns; 1615—73 tuns; 1624—45 tuns; 1634—159 tuns.

(b) For the period 1 November 1635 to Michaelmas 1636, see Table 4 above.

(c) Derived from Bourhis, 'Dartmouth, 1599–1641', 178 based on the E190 reference indicated.

## Imports at Barnstaple, 1600, 1636, 1647

| Year | French | Spanish | Total | PRO reference |
|------|--------|---------|-------|---------------|
| 1600 | 15 | 3 | 18 | E190/937/7 |
| 1636[a] | 114 | 23 | 137 | E122/198/7 |
| 1647 | 29 | 26 | 55 | E190/952/4[b] |

(a) For the period 1 November 1635 to Michaelmas 1636, see Table 4 above.

(b) See also W.B. Stephens, 'The Trade of Barnstaple at the end of the Civil War', *DCNQ* xxxi (1970), 169.

*Imports at Plymouth and Fowey, 1623–40*[a]

| Year | French | Spanish | Total | PRO reference |
|------|--------|---------|-------|---------------|
| 1613–14 | ? | 113 | ? | ?[b] |
| 1616–17 | ? | 86 | ? | ?[b] |
| 1617–18 | ? | 46 | ? | ?[b] |
| 1623 | 193 | 95 | 288 | E351/903 |
| 1624 | 282 | 65 | 347 | E351/904 |
| 1636[c] | 222 | 192 | 414 | E122/198/7 |
| 1637 | 222 | 209 | 431 | E351/906 |
| 1638 | 432 | 176 | 608 | E351/907 |
| 1638 | 309 | 60 | 369 | E190/1035/10 |
| 1639 | 616 | 0 | 616 | E351/908 |
| 1640 | 339 | 0 | 339 | E351/909 |
| 1641 | ? | ? | 324[d] | E351/910 |

(a)  Includes the other Cornish ports, except for 1638 (E190 ref.) which is for Plymouth alone.

(b)  Kent Archives Office, Cranfield MSS, U269/1/OEC39, M205, M206. These are for part years: October 1613–January 1614; Michaelmas 1616–25 March 1617; Michaelmas 1617–25 March 1618.

(c)  For the period 1 November 1635 to Michaelmas 1636, see Table 4 above.

(d)  Deduced from the duty paid.

# Fishing and the Commercial World of Early Stuart Dartmouth

## TODD GRAY

A shipman was there dwelling far by west,
for ought I know he was of Dartmouth . . .
he knew well all the havens as they were,
from Gottland to the Cape of Finisterre, ˙
and every creek in Brittany and in Spain,
his barge was called the *Magdelayne*.

> *The Canterbury Tales*,
> General Prologue,
> lines 388–9, 407–10

Blow the wind high, blow the wind low
It always blows fair to Hawley's Hoe.[1]

At the start of the reign of James I the memory of John Hawley in Dartmouth must still have been strong, although almost 200 years had passed since his death. His fame as a master mariner was strengthened by the tradition that he had been the inspiration for Chaucer's shipman. In 1622 Henry Hawley, perhaps a descendant of John, wrote a treatise on the promotion of national trade and dedicated it to James I. Written aboard the *Abigail* while *en route* to Java, it includes many of the great trade issues then under discussion: he wrote enviously of the Dutch, criticised monopolies and lamented irregularities in the making and selling of cloth. Hawley described Britain as being ideally situated for trade, lying midway

between the 'frozen north' and the 'scorching south'. His details of continental markets, and also of relations with the Dutch in the East Indies,
suggest personal familiarity. Most significantly for a Dartmouth man,
Hawley wrote of fishing that:

> I esteem [it] of more validity than all other trades whatsoever, not so
> much as it is the sea's free gift but in respect of the increase of men
> and shipping both enlarging other trades and accommodating the
> Commonwealth with coin more than all commodities else set them
> altogether.[2]

By the end of the reign of Elizabeth I Dartmouth's seafarers were familiar
with a range of ports unknown to Chaucer's mariner. This chapter is
concerned with the expansion of the port's ships and mariners into new
waters: the port's growth and prosperity was based on the development of
a range of coastal and overseas fisheries.

By 1600 Dartmouth had long been established as one of the South
West's principal ports (eclipsed only in the number of ships and mariners
by the cluster of havens which comprised maritime Plymouth) and
consequently was an important commercial centre, although never as great
as Exeter. In 1599, in the waning years of Devon's infamous 'sea dogs', it
was described by one Hortensis Spinolia as being:

> a large port [with capacity] for 600 vessels and at low tide, 5 yards of
> water. At the entrance [is] a bastion of earth with 6 or 8 pieces of artil-
> lery [and] further in, a castle with 24 pieces, partly of iron and partly
> of bronze and all in good order, and 50 guards and more inside and
> then another earth bastion with 6 pieces of iron all in good order. The
> place is not very large but not walled, the cliffs serving for walls, the
> people are warlike and constantly at sea with vessels to attack the
> Spaniards and other enemies. On the other side [of the river] there is
> a very beautiful village with good people. In the port are generally 30
> vessels of merchandise or war.[3]

The chief interest of this Italian visitor (or spy), who appears to have had
a more pleasant visit to Kingswear than to Dartmouth, lay in assessing
military potential. This accounts for his describing Dartmouth's inhabitants as warlike, particularly in view of what was then a very active interest
in privateering, or even piracy. He merely hints at the port's commercial
vitality, in contrast to John Leland, who had observed some 60 years
earlier that while Hardness was inhabited mostly by fishermen and some

merchants, in Dartmouth 'there be good merchant men in the town and to this have long good ships'. Tristram Risdon, an early Stuart topographical writer native to Devon, remarked that 'through the commodiousness of the haven the town is much frequented with merchants and furnished with fair shipping'. Likewise his contemporary Thomas Westcote noted that it was a 'fair town'. Both suggested that it had prospered because the river access to Totnes had become blocked with soil eroded from tin-workings further upstream.[4] It was claimed in 1606 that it was possible to wade across the Dart at Sharpham, several miles upstream from Dartmouth.[5] Notwithstanding, the river to Totnes was, as Westcote noted, busy with boats; in 1631 alone 37 boatloads of culme were brought to Totnes quay.[6] There were at least eleven bargemen residing in Totnes in 1619 while at Dartmouth there were lighters, small craft which ferried goods and passengers from ships at anchor to the shore. In 1583 there had been at least 12 lighters in the port: this included James Weren's little lighter and Mr Barter's 'houseboat'.[7]

Early Stuart Dartmouth had seen a great increase in population: Percy Russell noted that by 1642 half of those in Dartmouth bore surnames unknown there a century before.[8] The numbers of baptisms in Townstal parish rose from an average of 34 between 1587 and 1589 to 85 between 1641 and 1643.[9] There were only 76 able men mustered in 1569 while some 70 years later 808 men over the age of 16 took the Protestation oath of allegiance. This would suggest (although using a notoriously clumsy formula) that the population grew from approximately 760 to 3,232.[10] Dartmouth's 808 signatures in 1642 can be compared with 550 for nearby Totnes, 731 for Barnstaple, 1,440 for Plymouth and 3,447 for Exeter.[11] There are, however, additional factors to take into account when calculating a maritime community's population, as it could have had a greater proportion of young single men than other areas. In 1570, the year following the muster roll, there were only 28 seamen recorded for Dartmouth whereas in 1619, some 23 years before the Protestation Return, the number had risen to 446. If the population formula was roughly accurate, this would indicate that the proportion of seamen in the population had virtually quadrupled, but it is more likely that there were an abnormally high number of younger men resident there and also that the general population had not risen as high as is suggested. But, as will be seen below, the size of Dartmouth's own population may obscure its maritime importance.

In some respects Dartmouth was like many other English towns. The daily duties of the borough's officials were chiefly concerned with maintaining law and order. In 1615 the town officials were concerned about 'children whose parents are not able to maintain them and all such persons married and unmarried as are able to work and have no work nor any other trade'; they subsequently cited the Elizabethan statute made for the relief of the poor, and decided that there was to be provided flax, hemp, wool, thread, iron or 'any other necessary ware or stuff' for working on.[12] The business of the court leet included the maintenance of public ways, with one difficulty being the unlawful cleaning of fish.[13] The majority of the tasks, in fact, reflected the borough's maritime character: for instance, in 1619 three men were fined three shillings for employing ship's carpenters on 24 February (St Mathias day).[14] The water bailiwick's court was chiefly concerned with such issues as the unlawful use of seine nets, the obstruction of quays by discarded timber and anchors and ensuring that buoys were used to make anchors visible.[15] Percy Russell has suggested that the 'whole power and wealth' of the borough was focused on promoting fishing.[16] This is supported by the majority of the correspondence between the borough officials and their counterparts in Totnes, Exeter and Plymouth.[17] Correspondence with the Privy Council was often concerned with protection of trade and—like other towns when asked for money— reasons were given suggesting financial difficulties, such as in February 1626/7 when it was said that the war had halted trade.[18]

It was the maritime character of Dartmouth which distinguished it from many other English boroughs. The mayors' and receivers' accounts recorded a great number of French, Dutch, Spanish, Portuguese, Irish and Greek citizens who visited Dartmouth, and the parish registers show the considerable number of visitors who found their final resting place in the port. It was the first landing place in England of the Persian ambassador in February 1625/6, but unfortunately for the borough the festivities were soured by the misfiring of ceremonial gunshots which accidentally killed two local onlookers. In 1623, in response to a national inquiry into the number of superfluous alehouses, the mayor replied that he had suppressed as many as he could, taking into account the needs of the poor as well as of the great number of strangers who visited the port.[19] Only occasionally can glimpses of the transitory life of these seamen be found. For example, in April 1624 a coroner's inquiry into the death of Thomas Tozer, a seaman from a Flemish ship then riding in the harbour, offers some detail. Tozer, along with three other crew-members, spent an evening in which they consumed 12 pots of beer and afterwards attempted to return to their ship. They lit a candle in order to see their way down the cliff face at Southtown, but the wind blew it out and, although they were crawling on their hands and knees, Tozer fell and broke his skull. Visits of other sailors also had bloody outcomes.[20]

Even witchcraft accusations had a maritime character: dried fish was one of the items Margaret Foxe of Townstal allegedly sought from her neighbours in 1558 and amongst the evidence against Alice Trevisard in 1601 was that after an argument with John Baddaford, a sailor, she had advised him to go to Pursever Wood in order to 'gather up his wits.' Shortly afterwards, his wife testified, he returned from La Rochelle in the *Hope* of Dittisham in a state of madness from which he never recovered.[21]

By 1600 the Dart was one of the few navigable rivers in the South West whose entrance was not barred with sand or gravel. Only Plymouth, Fowey and the hamlet which was to become Falmouth were in a similarly enviable condition. Moreover, Dartmouth's riverfront provided extensive and deep anchorage which somewhat compensated for the steep hills about the borough which impeded traffic with the hinterland. While this restraint no doubt helped to slow economic growth in comparison with the greater commercial centres of Exeter and Plymouth, the borough was able to capitalize on the misfortune of the merchants of land-locked Totnes: a considerable portion of the goods which passed through Dartmouth, both inwards and outwards, were the property of Totnes men. Many Dartmouth shipowners must have prospered at their expense, but, as will be seen below, some Totnes men invested in ships of their own. Moreover, there were close family ties between the merchants of the two boroughs. Unlike other places, the corporation acquired effective, if periodically troublesome, control over the river. In 1333 the borough had leased from the Duchy of Cornwall the river rights, which included the collection of port dues as well as those of fishing and wrecks. The jurisdiction extended from Blackstone Rock at the mouth of the harbour to Totnes Bridge, seven miles above Dartmouth. Although it was merely one of several areas over which the Vice-Admirals of Devon and Cornwall had lost jurisdiction, the mayors of Dartmouth were involved in a series of disputes.[22] In 1532 the Vice-Admiral of Devon had tried to enforce his rule over the port, and after the Mayor's refusal, and his subsequent stay of several weeks in gaol, the corporation successfully fought in court for confirmation of Dartmouth's independence.[23] In 1558 the Mayor had been in dispute and according to one local man the corporation had been 'molested and troubled' three times in the previous 28 years by Admiralty officials.[24] By 1619, when the Duke of Buckingham became Lord High Admiral, there was a warning by Sir Henry Marten, Judge of the High Court of Admiralty, that authority had become greatly 'diminished' in the

South West.[25] It was at this time that a brief was drawn up suggesting seven steps to correct the 'almost utterly decayed' jurisdiction of the Vice Admiral on Devon's south coast.[26] The issue arose again in 1629 when the Mayor refused to acknowledge the legitimacy of the Admiralty's licence to a diver for searching for possible sunken ordnance; upon careful deliberation the Admiralty uneasily decided that because such diving was a recent innovation there was no precedent to establish jurisdiction.[27] The corporation continued to be troubled by the Admiralty.[28]

It was during the early seventeenth century that Dartmouth's three churches were rebuilt. Although as late as 1567 ships had been moored to the churchyard wall of St Saviour (located in the heart of the borough), the mud-flat was being steadily encroached upon for the building of merchant town houses and quays.[29] A map of the town drawn in about 1619 (see Plate 19) shows how the Fosse, the street which straddled the salt-water millpool behind the town and the river, initially connected the two halves of the borough. Approximately 150 houses are represented.[30] Hardness was, as Leland noted, home to many of the town's fishermen and their fishing smacks were moored there.[31] On the other side of the Fosse lay Southtown, Clifton and further on still, Warfleet. It was on this side of the millpool that the greater part of the new construction took place, including New Quay and the row of town houses, now known as the Butterwalk, which were built from 1634 to 1640 (see Plate 20). These new homes for the town's merchants demonstrate the port's prosperity. Some had elaborate plaster work which could well have been made with the plaster of Paris imported at this time from France. Some of the work was carried out by Thomas Ford, the local plasterer. Bricks, then a novelty for Devon, were also imported into Dartmouth: during the 1630s at least 36,000 'Flemish' bricks were imported from the Low Countries. These bricks were used for building the chimney stacks as well as the internal fireplaces in the Butterwalk.[32]

## Trade

Some local men traded exclusively in fish: in 1624 four merchants who were shipowners (who admittedly resided across the river from Dartmouth in Kingswear or Churston Ferrers) were variously described as dealing 'only in fishing voyages', 'their trading is in Newfoundland fish', 'they all trade as merchants for Newfoundland' and 'their trading is in Newfoundland fishing'.[33] Dartmouth's trade was fundamentally centred on the fisheries. However, Abraham Dawes, the government's surveyor,

*Plate 19*

Map of Dartmouth, 1619, drawn by Nicholas Townsend.

*Plate 20*

The old Butter Walk, Dartmouth, c. 1850.

reported in about 1625 that Dartmouth's main exports were cloth, tin and pilchards for the ports of France, the Atlantic Islands and the Straits of Gibraltar.[34] But Dawes' familiarity with the trade of Dartmouth appears to have been limited to an examination of the Exchequer's port books, the accounts of custom paid on goods entering and leaving port. His omission of any reference to overseas fish, the principal commodity, is a direct result of import duties not having been payable on fish. Nevertheless, the accounts hint at their importance: in 1624 fish was exported from Dartmouth with a value estimated at over £15,000, roughly a third of all exports. This, it will be shown below, was merely a portion of the amount of fish which the port's fishermen caught and traded. The great number and the diversity of imports were possible only because of the amount of fish sold in continental markets. It was principally to protect their access to such markets that the Dartmouth merchants, like many in the outports, struggled against encroachment by the London merchants; during the early seventeenth century they petitioned against monopolies involving their trade to France, Newfoundland, the Levant, Spain, Portugal and New England.[35]

Cloth exports consisted principally of Devon dozens mostly to Rouen and La Rochelle, 'pinwhites' to Rouen and St Malo and perpetuanos (mostly narrow with only some broad) to Rouen, La Rochelle and San Lucar. Tin was of declining importance as an export during the early seventeenth century, though occasionally Cornish tin was exported along with that produced in Devon. Curiously, one of the greatest exports was 'healing stones', the locally quarried slate used as roof tiles. While undoubtedly useful as ballast, slate stone was itself highly valued: in 1612 at least 770,000 slates were exported from Dartmouth.[36] Pilchards (otherwise known as sardines) were chiefly exported not only to the relatively nearby Iberian and French ports but also to Marseilles, as well as to Livorno in Italy. Other destinations were Alicante, Malaga, the Canaries and, surprisingly, Jutland. In 1634 over 1,000 hogsheads were exported. Rays were also sent to France and Guernsey.[37]

The traditional trading route for Dartmouth merchants was just across the Channel to the Breton and Norman ports as well as to those along the Bay of Biscay. Many local small vessels like the *Primrose*, a bark of about 20 tons, made the return journey to the French coast within a few days. One of the few local ship's masters who might have been of French descent was the owner of the *Primrose*, John Leprey, who was 46 years of age in 1619; the evidence for his being French (besides his surname) is merely that he was fined in 1619 for drinking and playing cards at home on a Sunday with a group of Frenchmen. Curiously, unlike Plymouth, there is no indication that Dartmouth had many French migrants, even during the war with France in the late 1620s.[38] French imports were dominated by two commodities, salt and cloth, which were needed for the fisheries. 'Bay' salt, crucial to the curing of fish, came principally from La Rochelle and Le Croisic, but there were a number of other ports involved. Cloth imports consisted chiefly of canvas, particularly 'vittery' from St Malo and brown Normandy from Rouen, as well as dowlas, lockram and greasecloth almost entirely from Morlaix, Treguier and St Malo. Other commodities included wine and also, to a lesser extent, wool cards, paper, occasionally rice and 'province' oil from Marseilles and, very rarely, whale fins.[39]

There was extensive trade with such Spanish ports as San Sebastian, Cadiz, Malaga, Bilbao and San Lucar as well as the Portuguese ports of Oporto, Lisbon and Viana. The corporation claimed in 1617 that it was at the Straits of Gibraltar and in the Mediterranean that the Dartmouth merchants had the best price for their fish.[40] From the Iberian peninsula commodities such as iron, wine and salt were especially important (though French salt was always more prevalent). Fruits, particularly raisins, prunes, figs, oranges and lemons, were imported in considerable quantities from both French and Iberian ports. There was also some commerce with the Dutch ports of Rotterdam and Horne, and coal was brought from Wales and Scotland. From Ireland came not only timber and herring but also wool, hides and occasionally yarn, stockings, blankets and rugs. Irish beef, tallow, pork and butter were also imported into Dartmouth, mostly for victualling the fishing fleet. Timber and pitch was also acquired from Norway and, from the 1630s, from northern New England. It was at this time that beaver skins were being brought from North America, aboard ships from New England and Newfoundland, and valuable cargoes of tobacco arrived, particularly in the 1630s from Barbados, the Summer Isles and St Christopher. Cotton wool was also imported from the West Indies. Occasionally other exotic goods, such as 'elephants' teeth' (presumably ivory), were brought from Guinea and, it was recorded, Brazil.

The interest in the West Indies was not new to Dartmouth. During the sixteenth century many ships had set sail from the port for the Americas: some simply because of its geographical position, others because it was home to Elizabethan adventurers such as Gilbert and Davis. The local interest continued with one of the earlier English trading expeditions to Brazil. On 10 February 1618 the *Laurel* of Dartmouth sailed to the Amazon, with a cargo which included knives, beads, spades and thimbles, and returned on 21 October with a freight of timber. The *Laurel* sailed again two months later for the Amazon[41] and was recorded in a survey of south Devon's ships in February of the following year as being in 'West India'. One of the entrepreneurs was one Thomas King of Dartmouth, who also resided in London, at least for a short period.[42] Dartmouth's interest in Brazil was, however, unusual and short-lived.

## The Fisheries: Inshore and Offshore

The usefulness of the customs accounts in gauging the trade of Dartmouth is limited because, as mentioned above, only commodities for which custom was due were recorded.[43] The greatest commodity with which Dartmouth was concerned, fish, was not included after 1563 except as an export. Nevertheless, the origin of incoming ships of Dartmouth was recorded, and from these records it can be seen that from 1620 to 1623 more than two-thirds of the overseas voyages were directly from the fisheries.[44]

It was during 1623 that the borough began the rebuilding of the fish market[45] and the great variety of fish available for sale reflected not just the amount of fishing carried out but the variety of places to which the seamen travelled. Dartmouth's fishermen had already expanded their activities from local waters to several North Atlantic fisheries, and the market would have served not only as a source of fish for local use but for continental buyers seeking fish caught from the North Atlantic. By 1600 pilchards were the greatest local fishery, but it may have been for salmon that Alexander Hammet and Richard Collins of Kingswear, as well as John Bowncer, George Davis and Richard Cosens of Dartmouth, were using seines in 1614.[46] Many men were involved in a wide variety of fisheries; Richard Davye was one Dartmouth fisherman who not only fished in the river Dart, in what was generally known as a 'home' voyage, but also 'at the main sea in other far voyages'.[47] During the early-fifteenth century, ships from Dartmouth had fished off Iceland, such as the *Christopher Courtney* in 1447, and there had been a regional interest in the North Sea fisheries in the 1550s. Also, Dartmouth, like many other ports in the South West, sent vessels to Ireland; for example, in the 1560s the *Trinity* of Dittisham made regular journeys to Ireland for herring.[48] The range of fishing interests was noted by the corporation in 1613, when it was claimed that 400 vessels and 12,000 sailors from the West Country went to 'Newfoundland, the deeps, Ireland & other places' and that from this 20,000 local people were maintained.

Dartmouth's greatest overseas fishery was for Newfoundland cod. This was the result of the European exploration of the Americas, with the port's particular interest being the discovery of new fish stocks. Thus, in May 1609 the mayor wrote to the Privy Council that:

> . . . the most part of the inhabitants of this town are owners of ships and trade not with any [of] the staple commodities of this kingdom but wanting other employments do set forth their ships to the Newfoundland in fishing voyages which are usually accomplished with extreme labours and industry. And by those voyages (though many times great losses do happen to the said owners in that fish in some places doth yearly fail and in the bad sales [of the fish] thereof many times when the same is transported) yet such benefit (besides the increase of his Majesty's customs) doth continually thereby redound to the Commonwealth and especially of these ports, that in this port and [in] the country adjoining not so few as two thousand families are chiefly and for the most part altogether relieved and maintained by the said fishing trade. And finding also by experience that of all the ships and barks belonging to this port (whereof the number hath of late years much increased) scarce three of them in a year are freighted by any merchant at all. Neither do these parts yield either merchants or merchandise by whom or where with the shipping of this port may or can be any other way employed. But that the said owners must be enforced of themselves to undertake the adventure and hazard of those fishing voyages.[49]

The mayor made several incisive points in this letter, understanding as he did that expansion had been the direct outcome of overcoming the deficiencies of the port by capitalizing on its asset. As noted earlier, the borough did not, unlike Plymouth and Exeter, have a large hinterland: Totnes was in a better position for the inland parishes of Dartmoor. Even the nearby havens of Salcombe to the west and Teignmouth to the east siphoned trade which could have come to Dartmouth. Moreover, although the mayor underestimated the number of ships chartered outside of the fisheries, it was true that the vast majority of voyages were associated with the fishing industry. The mayor also wanted to stress that the expansion involved a great deal of risk to all parties concerned.

Dartmouth's expansion was directly related to the European development of Newfoundland. Though this fishery was important throughout the West Country, for many ports it was an additional interest while for Dartmouth it became its 'life blood'.[50] While it is known that Devon men were involved at the start of the English interest in the fishery, from at least 1544 and probably earlier, and that a Dartmouth ship returned from there in 1554,[51] it is likely that it became of importance only from the 1560s onwards. According to several depositions made in the Consistory Court in Exeter it was not until 1563 that a Kingswear ship, which was owned by John Prowse and Robert Collins, first started to fish at Newfoundland. Several men testified that before that year they did not know of any vessels which fished there.[52] It was probably during the 1560s that the English began to increase their presence. By 1615 it was estimated by Richard Whitbourne, an Exmouth man, that as many as 250 vessels were there every year.[53] It was claimed by Dartmouth's mayor in 1630 that 40 of its ships were intending to resume fishing at Newfoundland after the wars with the Spanish and French and John Cutt, a Dartmouth mariner, testified in 1667 that from 1612 to 1622 as many as 80 ships had annually sailed from Dartmouth to Newfoundland each spring.[54]

Only eleven overseas port books survive for the port, but with the use of a series of petty customs accounts for 1619 to 1622 (which exempted free burgesses) it is possible to examine to some degree the Newfoundland voyages for five consecutive years. These were ships carrying 'train oil', the oil processed from cod livers, which was eligible for customs duty. There were 24 vessels returning directly from the overseas fisheries in 1618, 25 in 1619, 34 in 1620, 20 in 1621 and 22 in 1622 as well as 28 in 1624.[55] In addition, there were undoubtedly a great number of Dartmouth ships which first sailed to France, Spain or Italy from the fisheries, such as the ship owned by John Newman, a local merchant, which in about 1612 went from Newfoundland to Alicante on to London and thence back to Dartmouth.[56] Also, an indication of the overall number of vessels in the fishery is given by comparing the number of English ships recorded as entering the port with the number which were recorded as leaving: for the period from Michaelmas 1623 to Michaelmas 1624 there were 104 entries and only 39 departures.[57] A considerable portion of these 'missing' 65 vessels would have departed from the port for the fisheries and because they did not carry cargoes were not recorded as leaving in the customs accounts. Few of the port's vessels can be identified as not being involved directly in the overseas fisheries.

A comparison between a list of Dartmouth's shipowners in about 1619 and the customs accounts for the years around that date establishes that virtually all of the shipowners either freighted ships themselves, hired out their vessels or acted as masters of the ships for Newfoundland. Some of the Dartmouth ships were chartered by merchants of Totnes, Exeter and, in a few instances, Teignmouth. One of the few Londoners was Humphrey Slany, a leading member of the Newfoundland Company.[58] Curiously, in 1612 Nicholas Roope of Warfleet, a merchant who was very active in the overseas fisheries, chartered a London vessel, the *Edward Bonaventure*, for Newfoundland.[59] Roope was one of the principal fish merchants, but the fishery allowed—and needed—the participation of a wide range of individuals. It was standard practice in the West Country for profits to be divided into three parts: the first for the ship's owner, the second to the victualler(s) and the remaining third to be split between the crew, with the ship's officers having a larger share than the ordinary fishermen. This offered speculative opportunities for what could be a term of only six months with a return that could be very profitable: individuals could lend only a few pounds towards victualling at the ship's departure in early spring, and collect a substantial profit at the end of the summer.[60]

At the beginning of the seventeenth century, fish stocks were discovered further west and south than Newfoundland. When, in 1606, the North Virginia Company established the first colony in the region which became known as New England on the banks of the Kennebec river, one of its chief backers was Sir John Gilbert of Greenway, two miles upstream from Dartmouth. When a seasonal fishery, similar to that at Newfoundland, was established in northern New England, the Gilbert family continued to send vessels fishing there.[61] Indeed, the corporation claimed that 'they used to fish there many years before' the first successful colony of (new) Plymouth in 1620 and, moreover, that 'a ship from Dartmouth made a voyage on the coast of New England in *Anno* 1597'.[62] If true this was one of the earliest English voyages of discovery made there. Certainly Sir Humphrey Gilbert was familiar with the region.[63] A Dartmouth ship, the *Chudlegh*, owned by Sir Arthur Champernowne of Dartington, fished at New England during 1621 and 1622[64] and there were others.[65] Champernowne purchased a land grant for his younger son Francis, who emigrated there in 1636. Part of his land he named 'Kittery' after the 'quay, wharf, strand, court and courtelidges' of that name in Kingswear. In 1617 the property had been bought by Alexander Shapleigh, a merchant of Kingswear who was associated with Champernowne in several fishing journeys and who also sent a son to northern New England.[66]

By 1620 Dartmouth had developed a pattern of wide economic expansion: its fishermen had migrated to Iceland in the early fifteenth century, to the North Sea during the first part of the sixteenth century, to Newfoundland from the beginning of that century onwards and to northern New England from about 1600. The port's prosperity was built upon exploitation of fish stocks, but it was dependent upon profitable returns: unsatisfactory voyages, whether due to fish stock failure (which periodically happened everywhere) or political interference (such as occurred in Iceland, Newfoundland and New England), necessitated the discovery and initiation of new fisheries.

## Crisis Years: 1625–30

The continuation of fishing migration was dependent upon a secure and stable economic climate in Dartmouth. However, during the first years of the reign of Charles I Dartmouth experienced a series of economic setbacks. An increasingly serious problem was attacks by ships of the Maghrib (what are now the countries of Morocco, Algeria and Tunisia) which had become successful in taking English vessels. They were popularly known as 'Turks' because of the religious, and to some degree political, association between them and the Ottomans. Occasionally they were distinguished from the 'Moors' who were also to be found aboard some of the ships, particularly those vessels emanating from Morocco. In 1611 three Dartmouth ships were among the many vessels laden with fish which were captured and brought into Algiers.[67] On 5 July 1615 the corporation noted that ten Dartmouth ships had been lost to the pirates, or privateers, of Tunis and Algiers with an estimated value of over £8,000. This included Thomas Newman's new ship of 120 tons which was taken in the Straits of Gibraltar on its return from Marseilles.[68] Two years later the town's merchants wrote to the Privy Council that the North Africans had developed 'a strong fleet of well appointed ships, better ordered and united in their evil works'.[69] Also in 1617 the mayor of Dartmouth exchanged letters with Sir Ferdinando Gorges, the captain of the fort at Plymouth, regarding losses; Gorges noted that the corsairs were then in waters as close as those off northern Spain.[70] In 1619 the mayor recorded that over 50 Dartmouth men had been taken captive by the 'Turks'.[71] In June 1622 the mayor wrote to the Privy Council, informing them that six ships with 130 seamen had been taken in the past year by the Algerians and that the borough had to support the families of the men who had been lost.[72] It was possibly from one of those ships that two Dartmouth sailors, Thomas Chickley and Andrew Tucker, were captured, only to escape back to England. Returning sailors were suspected of collaborating with their captors and becoming 'renegades'.[73] The attacks continued through the early 1620s, and when the North Africans suddenly, and unexpectedly, appeared off the English coast in the spring of 1625 the corporation was one of many in the South West which wrote to the Privy Council pleading for help. One of the first vessels reported to be taken was a Dartmouth ship in Plymouth harbour in April.[74] Some vessels were taken back to the Maghrib, while others were scuttled or left drifting at sea. The *Hopewell* of Dartmouth was one such ship which was found crewless off the Lizard peninsula in Cornwall; a pair of 'Turkish' shoes was found aboard.[75] In the following spring it was reported that the town had lost three barks bound for the Newfoundland fishery.[76] From 1629 to 1638 eight Dartmouth ships, with more than 116 seamen, were captured and brought into Algiers, and between 18 May 1639 and 15 January 1640 a further six were taken there with 71 seamen aboard.[77] In 1637 23 Dartmouth men were rescued by the Royal Navy from captivity in Morocco.[78]

Undoubtedly many captives never returned home. Financial losses were high in terms of both ransoms and loss of ships and cargoes. Dartmouth captain John Newman paid a ransom of £200 after being imprisoned for a year.[79] One Dartmouth merchant estimated that at this time Exeter, Plymouth and Dartmouth had lost as much as £54,000 because of the ships from Tunis and Algiers, and that over £100,000 had been lost throughout the counties of Devon and Cornwall.[80] He himself claimed to have lost, through the 'Turks' as well as shipwreck, £5,484.[81] Probably a fifth of the port's shipping was lost to the corsairs.

In August 1625 the corporation increased the watch of the borough 'by reason of the dangerousness of these times, both in regard of Turkish pirates by sea and the contagious infection which is in divers places throughout this kingdom'.[82] Unfortunately for the borough, the arrival of this epidemic had coincided with the appearance of the 'Turks'. Bubonic plague and viral infections were responsible for mortality crises in some parts of Devon at least once, on average, in every decade from 1540 to 1650. In 1590 plague was noted in the burials in the parish register of St Saviour's, first in the household of one John Gould, and then spreading to those of Roger Barons and Andrew Macy. Between the three households 13 family members died, including an apprentice. It may have been the plague which caused the deaths of seven Dutch seamen who arrived in an East Indies ship in May 1610. There were outbreaks in Dartmouth in 1602, possibly in 1615, in the late 1620s, 1636 and during the Civil War.[83] There was also disease just across the river at Kingswear in 1604 and 1605.[84] During the late 1620s several epidemics were caused by the naval expedition of 1625 for Cadiz, which was based at Plymouth, as well as by the return of the fleet from the Isle of Rhé in 1627. Sickness spread throughout Devon.[85] In February 1626/7 the mayor of Dartmouth reported that the seamen there were ill; many men from outside of the South West, particularly from East Anglia, were buried in St Saviour's churchyard.[86] Burials at St Saviour's increased from an average of 43 during 1616 to 1625, to 125 in 1626 and 90 in 1627. In June 1627 the mayor wrote to the Privy Council that 'most men of ability in body and purse have left that town for fear of the plague', although only ten houses as yet were infected. Less than a month later, when money was raised by the justices at the Quarter Sessions in Exeter for the relief of Dartmouth, the mayor reported that only fifteen houses then had plague.[87] In September the mayor wrote of the deaths of 'a great number of the inhabitants' caused by sickness and the war.[88] The vicar of St Saviour's noted in his parish register that 57 of those who were buried between 21 May and 17 November 1627 died of plague by recording a letter 'p' next to their names.[89]

However, in a report on the borough's trade in 1627, the mayor was more concerned with the effects of the hostilities with Spain and France.[90] The arrival of the north African ships had also coincided with the deterioration of relations with those countries. Because of the hostilities a significant number of Spanish and French privateers appeared periodically off the English coast. Ships from Dunkirk were a particular problem; one letter from Dartmouth informed the Privy Council that the Dunkirk and Biscay ships, as well as French 'pirates', had taken five Dartmouth ships and that shipowners refused to put their ships to sea. Moreover, a year after hostilities had ceased, in 1631, crew from a small fleet of French ships, after victualling at Dartmouth, went ashore in broad daylight and, after stealing 12 sheep and an ox, robbed the fishermen even of their clothing.[91] Occasional problems with Spanish vessels persisted, as in August 1636 when the *Medusa* of Dartmouth was robbed of its cargo of slate stones, eight coloured kerseys, four rolls of tobacco (which weighed 40lbs apiece), three Flemish jugs and the crew's clothing.[92]

In 1628 the government requisitioned nine Dartmouth shallops (or small) vessels, to serve in a small fleet of fireships for the campaign at La Rochelle, and eight years later the owners were still seeking compensation for two of these as well as two others.[93] The shipowners had been reluctant to have their vessels used by the Crown: 'it is nothing else but warrant and command that must draw them to it.' There were also difficulties in impressing Dartmouth seamen.[94] The war, which did not end until 1630, greatly disrupted Dartmouth's traditional trade routes. Virtually all of Dartmouth's fish exports in 1624 had been to France or the Iberian countries, and the closure of both these markets during the war was disastrous. Thus, in 1627 more than 20 Dartmouth fishing vessels were said to have remained inactive in the harbour, instead of fishing overseas, and more were expected to do the same in the following season.[95] To some extent efforts were made to expand the Italian trade, which had been a popular destination (particularly to Livorno) through the late sixteenth century. Whereas in 1624 two ships had exported £320 worth of fish, in 1628 six vessels took fish worth £5,890.[96] By the war's end the fleet was impatient to resume fishing and proceed to the continental markets: as mentioned earlier, in March 1630 forty vessels from Dartmouth waited for permission to leave for Newfoundland.[97]

To compensate for the disruption some shipowners and mariners turned to the opportunities of privateering. Dartmouth was one of the leading ports. One prize ship brought in was the *Fortune* of Lubeck, taken by Captain Andrew Fulford of the *Chudley* of Dartmouth, which was valued at £1,325 5s. 3d. Of greater value was the Portuguese ship the *Nuestra Senora de Rosaria*, which was brought in by the captain of the *Dolphin* of Dartmouth and was valued at over £7,000.[98] However, the war did not stop one act of co-operation between William Hammett, the master of the *Francis* of Dartmouth, and the master of a ship from the Bay of Biscay: while both vessels were fishing in Conception Bay at Newfoundland during the summer of 1627 a hat, some tobacco and a pistol were exchanged by Hammett for four 'shallops' (most probably a silver coin worth about 18 shillings) from the Basque mariner.[99]

## Maritime Employment and Shipping

On 1 September 1623 the mayor of Dartmouth declared in a letter to the Privy Council regarding local men impressed for the navy that:

> Those formerly sent are mechanical men & husbandmen it is true [but] that there are very few mariners in these parts but are husbandmen & in the winter time employ themselves in ['labour of husban' crossed through] the common labours of the country and although there be a great number of mariners that usually sail out of this port to the Newfoundland, yet there are not the tenth part of them dwelling in this town.[100]

The mayor must have been aware of the Admiralty's recent survey of south Devon which had been commissioned by the Duke of Buckingham, the Lord High Admiral of England, possibly as one of the steps to reassert the authority of the Vice-Admiral in south Devon.[101] The report recorded that along that coast there were 3,653 seafarers, of whom only 446 resided in Dartmouth itself, while across the river in Kingswear there were a further 93 seamen. Most of those listed in Dartmouth were mariners and sailors: there were 33 mariners and 281 sailors 'at home', 40 shipwrights, 14 coopers 'for the sea', 3 surgeons at sea, and 57 mariners and sailors 'from home'. There were also 18 sailors in Townstal.

Of far more significance, in support of the mayor's comment regarding the number of mariners residing outside of the borough who worked aboard the local overseas fishing fleet, are the number of seamen listed as residing in nearby parishes. The report shows that the number of seamen in the borough and in Torbay far exceeded any other area of south Devon: there were 1,538 mariners in the Dartmouth area, comprising 42 per cent of the overall number. For example, there were 153 seafarers in Brixham, compared with only 43 in 1570, and in the three Torbay parishes of Paignton, St Marychurch and Tormohun (including Cockington) there were 363 seamen, compared to 102 in 1570.[102] These communities served as dormitories for the fishing fleet. Dartmouth's importance as a centre of overseas fishing was directly related to the increase in the mariner population of these surrounding parishes.

As mentioned earlier, Dartmouth's muster of able men in 1601 comprised only about 500 individuals, a figure only slightly higher than the 446 seamen recorded in the borough 18 years later. Notwithstanding Dartmouth's growth in the intervening years, the figures reinforce the importance of the maritime ventures in employment to the port. Although Buckingham's survey does not show a wide variety of maritime trades in the port, this was due to its recording seamen in more general occupational terms. Certainly a great number of men in more specialized trades, such as pilots and trumpeters, resided in the port. Some apprentices came from considerable distances to become indentured to Dartmouth merchants to learn the 'trade and occupation of a sailor', such as William Tyner of Hatfield in Hertfordshire.[103]

In 1623 seventy-six Dartmouth 'merchants, owners of shipping, adventurers and mariners' signed a petition against the erection of a lighthouse on the Lizard peninsula.[104] A comparison with Buckingham's survey shows that the signatures were chiefly of the port's shipowners and comprise about a sixth of the total number of seamen. It highlights the considerable number of men who owned ships in the port. As claimed in the letter of the mayor of Dartmouth in 1609, and verified elsewhere, the number of ships had at that time greatly increased.[105] Dartmouth emerges in the 1619 report as the leading port in the number of ships, with Plymouth taking second place. Only by adding shipping at Saltash and other Cornish communities on the river Tamar to Plymouth's figure is Dartmouth relegated to second place. Dartmouth had a total of 93 vessels which comprised 38 per cent of South Devon's 247 ships. The port's 3,916 tons was 39 per cent of the total tonnage listed for the south coast. Included as being of Dartmouth were five vessels 'in the harbour of Dartmouth the owners of Totnes', four likewise of Dittisham, five of Kingswear, three of Churston Ferrers and nine of Torbay. Six ships of Cockington and two of Tormohun were also recorded as 'of Torbay'. There were 57 ships accredited to Dartmouth itself. Few ships were recorded as carrying ordnance and the oldest were the *John Baptist* and the *Swyft-sure*, both listed as being 40 years old.

In a separate listing of ships, undated but clearly contemporary with Buckingham's survey, are the names of the shipowners of Dartmouth and Salcombe and the number of shares for each vessel. There are slight differences between the two surveys concerning the 'home' locality of the vessels: for instance, the ships of Churston Ferrers are listed as being of Brixham, and two of the ships in Buckingham's survey recorded as from Dittisham are listed under Cornworthy. The two lists show that while the majority of Dartmouth's shipowners resided in the borough itself, a considerable number of the vessels were owned by men in the surrounding parishes. While it may have been standard elsewhere for vessels to have had multiple ownership there is little evidence of this for Dartmouth.[106]

Dartmouth's trading community and shipowners were largely identical. The shipowners were also traders, and, though not all of the merchants were shipowners many must have invested in the fisheries as victuallers. This is not to say that the town's residents were not involved in a wide variety of occupations. These included not only the traditional maritime trades such as mariners, sailors and fishermen but also surgeons, gunners, coopers, cordwainers, joiners, sail-makers and shipwrights. The trading community was large, and the borough's records show that in 1611 included amongst the traders who were keeping shops were linen-drapers, weavers, tailors, glaziers, barbers, chandlers, haberdashers, brewers, bakers, mercers and at least one goldsmith.[107] The records also mention Thomas Adams and Nicholas Townsend, both described as painters.

Townsend drew the map of Dartmouth in 1619 (see Plate 19).[108] Few merchants did not have interests in shipowning. The importance of commerce led Dartmouth, like many other boroughs, to choose merchants for its representatives in Parliament, such as Roger Mathews, who repeatedly sat for Dartmouth. Mathews regularly sent his vessel, the *Prosperous*, to Newfoundland, and along with William Neale was outspoken in Parliament about the fisheries. Merchants clearly dominated the running of the borough: between 1603 and 1642 all of the mayors were involved in trade and the majority of them were shipowners.[109] Forty-one of the 92 inhabitants who contributed to the benevolence of June 1622 are known to have traded overseas within the previous three years. Moreover, the vast majority of these merchants, particularly of those who contributed most heavily, were shipowners.[110] Few merchants in Dartmouth failed to recognize the benefits of shipowning.

In 1619 there were 168 shipwrights recorded in South Devon, with five in Kingswear, 15 in Stoke Fleming and as many as 40 in Dartmouth. The port was a shipbuilding centre of sufficient size to attract a number of apprentices, including John Lay, the son of an East Budleigh miller. In 1619 Lay was apprenticed to John Tricky of Hardness, who already had another East Budleigh apprentice.[111] A dispute in 1627 between the Corporation and the Company of Shipwrights at Ratcliffe near London suggests the character of shipbuilding and repair in the port. The mayor claimed that 'sundry poor shipwrights dwelling in divers villages near the sea coast to the eastward of Teignmouth . . . always used to work building, repairing and dressing' their ships, but that the London company had sought to restrict that work and that there were not enough shipwrights at Dartmouth to work on the ships during 'seasons convenient'.[112] The only shipwrights recorded in 1619 as residing east of Teignmouth were in the parishes of Woodbury, Colaton Raleigh, Withycombe Raleigh and Otterton. This was the third greatest centre on the south coast.[113] It would seem there was close co-operation between the two areas.

While there was some wood available locally, for in 1579 Norton Wood in Townstal parish had provided 'some timber for small boats',[114] there are nevertheless few records of large ships being built between 1600 and 1642 in Dartmouth or even in Devon as a whole. The need to import timber must have handicapped shipbuilding. In only a few instances was the Admiralty under James I obliged to award a royal bounty, a subsidy given to promote native shipbuilding, for Dartmouth ships: in 1610 for the *Trial* of 238 tons, in 1613 for the *Handywork of God* of 230 tons and in 1615 for the *Rose* of 200 tons. In 1626 the *Merchant Royal* of Dartmouth was built, together with the *Resolution* of Exeter, constructed by John Bayley of Otterton.[115] Many of the larger ships were probably bought from the Dutch, but some were also acquired from the Vice-Admiral: between 1624 and 1627 at least three vessels seized by Sir John Eliot were sold to Dartmouth merchants.[116] It appears that most of the local work was in repairing vessels and in building smaller boats.

## Conclusion

Dartmouth's position in the early seventeenth century as a leading shipping port, not only within the region but also in the country as a whole, was a direct consequence of its involvement in fishing. The character of the port seems to have changed quite drastically from the days of John Hawley. Many of its other imports and exports related directly to this principal interest. When that shipping base was under threat, so too was its involvement in fishing and therefore its continued prosperity. With the end of the Spanish and French wars of the late 1620s, Dartmouth re-invested in its fishing operations, with more ships being recorded as returning directly from Newfoundland to Dartmouth in 1633 than in any previous year.[117] While this could have been due to reluctance on the part of shipowners to sail on directly to the continent, and thus risk being taken captive by the north Africans there, the number of ships at Newfoundland also demonstrates the port's resilience after the deprivations of the war years. 'Wanting other employments' (as its mayor wrote in 1609), unlike its near neighbours and close competitors, Plymouth, Exeter and even Barnstaple, Dartmouth had no other trade or easily defined hinterland to develop. It was forced to exploit its principal natural asset, which was its good harbour. The key to success lay also in taking advantage of close proximity to continental markets and exploiting a large local workforce, much of it resident outside the town proper. But Dartmouth also helped to develop new fisheries through exploration and colonization. The discovery of the Americas had presented the port with fresh opportunities: a traditional interest in the fisheries of Ireland, and even Iceland, was extended to those in Newfoundland and then northern New England. To the mariners of Dartmouth the fisheries had become an industry and the focus of their commercial world.

## Notes

I would like to thank Dr Jonathan Barry for his many useful comments on early drafts of this paper.

1. Percy Russell, *Dartmouth: A History of the Port and Town* (1950), 15. I would like to acknowledge my great debt to Percy Russell, whose work has set the stage for all subsequent studies of Dartmouth.

2. DRO, DD62059.

3. PRO, SP12/270/77. I am grateful to Dr Sandra Cavallo for her translation, which clarifies ambiguities in the nineteenth-century calendar.

4. L. Toulmin Smith (ed.), *The Itinerary of John Leland the Antiquary* (1906–8) i. 220; George Oliver and Pitman Jones (eds), Tristram Risdon's *The Chorographical Description or Survey of the County of Devon* (Exeter, 1845), 168–9; Thomas Westcote, *A view of Devonshire in 1630* (London, 1811), 424–5.

5. PRO, E134/3 James I/Hilary.

6. DRO, 1579a/13/16.

7. Todd Gray (ed.), *Early-Stuart Mariners and Shipping, The Maritime Surveys of Devon and Cornwall 1619–1635* (DCRS New Series, 33, 1990), 23; DRO, DD61461, 76.

8. Russell, *Dartmouth*, 82, 108.

9. DRO, St Saviour parish register. The first complete year in the register is 1587.

10. DRO, DD61941. A muster of 1601 also suggests sharp growth: 504 men were mustered in the six wards of the town, which could imply that the general population had increased to about 2,000 persons.

11. A.J. Howard and T.L. Stoate (eds), *Devon Muster Roll for 1569* (Bristol, 1977), 196; A.J. Howard (ed.), *Devon Protestation Returns* (Bristol, 1973), 192, 119, 389, 313–37.

12. DRO, DD61887.

13. DRO, DD61890 and DD62098.

14. DRO, DD61790.

15. DRO, DD61877. See also Russell, *Dartmouth*, 7, 30, 56, 60.

16. Russell, *Dartmouth*, 82.

17. For one example see DRO, DD61903, 'to Mr Thomas Gourney and Mr William Nyll their charge at Exon about the setting forth against the Turks'.

18. PRO, SP16/53/25.

19. PRO, SP14/138/40; DRO, DD62211.

20. DRO, DD62093.

21. Todd Gray and John Draisey, 'Witchcraft in the Diocese of Exeter: Part II, East Worlington (1558), Townstall (1558) and Moretonhampstead (1559)', *DCNQ* xxxvi, 282–5; Todd Gray, 'Witchcraft in the Diocese of Exeter: Dartmouth 1601–2', *DCNQ* xxxvi, 231–2; Michael and Alice Trevisard were later brought to Exeter to appear before the justices: DRO, DQS Bundle Box 10 (1601–2), March. I am grateful to Mr Mark Stoyle for this reference.

22. Russell, *Dartmouth*, 30, 56–7; R.G. Marsden, 'The Vice-Admirals of the Coast', *Economic History Rev.* xxiii (1908), 738. Among the Duchy's other interests were the rights to the river Tamar, and other landholders laid claim to Admiralty jurisdiction to certain sections of the Devon coast, including parts of the coast of the South Hams.

23. Russell, *Dartmouth*, 56–8.

24. PRO, HCA13/12, fols 106–13, 245–8.

25. PRO, SP14/111/38.
26. PRO, SP15/42/33.
27. PRO, SP16/162/75, 166/31, 167/19 and 57, 150/9 and 41.
28. PRO, SP16/381/77.
29. DRO, DD61429; Russell, *Dartmouth*, 92–105 and 'The Building of the New Quay at Dartmouth, 1584–1640', *DAT* lxxxii (1950), 281–90.
30. DRO, R9/1/Z/33.
31. DRO, DD61877.
32. Russell, *Dartmouth*, 97–9; DRO, DD61790; DCO, Dartmouth Petty Customs, 1630s; Peter Beacham, 'Local Building Materials and Methods', 27, and John Thorp, 'Town Houses of the Late Seventeenth and Early Eighteenth Centuries', 119, in Peter Beacham (ed.), *Devon Building* (Exeter, 1990).
33. PRO, E134/21 James I/Trinity 13. The merchants were Nicholas Lewys, Alexander Shapley, William Kent alias Kempe and Alexander Hammett.
34. PRO, SP16/522/130. The other Devon ports mentioned were Exmouth 'a place of great trade for France and Brittany and the [Atlantic] islands whose vent is kerseys and such like and return linen cloth', Barnstaple 'whose commodities are bayes, kersies and places of trade the islands, Spain and France' and finally Plymouth 'the chief port whose commodities are tin, kersies and pilchards and trade for France, Spain [and the] islands'.
35. DRO, DD61832, DD61846, DD61848a–49b, SM1989, DD61927, fol. 26, DD61921–4.
36. DCO, Dartmouth Petty Customs, 1612.
37. Jean Jacques Bourhis, 'Le Trafic du port de Dartmouth, 1599–1641' (unpublished PhD thesis, University of Brittany, 1972), i. 43, *passim*; DRO, DD1927, 1989, fol. 26; Gillian T. Cell, *English Enterprise in Newfoundland, 1577–1660* (Toronto, 1969), 137.
38. DRO, DD61969; Gray, *Early-Stuart Mariners and Shipping*, 20, 97, 104. There was one alien living in Brixham in 1581: T.L. Stoate (ed.), *Devon Taxes: 1581–1660* (Bristol, 1988), 61.
39. Much of this and the following information has been obtained from the Dartmouth Petty Customs housed in the Duchy of Cornwall Office as well as the Dartmouth Port Books at the Public Record Office, Series E190.
40. DRO, DD61967.
41. Joyce Lorimer (ed.), *English and Irish Settlement on the River Amazon 1550–1646* (Hakluyt Soc. 2nd Series clxxi, 1989) 188–9. It set out on 22 December.
42. Gray, *Early-Stuart Mariners and Shipping*, 25; BL, Cotton MSS, Otho E VIII, fol. 250. 'This King of Dartmouth lodgeth at a Boddymakers house, next to the gun[?ner] in Chancery Lane near Holborne'.
43. See Alison Grant, 'Port Books as a Source for the Maritime History of Devon', in David Starkey (ed.), *Sources for a new Maritime History of Devon* (Exeter, 1987), 57–69; J.H. Andrews, 'Two problems in the Interpretation of Port Books', *Economic History Rev.* ix (2nd Series, 1956), 119–22.
44. DRO, DD61979, DD62038a, DD62056b.
45. DRO, DD62109, fol. 12.
46. DRO, DD61877.
47. DRO, Chanter 860, fol. 88–91.

48. Wendy R. Childs, 'Diverse Lands Far Beyond the Seas: The Overseas Trade of the South West in the Later Middle Ages' and this author's 'Tithes in the Development of the "Home" and "Far" Voyages, 1540–1642' in Stephen Fisher and Todd Gray, Exeter Studies in Maritime History, vol. viii, forthcoming; DRO, Chanter 855b, 179–81.
49. DRO, SM1989.
50. W.B. Stephens, 'The West-Country Ports and the Struggle for the Newfoundland Fisheries in the Seventeenth Century', *DAT* lxxxviii (1956), 92.
51. John J. Beckerlegge, 'Plymouth muniments and Newfoundland', *Transactions Plymouth Institution* xviii (1936–7), 3; DCO, Dartmouth Petty Customs, 1554.
52. DRO, Chanter 855a, fols 45, 65, 478–9 and Chanter 855b, fols 13–14.
53. Cell, *English Enterprise*, 100.
54. PRO, SP16/531/15; WDRO, W360/74.
55. Cell, *English Enterprise*, 132, 136, 140; DRO, DD61979, DD62038a, DD62056b; Laura Nicholls, 'The Trading Communities of Totnes and Dartmouth in the Late Fifteenth and Early Sixteenth Centuries' (unpublished MA thesis, University of Exeter, 1977), 96.
56. PRO, REQ2/406/67. Such a voyage would subsequently have been recorded in the customs accounts as coming from one of those ports and not Newfoundland.
57. Bourhis, *Trafic*, i. 21.
58. Gray, *Early-Stuart Mariners and Shipping*, 103–5; DCO, Dartmouth Petty Customs; PRO, E190/944/2 and 947/1; DRO, DD61979, DD63038a and DD62056b; Cell, *English Enterprise*, 54, 55, 58, 60, 77.
59. DCO, Dartmouth Petty Customs, 5 October 1612; Gray, *Early-Stuart Mariners and Shipping*, 24; Russell, *Dartmouth*, 105–6. This vessel may have been later known as the *Edward Bonaventure* of Dartmouth.
60. Cell, *English Enterprise*, 3–21, 150–1.
61. Charles M. Andrews, *The Colonial Period of American History* (New Haven, 1934) i. 91–4; DRO, SM1988, fol. 181. In 1628 the *Command* of Dittisham was sent by Lady Elizabeth Gilbert to Newfoundland.
62. DRO, DD61616.
63. D.B. Quinn (ed.), *The Voyages and Colonising Enterprises of Sir Humphrey Gilbert* (Hakluyt Soc. 2nd Series lxxxiii, 1938), and with A.M. Quinn (eds), *The English New England Voyages, 1602–1608* (Hakluyt Soc. 2nd Series clxi, 1983).
64. C.E. Champernowne, *The Champernowne Family* (typed MS at the Westcountry Studies Library, Exeter, 1954), 256–64; F. Tuttle, 'Captain Francis Champernowne', *New England Historical and Genealogical Institute* xxviii (1874), 80–1.
65. DRO, DD61944.
66. DRO, DD12022. See also DD12006, DD12019; Russell, *Dartmouth*, 107.
67. Russell, *Dartmouth*, 89–90; Gray, 'Turkish Pirates and Early Stuart Devon', *DAT* 121 (1988), 159–71; PRO, HCA1/47/261. One of these, the *Grace*, was reportedly bought with the consent of the vessel's master.
68. DRO, DD61927, fol. 3.
69. DRO, DD61922.
70. DRO, SM1989, fol. 26.
71. DRO, DD61947, fol. 12.
72. DRO, DD62067.

73. PRO, HCA13/44/66-7.
74. PRO, SP16/1/69.
75. PRO, HCA13/53, examination 169, May 1637.
76. PRO, SP16/25/78.
77. PRO, SP71/1/157; HLRO, Main Papers, 5 March 1641.
78. John Dunton, *A True Journall of the Sally Fleet* (London, 1637); also, PRO, SP71/13/29.
79. PRO, SP16/297/33-4.
80. BL, Harleian 296, art. 56.
81. PRO, REQ2/406/67.
82. DRO, DD62202; H.W. Hodges and E.A. Hughes, *Select Naval Documents* (Cambridge, 1927), 43-4: They petitioned the Privy Council for ordnance in July 1626.
83. Paul Slack, *The Impact of Plague in Tudor and Stuart England* (1985), 83-99; DRO, St Saviour parish register, 9 December 1590-9 May 1591, 17 May 1610; N.C. Oswald, 'Epidemics in Devon, 1538-1837', *DAT* 109 (1977), 73-116, 87.
84. DRO, DQS OB1/2, Pas.1604 & 10 January 1604/5.
85. Slack, *Plague*, 97.
86. DRO, St Saviour parish register. This included men from Lyme Regis, Bristol, London, Ipswich, Newcastle, Limehouse, Aldborough, Colchester, Boston and Oxford; PRO, SP16/53/25(i).
87. R.M.S. McConaghey, 'Medical Records of Dartmouth, 1425-1887', *Medical History*, iv, no. 2 (April 1960), 98-100; PRO, SP16/526/81; DQS, OB 1/6, 113.
88. PRO, SP16/78/21.
89. DRO, St Saviour parish register.
90. PRO, SP16/53/25(i).
91. PRO, SP16/149/26 and 201/59.
92. PRO, SP16/334/11.
93. PRO, SP16/116/69a printed in Gray, *Early-Stuart Mariners and Shipping*, 114-15; PRO, SP16/340/68. See also 133/45.
94. PRO, SP16/80/77 printed in Gray, *Early-Stuart Mariners and Shipping*, 110; PRO, SP16/60/15.
95. PRO, SP16/53/25(1).
96. Cell, *English Enterprise*, 137.
97. PRO, SP16/531/15.
98. PRO, HCA4/2, 24 January 1629 and 23 February 1628.
99. DRO, SM1988, fol. 23; R.C. Anderson (ed.), *The Book of Examinations and Depositions, 1634-39* (Southampton Record Society iii, 1934), 21-2.
100. DRO, DD62093, printed in Hugh R. Watkin, 'Press-gang in South Devon in 1623', *DCNQ* xiv (1926-7), 179.
101. PRO, SP15/42/33.
102. Tormohun (60), Paignton (100) and St Marychurch (144): Gray, *Early-Stuart Mariners and Shipping*.
103. DRO, DD62013.
104. DRO, DD62087.
105. PRO, E134/3 Jas I/Hilary.
106. Gray, *Early-Stuart Mariners and Shipping*, 18-25, 96-8, 103-5.

107. DRO, DD62184, DD61810, DD62047.

108. DRO, DD61929.

109. Russell, *Dartmouth*, 107, 109; Robert C. Johnson, Mary Frear Keeler, Maija Jannson Cole and William B. Bidwell (eds), *Commons Debates 1628* (New Haven & London, 1977), 201, 209, 512; Gray, *Early-Stuart Mariners and Shipping*, 97. For example, the *Prosperous* was in Newfoundland in 1627: PRO, E190/947/1.

110. DRO, DD62056a.

111. Gray, *Early-Stuart Mariners and Shipping*, 18, 22, 28; DRO, DD62097.

112. DRO, DD61946.

113. Gray, *Early-Stuart Mariners and Shipping*, 37, 46–7, 48, 49. That the two East Budleigh boys came to Dartmouth as apprentices, when there already were such a large number of shipwrights across the river Otter, suggests a considerable annual migration of workers from that area to Dartmouth.

114. DRO, Chanter 860, fol. 169.

115. Brian Dietz, 'The Royal Bounty and English Merchant Shipping in the Sixteenth and Seventeenth Centuries', *Mariner's Mirror* 77, No. 1 (February 1991), 18–19; PRO, SP16/16, fols 43, 89. The 120 ton ship was built by John Shapleigh, shipwright, for John Shapleigh, sen., a Totnes merchant and John Shapleigh, the younger, a Dartmouth merchant.

116. R.W. Unger, *Dutch Shipbuilding before 1800* (Amsterdam, 1978), 44; Harold Hume (ed.), 'Sir John Eliot and the Vice-Admiralty of Devon', *Camden Miscellany XVII* (Camden Soc., 3rd Series, 64, 1940), 44–8.

117. Cell, *English Enterprise*, 140.

# The Clergy in Devon, 1641–62

IAN GOWERS

Church life in England did not disappear with the collapse of episcopal authority in the 1640s.[1] Attempting to track its probable course is full of interest, as well as having more than its fair share of methodological pitfalls. In large measure we must rely on the Walker MSS retained in the Bodleian Library, Oxford. However, following the example of A.G. Matthews, who published his *Walker Revised* in 1948, it is evident that Commonwealth Church material preserved mainly in Lambeth Palace and at the Public Record Office can also provide important clues as to the personnel not only serving parishes that had their clergy sequestered but also those officiating where a natural vacancy had occurred. Sometimes we can glean what kind of patronage they enjoyed, at least initially.[2] There will always be gaps in the evidence, but the search for that missing information is bound to improve the quality of the questions we ask about individual parishes.

Dr John Walker's prime motivation in publishing his *Attempt*[3] in 1714 was to reply to the nonconformist propaganda of the time that might suggest to later generations that only their clergy had suffered from the upheavals of the mid-seventeenth century. His systematic enquiry about the state of every parish after 1642 appears to have been sent via archdeaconries throughout the whole of England and Wales. There were plenty of incumbents who for one reason or another did not see fit to reply. In some cases relatives of sequestrators or intruders or other key figures were still alive and were therefore unwilling for embarrassing reminders of the past to resurface. To talk of such events was one thing: to find them in print quite another.

In Devon, which Walker as rector of St Mary More (Major) in Exeter knew better than most counties, he only received information about some 204 parishes or 43 per cent of the total. Moreover, surviving correspondence only relates to 189 of these and normally gives a second-hand and very incomplete account of Interregnum developments within the relevant parish. Usually the replies were heavily prejudiced against the intruders, those individuals, ordained or not, who were appointed to replace the sequestered clergy. Some informants offered facts only very tentatively, and just occasionally, where they were categorical, they can now be proved to have been wrong from other surviving archive material. Yet for all these weaknesses the overriding Walker MSS evidence is local and personal, offsetting the far colder detached material to be found in central government sources.[4]

Relevant Commonwealth records reveal when and how vacancies and sequestrations were filled. They also deal with the augmentation of selected clerical salaries, made possible by the requisitioning of episcopal and capitular assets. Political issues surface in petitions and State Council orders, and the minutes of such committees as that for Plundered Ministers, and later that for the Approbation of Public Preachers include numerous references to Devon. In 1650 a nationwide survey of the Church was commissioned and though it seems to have been fairly generous to existing clergy, whether Anglican or otherwise, it still represents a useful yardstick for measuring the state of the county's clergy as a whole. An Exchequer list of clergy in 1652 is incomplete and is inclined to mangle the incumbent's name as if spoken rather than written, but it can still be used as another indicator of constancy or change.[5] Away from London, Quarter Sessions material and parish records can occasionally confirm or question other evidence.

This enquiry into the wide range of sources here outlined is an attempt to discover how resolutely Devon Anglicanism survived through the twenty years of uncertainty; how effective in the county was any State-approved alternative to the traditional Church of England; and how significant was the role played by the influential laity of Devon in determining the kind of church that prevailed during the Civil Wars and Interregnum. Further, to summarize and clarify the situation of the clergy, a statistical table has been devised, its data drawn from these sources; though considerable problems have emerged in giving proper labels to the large numbers of the clergy and substitutes involved, it should still prove to be an important focus for any further debate about the state of the church in Devon between 1641 and 1662.[6]

Established church authority in the mid-seventeenth century became eroded over a period of some six years. Episcopal courts lost their effectiveness—such as it was—in 1641, but the last episcopal admission to a Devon parish was made as late as 2 June 1646.[7] Meanwhile, the Parliamentary Committee for Plundered Ministers had been empowered in July 1643 to sequester scandalous clergy and replace them with deputies more sympathetic to the Parliamentary cause. Their impact on Devon cannot be traced for certain before August 1644 when Richard Reynolds, rector of Stoke Fleming, was ousted in favour of William Bayly. On the outbreak of war Bayly had deserted his vicarage at Tamerton Foliot and run away to London. When he returned to the west, with Parliamentary support, it was to the much more lucrative rectory near Dartmouth, although military considerations may well have delayed the start of his effective ministry there.[8] Seventeen other Devon clergy are known to have fled from royalist forces, and one other, Francis Burnard of Ugborough, was taken prisoner. Some of the former were given sequestrations in London or Kent. Most, however, returned to livings in Devon.[9]

Curates are best located from visitation records, but of course there were no episcopal visitations between 1638 and 1662. Evidence from one archidiaconal visitation of 1645 has survived. More importantly in this respect, the Protestation Returns of 1641 have been of some use. Even so, assessing the number of curates, never mind their political sympathies, has to remain largely a lost cause. Ames Short, who served Topsham in 1645, is a notable exception. He subsequently committed himself wholeheartedly to the Presbyterian cause throughout the Interregnum and beyond. The Topsham curacy was normally a Dean and Chapter appointment.[10]

The ousting of Anglicans loyal to King and Prayer Book did not occur in some comprehensive purge once the military might of Parliament had prevailed. There was protracted harrassment that lasted until after the Penruddock Rising of 1655, and in a few cases the local correspondent replying to Dr Walker's enquiries suggested that the incumbent concerned might well have been better off had he suffered formal sequestration. There appear to have been at least three reasons for the prolonged vexation. Firstly, there was a shortage of good, replacement clergy. Secondly, regularly appointed clergy often enjoyed more local gentry support than made sequestration a straightforward option. Thirdly, repeated references to arbitrary acts of bribery or plunder on the part of Parliamentary soldiers show how profitable it was for some to keep suspect clergy under long-term threat. This is not to deny that sometimes there were genuine grounds for considerable ideological frustration among zealous revolutionaries.

'Scandalous' was a term used across several preceding decades to describe ministers who were either negligent in preaching or remiss in personal conduct. In the 1640s, however, it also came to mean those who supported the King in his armed struggle against Parliament. Indeed, moral failure became a minor factor in dislodging Devon clergy from their livings. Within this category William Lange, vicar of Bradworthy, appears to have been a colourful rogue: admitted in 1622, he was fortunate to have survived the years of episcopal discipline.[11] Five others in Walker's list were criticized for varying degrees of unworthiness, drunkenness being the most common. The unfortunate James Bache, vicar of Egg Buckland, was deliberately enticed into a public house, and those who then informed against him became principal benefactors from the ensuing sequestration.[12] Charles Churchill, rector of Feniton, had a ruddy complexion by nature. His political offences were compounded with an alleged lack of sobriety to make up 'a sort of Accumulative Scandal'.[13] When James Burnard, the pluralist vicar of Awliscombe and Upottery, was accused of being the father of a base child in Honiton, contemporary opinion was divided upon his guilt or innocence.[14] Sometimes rumour could do as much mischief as fact.

Far more honest, we may feel, were the avowedly political charges brought against the royalist clergy. Quite a few like Robert Chaplain and Richard Pote had served in the King's army. Theophilus Powell and William Harvey were remembered for their royalist preaching. Roger Trosse and Anthony Gregory were punished for contributing horses as well as money to the King's cause. Yet even in these cases some moral blemish was added if at all possible. The rector of Upton Pyne's real offence in 1655 was to send gifts of food and cider to Penruddock and Grove after their abortive uprising, but he was branded 'insufficient', another convenient term of unspecified abuse.[15]

By the rules of sequestration a fifth of the victim's income was reserved for the upkeep of the family so long as the change was effected peacefully. Great was the difference between those intruders who promptly paid their fifths and the apparent majority who found some reason for delaying or denying this legal right altogether. At Molland, Daniel Berry seems to have been reasonably dealt with in this regard, but at Aveton Gifford, William Lane and his family were reduced to dire straits. Lane lost his temporal estate as well as both his livings, Ringmore being his other rectory. While his own misfortunes and death have been summarized by

Matthews, no mention was made there of Mrs Lane's additional distress. Her lawful retention of certain mills in Aveton Gifford was twice interfered with by Francis Burnard, the intruding minister, who diverted the water supply to his own advantage. An appeal to Cromwell eventually succeeded, but we may well wonder at what cost to themselves and their friends, especially when we learn that Lane died on the journey back from London.[16]

Not all Anglican casualties were such heroic loyalists. William Satterley, curate of Ide, had character defects over and above imbibing too much. The very scandalous life of John Nicholson at Churchstow has nowhere been spelt out in any detail. However, Christopher Hammond at Cornworthy was said to have 'kept a whore' publicly, and John Padfield, rector of Huntsham, was another clergyman charged with fathering a bastard child. Regrettably, such irregular behaviour or allegations thereof can be found too among the reforming clergy, some of whom also succumbed to the grosser temptations, as will be shown below.[17] By comparison the reliance of Henry Wilson on homilies rather than on sermons at Buckland Filleigh would seem to be the mildest of blemishes. Similarly, Matthew Bennet in Exeter was noted only to have been a reading minister.[18] From Stoke Fleming there were complaints of persistent neglect over thirteen years at the hands of pluralist Richard Reynolds. The new authorities tried hard to end the tradition of holding more than one parish, but practicalities obliged some Commonwealth appointments to become virtual pluralities, if only by default.[19]

Thomas Bedford, the Plymouth lecturer foisted on the town's corporation by king and archbishop in 1635, was accused of Arminianism. An examination of his 1639 *Treatise of the Sacrament* reveals nothing that might offend its dedicatee, Bishop Joseph Hall. Though Bedford argued against Calvin's requirement that every sacrament should be preceded by a sermon, his main thrust was against the continental theologian Bellamine and the Catholicism he so stoutly defended. At Paul's Cross the previous year Bedford had condemned tavern haunting in one section of his oration and the fawning flattery of the ambitious in another. His tenor throughout was one of moderate Anglicanism.[20]

Edmund Read of Mariansleigh had eagerly supported the Book of Sports and sometimes played bowls on Sunday, but the most Laudian testimony in Devon appears to have come from Anthony Short, rector of Ashreigney and Drewsteignton. His stand was not only in defence of monarchy but also in support of genuflexion and an aggressive expectation of law and order. Though he denied some of the charges in 1647, he attended Penruddock at his execution in May 1655 and was not generally known for taking any half measures. Even so, the objections to his ministry still appear more political than ecclesiastical.[21]

At Talaton the Book of Common Prayer was torn in pieces and the pulpit fall defaced, but in Whimple there was even greater iconoclastic fervour when its self-styled reformers burned the prayer book and altar rails and smashed painted windows, statues and the organ. Moreover, Dr Cotton's curate there was pulled out of the pulpit. This was probably the John Phare listed by Walker; if so, he moved quickly to the curacy of Bradninch, whence he was evicted for refusing the Solemn League and Covenant.[22]

Between December 1642 and June 1645 Parliament claimed the right not only to enforce sequestrations but also to present new clergy to vacancies where patronage had formerly belonged to bishops, delinquents or the Crown.[23] Later, two more restrictive clamps were fastened on the clergy nationwide, as a result of post-war political developments. In order to establish an effective Presbyterian system, all incoming clergy from 1648 onwards were expected to adhere to the Solemn League and Covenant. Then, following the execution of Charles I, the Army required those in authority to take the Oath of Engagement, an oath of loyalty to the existing state without either monarch or house of lords. Had the former been applied rigorously it would have left Devon with little more than a quarter of its clergy. Had the latter been enforced, the survivors would have been few indeed.[24]

The haphazard tendering of the Covenant and Engagement was manifestly unjust. Though the overwhelming number of Interregnum sufferers were Anglican, not all were. Increasingly, one suspects the parish brand of religion was determined by the influence of the local gentry, together with the fitful interference of an aggrieved army.

The stubborn adherence of some clergy to the Prayer Book, despite its use being strictly forbidden by Parliament as from 1645, shows the strength of continuing support for Anglicanism in some parishes. Throughout the county some 22 churches were said to have made deter-mined efforts to retain the Book of Common Prayer.[25] At Stoodleigh, for example, John Abraham kept his rectory throughout our period and was described in the Parliamentary Survey of 1650 as a 'painfull preaching minister', yet Walker's informant claims that he stayed loyal to the Prayer Book and was neither molested nor ejected.[26] At Clayhanger parishioners kept watch while Anglican forms of worship were observed. On one occasion a nearby landowner, Mr Nutcombe, had to bribe soldiers to stay away. The vicar of Brampford Speke, William Norris, was said to have read Common Prayer all the time, but on his death in 1654 he was replaced by the Independent, Henry Hallett.[27] The curate of Slapton, Weymouth Stert, was reported to have 'used the service book as often as required'. The rector of Dodbrooke, John Waltham, was noted as having preserved the parish from 'the infection of those times'.[28] Such generalizations defy exact analysis, though they imply a brave defiance towards contemporary fashion. Erisy Porter, rector of Butterleigh, had the prayer book snatched out of his hand while conducting a funeral, but the service continued, it was said, from the loyal man's memory.[29] These examples might suggest that the countryside around Tiverton was more stubbornly conservative than elsewhere. Although each archdeaconry is reasonably represented within the aforesaid 22 places, the deaneries of South Molton and Chulmleigh are noticeably above average and offer a possible contiguous area of like-mindedness.

The situation at Poughill and Cruwys Morchard was somewhat curious. Though the pluralist rector was obliged to forego both parishes, they were then served by his son and son-in-law respectively. Since the latter, Jonas Holmes, was more amenable to the favoured practice of those times, a select party of Anglicans went regularly from Cruwys Morchard to Poughill for holy communion. William Frank, the rector, was never formally sequestered but suffered considerable loss of tithe. While one source says he was obliged to preach elsewhere for a livelihood another claims that he was permitted to retain his temporal estate and that he 'liv'd very comfortably, notwithstanding all their spight and cruelty'. He was harrassed rather than silenced. The uncertain situation allowed his patron (termed his greatest enemy by one informant) to take economic advantage for himself, especially as regards tithing. The same influence, namely Henry Cruwys, also leaned on Holmes to preach down the Lord's Prayer.[30]

Personal animosities were yet another factor in causing problems for Anglican loyalists, even extending to outright sequestration. In the case of Henry Wilson, rector of Buckland Filleigh, the trouble went back as far as 1614, when his appointment by Bishop Cotton was resented by the then Earl of Bedford. Incredibly, this grievance was not only remembered around 1648, when Wilson was replaced for 12 years, but even into the next century, when John Walker was soliciting local recollections. The same source added this significant comment:

If the great man of the parish shall make it his business (upon some grudge or prejudice how unjustly soever taken) to run down and vilify his Minister, he must needs sink very much in the esteem of the plowman and the farmer who having but little judgement of their own are in most things of the same mind and opinion with their Landlords.[31]

It was a principle that could embarrass parliamentary committees as well as bishops sometimes.

At Brixham the prime cause of John Travers' fall was said to have been the animosity of a certain lady formerly censured by the ecclesiastical courts, while Richard Reynolds owed some of his problems at Stoke Fleming to one whom he had earlier rebuked for oppressing a widow.[32]

Of the 207 names listed for Devon in *Walker Revised* only 161 are known to have held a living or curacy there between 1641 and 1646. The rest are later claimants to parishes, or else schoolmasters or clerical refugees from elsewhere. Within these 161, eleven died before the end of 1646 and only one of these, Bernard Herniman of Lifton, was ever formally replaced or sequestered so far as we know.[33] Horsham and Stucley were nonconformist victims of 1662 and are glaring misfits in a list of Anglican sufferers. However, they can be replaced by two that Walker himself never detected, namely Samuel Randall of Bradstone and George Williamson of Halberton, though Matthews came to suspect the latter.[34] Altogether 94 clergy were sequestered, though ten of these were pluralists and allowed to retain a single parish. Six were evicted from curacies or the like. Thirty-three were harassed but not evicted. Nearly 20 have little known reason for being included among the sufferers. Even the revised figure of 123 or 133, however, though well below the grand total of 207, still represents a widespread and painful persecution.

The fate of those cast out of their livings varied considerably. We have noted the fate of William Lane. Some, like John Strode and Daniel Berry, were permitted to retain their personal estate.[35] John Trosse and Augustine Osbourn were among seven known to have become schoolmasters, with presumably all the loss of status and of income that that would imply.[36] Philip Hall turned to carding wool, and Robert Ball was found hedging and gap-stopping.[37] Jonas Stiles went to Padua University to study medicine. Thomas Jones died in exile while Richard Hall turned papist overseas but relented at the Restoration.[38] Robert Herrick relied upon the charity of friends in London, and Richard Kay turned household chaplain for some of the comparatively short time that his living of Holne was sequestered. George Pierce served a similar role for Sir Thomas Allen in London.[39]

At least 25 clergy found alternative parishes to serve. William Slater may even have been happier in his London charge of St Peter Poor than he had been in Cullompton.[40] Emmanuel Sharp, having been the incumbent of Mortehoe before the war, was then sequestered from Bathealston in Somerset around 1649. He subsequently served three more Devon parishes in quick succession, but his preaching was too near the political bone for the times, and without the protection of Sir Edmund Fowell he would probably not have survived, even in a relatively minor parish such as Marldon.[41]

Thomas Brook and William Norris both benefited from the protection of Hugh Peter, the Roundhead luminary, who had a sister living in Bampton.[42] Edmund Reynell supported William Satterley at Sherford, while James Burnard was defended by Henry Fry Esquire in his unofficial parish of Burlescombe.[43] Richard Newte was fortunate enough to have the support of Robert Shapcote and Arthur Basset, both colonels but on opposing sides in the first Civil War. Even so, his earnings—first at Ottery St Mary and later at Heanton Punchardon—will nowhere near have compensated him for the loss of his two portions of Tiverton rectory.[44] William Battishill only suffered a few months' sequestration after appealing to his own brother-in-law, Captain Philip Francis, a member of the influential County Committee. When Edmund Ellis survived the local inquisition, thanks to the support of Sir John Bampfield and Justice Beare's grandfather, the Presbyterian doorkeeper cried out in despair 'Let this man go, let all go.'[45] Here the moderating voices of note were both on the Parliamentary side.

In several instances, besides that of William Frank cited above, threatened clergy sometimes resigned in favour of a relative. For example, the vicarage of Heavitree in 1646 passed from John Bury to his son-in-law, William Banks. John Bragg at Thorncombe was replaced by William, his son. Bartholomew Parr surrendered Rewe to his son Edward while retaining his other parish of Clyst St Mary. At least four other clergymen enabled a son or relative to succeed them quite legitimately.[46] The most curious of situations to emerge from surviving evidence relates to Ideford where the rector, Francis Strode, found it expedient to withdraw for the greater part of the year lest visitors to the spa there should detect his true loyalties and force his removal. We may well wonder who served the cure during his prolonged absences.[47]

Thus it will be seen that Anglican 'suffering' embraced everything from temporary and minor inconveniences to protracted persecution or even death from heart-break. The hammer blows fell more noticeably on wealthier livings, since with the poorer vicarages and curacies, as one correspondent so cogently expressed it, 'their poverty was their protection'.[48]

What, then, is worth noting about the intruders, those who replaced the episcopally appointed clergy after 1646? After July 1643 no one was supposed to enter a sequestrated benefice unless he had first been examined and approved by the Westminster Assembly of Divines. Although a few Anglicans and Independents were invited to this large, consultative body, the overwhelming membership was that of English Presbyterians. In March 1647 Parliament ordered that sequestrations be given only to those who had first taken the Covenant.[49] Ironically, such restrictions served in part to help remaining Anglicans, since County Committees were then harder-pressed to find acceptable substitutes for those they outsted. Hence the delayed displacement of many 'delinquent' Anglicans.[50]

Before 1646 there were some 41 episcopally ordained clergy who showed themselves to be staunchly Presbyterian when opportunity allowed. Most of these openly declared their support for *The Joint Testimonie of the Ministers of Devon whose names are subscribed . . . unto the truth of Jesus . . . In pursuance of the solemn League and Covenant of the three Nations.* The names of 73 ministers were printed with this. One of these, Treise of St Mabyn, belongs to the Cornish story.[51] Some might be branded as fellow travellers. While 15 were dead by 1662, no fewer than 17 of the rest opted to conform after St Bartholomew's Day. More surprisingly, there were at least 12 clergymen within the county towards the end of 1648 who subsequently suffered for their Presbyterianism, but who did not apparently subscribe to this public call for the prompt establishment of an effective Presbyterian Church government nationwide.[52] Most of the intruders and those formally appointed to vacant livings from 1646 to 1648 were Presbyterian. Of them, 33 subscribed to the *Joint Testimonie*, though nine subsequently conformed to the restored Church of England. Nine others were Independents. A few Anglicans, like George Palfry at Upottery and Benjamin Devenish at Down St Mary, do appear in the Parliamentary Survey of 1650. No record survives of any regular admission for them, yet they apparently served their parishes up to and beyond 1662.[53]

From the statistical table at the end of this paper it will be seen that the decline in the number of Anglican clergy between 1646 and 1650 was marginal. The Presbyterian gain of 31 was largely at the expense of parishes where the 1646 situation remains unknown. It could be argued that sequestrations did not bite seriously into the county's Anglican strength until after 1649 when Presbyterianism was in nationwide political decline.

The dubious quality of some intruders was frequently highlighted by those individuals replying to John Walker's enquiries. Richard Morse, for example, used to talk 'very frivolously and impertinently in the pulpit' at Yarcombe. At Bovey Tracey John Tucker regularly preached with a sword at his side, while Brixham's John Kempster would whine and cry in his delivery; moreover, it was believed that he used Dr Gurnall's sermons rather than his own. Joseph Edgcombe, a later Bovey Tracey intruder, was such a mean scholar that he was said to have brought away from Oxford only what he took. Robert Gaylard of Ide, another Oxford graduate, was dubbed 'a very ordinary fellow', while Robert Stidson of St Marychurch was damned with faint praise that he was 'not so bad as the Rest of His bigotted fraternity'.[54]

For all the earlier Puritan criticism of some Anglican unworthiness, their own side was also tainted at least by rumour. Thus Richard Cresson, mistakenly listed by Matthews among his Anglican sufferers, had to move away from Axminster to avoid scandal, and in 1655 Thomas Jackson of Mary Tavy was apparently ejected for some indeterminate misdemeanour. He died there almost immediately.[55]

The oddest intruder was undoubtedly Christopher Jellinger of South Brent. He arrived there in 1647 to replace the sequestered John Gandy. Correspondents for miles around had their own Jellinger anecdotes. One of them restrained himself enough to write 'The many ridiculous sayings and doings of Gillinger it was put into the place of the said Dr I think are fitter to be buried in oblivion than to walk up and down in print.' Others could not forbear telling of his visits to married couples late on their wedding night. He once claimed to have met Jesus Christ on the road from Plymouth. He argued strongly against the wicked practice of usury, and sometimes conducted four hour services, thereby keeping menials from their work. Even half a century later he was remembered as 'a very ridiculous fellow and a meer Jackpudding in a pulpit'. Fortunately for Presbyterianism there were others of their kind who won praise and admiration, even from those unsympathetic to their cause.[56]

The 1650 Parliamentary Church Survey covered 363 Devon parishes out of a possible 467. Most of the missing ones—for some reason—were in the Christianity, Dunsford and Moreton deaneries. When compared with the

Puritan surveys of 1584, its comments on serving clergy were moderate indeed. Only very rarely was there criticism as at South Molton: 'John Coren it is not well supplied.' Even here the attack may be aimed more at the miserly impropriator than at the minister. Cornworthy's 'Christopher Hammond fit to be removed' was more specific. Occasionally even a godly cleric suffered rebuke. Thus at Goodleigh Thomas Downe 'hath not supplied it constantly this 3 years.' Almost certainly he was concentrating on his ministry at St Paul's in Exeter and hoping to retain the bulk of his Goodleigh income as well. Where a name is given without comment it may still imply some measure of criticism. For many curacies it is an invaluable source for indicating whether or not there was any regular worship attempted and, if so, by whom it was conducted.[57]

With the appropriation of episcopal and capitular lands in 1646 and 1649 respectively, the revolutionary government had plenty of disposable wealth to hand out by way of augmentation. Across the 1650s it can be shown that it was intended to supplement the revenue of no fewer than 75 parishes this way. Alongside this process were recommendations to unite some parishes and divide others. Such reforms would doubtless have improved the overall church finances in the county, but only at the considerable expense of traditional Cathedral worship and of most episcopal government.

Even so, the operation of the augmentation system was far from equitable. John Howe, the favoured Independent preacher, though apparently often absent from Torrington, still received £100 annually while the vicar of populous Plymstock, despite being put in by the County Committee and by the election of the parishioners, received only £10 a year. On the other hand, the likes of Theophilus Alford, Anglican curate of Wembury, could receive £50 annually without ever obviously supporting either the Presbyterian or Independent cause. It would be very instructive to learn more fully upon what basis the considerable largesse was distributed.[58]

Adequate financial support was often hard to secure. It was said of Christopher Baitson, rector of Chulmleigh, that during the troubles all but two of the parish refused him tithes. Less drastic by far was the estimated drop in the value of Stoke Fleming's tithes from £240 to £140 a year. At Lydford the loss in tithe value lasted well beyond the Restoration, but the alleged problem of collecting tithes in Thorverton may well have been linked to local reaction at their vicar receiving a £50 augmentation that no predecessor had ever had.[59] The six 'clergymen' that Cadbury had in quick succession after the death of their elderly James Bradford around 1651 were probably the consequence of uncertainties regarding their material recompense. One letter to Walker refers to tithes being more easily impropriated when there is no settled minister. It goes on to state that the next vicar, Robert Heycroft, admitted in 1661, had to sue for his rights in the Court of Exchequer. As if to confirm the nature of the problem, another correspondent, from Cadbury, testified that the original replacement there, a schoolmaster named Pattin, was paid by Mrs Fursdon. Without formal inductions and visitations who was to know by what right the newcomer had been appointed? At Virginstow the lay sequestrators were thought to regard all ministers as unwelcome, since presumably they were the chief beneficiaries of any vacancy.[60]

Several Anglicans were removed because they would not adhere to the Solemn League and Covenant. Largely overlooked have been the misfortunes suffered by Presbyterians who objected to the Engagement. Soon after the 1650 Parliamentary Survey John Forward left his Ottery St Mary vicarage of officiate at Sandwich in Kent. Walker's correspondent says that Forward could not 'swallow the Engagement', but in fact he subscribed to it on 28 June that year. Could it be that his willingness to conform lost him vital lay support in the locality—hence his eastward removal for the time being? He came back to his Devon parish by 1657.[61]

Thomas Ford and Ferdinando Nichols were the subjects of a high level investigation at Exeter. In a peevish letter sent to Major Blackmore on 1 April 1650 the Council of State complained of 'intemperate declamations and seditious invectives of some men in their pulpits'. The letter went on to assert that:

> the Commonwealth cannot be safe if they be suffered under the veil and disguise of their learning and knowledge and their pretended calling to abuse and mislead the people. Among others creating these dangers to the Commonwealth we are informed that Mr Ford and Mr Nichols, preachers at Exeter, have been and are principly active.

It then called for the justices to investigate and report back.

If there was any interrruption to their ministry it does not seem to have been for very long.[62] Though Calamy maintained that William Yeo of Wolborough lost an £80 augmentation for refusing the Engagement, official Commonwealth records show that Yeo received £50 a year both before and after 1650. Any hiatus (if true) may again have been of short duration.[63]

By and large it is very difficult to come across any overtly political comment in sermons or biographical notes. Hugh Gundery, probably when returning to where he had been curate, was remembered at Ottery St Mary for saying:

> There is a nation called Cavaliers and they hope, hope, hope for a time but before the time come, I hope their eyes will drop out of their heads.

Was this the sort of declamation the then Council of State wished to be used in the pulpit? The more usual Presbyterian practice was to avoid all political comment, as appeared clearly in the seventh rule for the Exeter Assembly in 1655. It stated that 'in our consultations and debates we will not meddle with Civil or Secular matters'.[64] Just how difficult this was can be seen in a sermon preached by Richard Saunders, a Presbyterian, in front of those same justices less than a year after the Ford and Nichols enquiry. 'I seldom engage in State-Divinity,' he said, 'the work of a Gospel Minister being to win souls.' Even so, he then went on at some length to argue the legitimacy of existing government, however 'inconvenient it might be to have a standing army'.[65] Two Anglican clergy, Nicholas Bryan and Robert Bradford, lost their augmentations, the latter almost certainly for refusing the Engagement.[66]

The early 1650s in Devon saw a notable decline in the number of known or suspected officiating Anglican clergy. Sequestrations, resignations and deaths will not account for all, but the considerable rise in the unknown column reflects the greater difficulty of ascertaining just who did have the cure of souls by then in many parishes. The modest rise in the ranks of Presbyterian and Independent clergy again reveals the considerable problem of finding reliable substitutes to take over vacant charges.

The Exeter Assembly of October 1655 was a belated attempt to set up a voluntary Presbyterian system in Devon. It was realized that many parishes would not co-operate, and that without discipline irregularities would persist even in supportive areas. However, if one third of the serving clergy could be persuaded to give some lead in ecclesiastical authority, it might yet save the country from anarchy. Calamy later commended George Hughes for inducing ministers of episcopal and congregational persuasion to support the project alongside Presbyterians.

The 133 names hitherto given as participating in this development is incomplete. The Walker MSS reveal a Great Torrington presbytery that operated from at least 1657, involving a further ten clergy. Yet another

Bodleian manuscript can add four more. The county appears to have been divided into eight, and then nine, sub-divisions. Four Independents included in the revised total of 147 signed only qualified acceptance of the organization and its principles, yet four others seemingly made no such reservation. About 63 signatories may be regarded as outright Presbyterians.[67] Typifying those wanting some unity and organization rather than none was Francis Fullwood of West Alvington. Though he subscribed to the Exeter Assembly, after the Restoration he soon became Archdeacon of Totnes. His published writings before and after 1660 show a consistency of moderation.[68] Others may have temporized less honourably, but there was by then widespread concern about the spontaneous growth of Baptists and Quakers. John Quick later testified that:

> from the years 1649 & onwards the glory of God was sensibly departing from their Congregations . . . that their people had itching ears . . . unto wicked Schisms.

Such developments made the Exeter Assembly and its like that much more necessary.[69]

Among the Anglican supporters of voluntary presbyteries were Elias Eastway of Bradworthy, Baldwin Acland of Tedburn St Mary, Roger Ashton of Stowford and William Miller of Christow. Though ousted from South Brent, John Gandy nevertheless participated as the Commonwealth rector of Bridford. It is just as baffling to find 16 resolute Presbyterians serving in Devon at the time who were not linked in any known way with this voluntary organization. Fourteen of them became nonconformists in 1662: the other two died before 1660.[70]

What further evidence survives of other Presbyterian activity before 1660? Twenty-one ministers serving a Devon parish during the Interregnum were ordained the Presbyterian way by a group of senior brethren. Up to 1657 such events took place in London or Salisbury. In the last three years of the Commonwealth, however, local ordinations were conducted at Exeter, Hatherleigh, Holsworthy, Dartmouth, Plymouth, Feniton and Wolborough. Fourteen of those who were made ministers in this way shortly afterwards became nonconformists, but five conformed, presumably submitting first to re-ordination. One other died and the whereabouts of the last after 1660 remains unknown.[71]

References in contemporary records to the Presbyterian Directory or Prayer Book are exceedingly rare. Thus, although the Book of Common Prayer was officially banned as from 1645, little is known about what replaced the old order. A Quarter Sessions certificate testifies that a Talaton couple were married in the presence of Edmund Hunt, curate 'according to the order contained in the directory'. At Little Hempston Thomas Friend was said to have used the Assembly catechism and common prayer. At Plymouth Francis Porter, according to Quick, was the first to set aside the liturgy but the first to resume it at the Restoration. Porter subscribed both to the *Joint Testimonie* and to the Exeter Assembly, but otherwise appears only as a nonentity completely overshadowed by the very influential George Hughes.[72]

Specific references to lay eldership are hardly more numerous. Ottery St Mary kept a presbytery for 12 years. West Alvington had lay elders and Stoke Fleming had at least two. Considerable irritation was caused at Northam, it would seem, when a barrister of blameless morals was denied the sacrament until he had been examined by 'a very silly fellow as most thought', a weaver by trade. One is left to assume that he was an elder. The autobiography of George Trosse cites an occasion in Exeter when he was examined by a minister with a lay elder present.[73] Unfortunately, the major part of the Presbyterian story in Devon at this time has been lost beyond recall. The organizational presbyteries in Devon never seem to have included any lay element, so fundamental to pure Presbyterian intention.

What has survived is the agonizing debate as to the proper conduct of communion services. Both in the deliberations of the Exeter Assembly and of the Torrington presbytery, the problem of who should be allowed this sacred ritual was never satisfactorily resolved. Anglicans had offered bread and wine to all who were not formally excommunicated by the Church courts. In more normal times charges were levelled against those of the laity who neglected to receive the elements at least once a year. The alternative Presbyterianism agitated for greater local control of the parish and worked towards having an effective discipline there subject only to a higher synodial authority, such as that of the Exeter (i.e., County) Assembly. Without some agreed structure many reforming clergy either held occasional communions or none at all. At Dunsford William Pearse excused his neglect of the communion on the grounds that 'the people were unworthy'. At Ottery St Mary a select communion was the only one available for 12 years. The Torrington presbytery thought only those who 'have a competent understanding of the Gospell Covenant and of the other fundamental doctrines of the Christian Religion' should communicate.[74] The intruding rector of Drewsteignton only served those parishioners who received the elements either standing or sitting, while at

Bratton Fleming Anthony Palmer conducted but one communion service in 12 years. Presumably he judged it a failure.[75]

With so little agreement on the issue, even among reforming clergy, most laymen were bound to remain unconvinced and probably resentful. Similarly the transforming of marriage into a purely civil ceremony performed by Justices of the Peace probably redounded more to the advantage of traditional clergy than of those who replaced them. Meanwhile, old-time customs persisted. A Quarter Sessions order of April 1658 required every parish church in the county to publish a ban on revels— surely an effective testimony to their widespread survival.[76]

Some Presbyterian clerics were less than tactful in their relationships with local gentry. For example, when a funeral sermon by Alexander Grosse, vicar of Ashburton, failed to satisfy one of the mourning sons, the former was reported as saying to the latter: 'Hold thy tongue young man, one Eagle seeth farther than ten Owls.' Humphrey Saunders at Holsworthy refused communion to some of his gentry, while at Kingsbridge in 1656 Nicholas Tripe, gent., was sufficiently incensed as to interrupt one minister and congregation on lecture day. The clergyman in question was likely to have been Anthony Loveis, the intruding rector of nearby Charleton. There was a Nicholas Tripe among the Exeter Quakers of 1661.[77]

Complimentary remarks about some Devon Presbyterians can be found even in the Walker MSS. For instance, Thomas Ford of Exeter was summarized as well-read and a man of good morals; Nathaniel Durant of Cheriton Fitzpaine was reckoned to have been a good scholar and a sober individual. Though Ferdinando Nichols of Exeter was episcopally ordained and a man of good life, he was termed an indifferent scholar. All these comments are to be found in Dr Walker's own difficult handwriting. In his published *Attempt* he adjudged Thomas Friend of Little Hempston an honourable man, despite his denying communion to the parish for nine whole years. The local correspondent had described Friend as 'of a very honest, sober and peaceable conversation'. Anthony Downe of Northam was still held in high regard long after his 1662 deprivation. Joseph Squire was called a very able divine for his ministry at Lifton, while similar praise was bestowed on John Herring of Marystow.[78]

A more qualified commendation was afforded the mid-century vicar of Plymouth. In 1703 James Yonge wrote that George Hughes 'was more of a gentleman in his deportment and way of living than any of that gang I ever saw'. However, he goes on to scorn his philosophy, divinity and logic. An examination of Hughes' published works hardly substantiates

Yonge's derision, though to some extent unwitting testimony in John Quick's biography of Hughes may. There the principal upholder of Devon Presbyterianism was said to have advised young ministers not to refer to the Church Fathers or to Schoolmen concerning problematic matters 'for the one never understood Scripture & the others were utter strangers to our present controversys'. The latter might be obvious, but not so the former. On another occasion Hughes advised that honest hearts and weak heads remained among the laity! Elsewhere he defended usury against the arguments of Jellinger. Regularly he preserved a good relationship with Plymouth magistrates and had Anglican clergy as friends both before and after the Restoration. His daughter married the eminent Independent preacher, John Howe, in 1657, and the breadth of ecclesiastical support for the Exeter Assembly already shown testifies to his considerable influence. One writer described it as 'a kind of papal sway'.[79]

Devon Independent ministers were still growing in number by 1660, but their cause remained significantly harder to sustain than that of their Presbyterian rivals. Their numbers were few, their publications almost non-existent and their education markedly inferior. Their most illustrious individual, John Howe, was quickly summoned to preach before the Lord Protector so that Torrington was promised supply preachers in exchange. We have little hope of discovering how well such a promise was kept, apart from the brief ministry of Increase Mather and short-lived attempts in 1659 to replace him with John Bullock.[80]

At the lower end of the ability scale, Walter Shute of Cornwood offered this observation from the pulpit on hearing of the death of Charles I: 'Now I plainly see yt Hell is pav'd with the Skulls of Kings and Princes.' Designated an ignorant and gluttonous person in Walker's correspondence, he nevertheless managed to conform and remain vicar there after St Bartholomew's Day, 1662.[81] The most reprehensible cleric, however, was probably Thomas Larkham, vicar of Tavistock from 1648. In 1892 Mrs Radford outlined what was then known about this controversial refugee from an earlier Laudian discipline: along with several other exiles he returned from North America once the Civil War outcome had given new hope of winning promotion within a reformed Church this side of the Atlantic. Recently found has been a Quarter Sessions order of July 1653, releasing one Joan of Clayhanger from being bound to Thomas Larkham but without giving reason for the discharge. Was she yet another victim of this man's amorous indiscipline? (He was reputed to have fathered two bastards previously.) The stormy nature of his Tavistock ministry makes it all the more surprising that it was not until 1659 that the local Presbyterians saw fit to establish a rival mid-week lecture to his. Testimony to the bitterness of the row Larkham then had with the layman Nicholas Watts was cited by a Walker corresondent. However, according to Calamy, Watts later confessed that his attacks on Larkham had been 'idle and wretched'. The fifth Earl of Bedford may well have delayed his stipend at some point and even have forced his resignation at the end of 1660, but he still allowed him and his fellow Independents to use the refectory of Tavistock abbey for their protected meeting after 1662.[82]

The nature of the quarrel that afflicted the Exeter Independents just prior to the Restoration has done little to aid their reputation with posterity. Susanna Parr had broken ranks by going to hear the Presbyterian Thomas Ford, perhaps on the other side of that infamous wall in the cathedral separating Independents from Presbyterians. The lady was excommunicated as a consequence, but fought back by setting out her case in print. Her defence managed to blacken the reputation of Lewis Stucley in the process. It seems he was a schemer too, often absent from Exeter and excessively engaged in law-suits. He certainly had a prolonged legal struggle with Richard Newte over the Tidcombe and Clare portions of Tiverton rectory, but with an augmentation of £200 a year Stucley could well afford a protracted and expensive quarrel.[83]

Without any formal organization among the Independents, their number—and even their identity—is that much harder to assess. If 30 was about their true number by 1660, the nonconforming total of 27 still shows a commendable commitment to conscience. Not included in the latter figure is Edward Byne, who, after moving successfully in 1662 from Upton Pyne to Pyworthy, still had his conformity very much in question nine years later when he was suspended from the latter living.[84]

Soon after the return of Charles II, eight Devon Independents composed a humble address to their new ruler. It began:

> Most dread Sovereign. It hath pleased the All-wise god for many years to make darkness his pavilion and secret place, the Lord hath with a strange mysteriousness so balanced affairs that oftentimes his own people have stood amazed and unresolved . . .

About the same time in Lyme Regis the former curate of Topsham, Ames Short, was rejoicing at the prospect of not being oppressed by his neighbours or being subject to 'the aspiring attempts of proud and ambitious men to exalt themselves to the highest place of power and authority'.[85] Presbyterianism had a far more consistent attitude to monarchy than did Independency, but neither avoided the ensuing exclusion and disappointment.

The nature and mood of the Restoration Church can well be understood from the writings of John Gauden, briefly to become bishop of Exeter before moving on to Worcester. His writings in defence of Anglicanism, while admitting minor blemishes within the old Church, allowed no credit whatsoever to the radical reformers. To him they were but

> Levellers of the Ministerial duty and dignity . . . [who promoted] infinite swarms of mechanick rivals . . . into desks and pulpits. . . . [Their] pitiful preaching . . . consisted not in study meditation and reading but in a bold look, confident spirit and a voluble tongue.[86]

Though some 124 clergy or thereabouts were removed from their clerical function in Devon between the Restoration and the Bartholomew Day subscription requirement of August 1662,[87] 87 of these had degrees and 27 of the total had served pre-war Anglicanism. The rag-tag and bobtail preachers were more often those set up to fill the gaps caused by the insufficient supply of qualified substitutes or the local interference with income or, of course, both. Those formally intruded or presented were not, as a rule, either incompetent or irresponsible, apart from the controversial tendency already noted of not administering a regular communion.

If it has been far from easy to track down the movements and motivation of the clergy, the role of influential laymen must be significantly harder to identify. The composition of the County Committee up to 1653 can be derived from several specific references to it in the Walker MSS. Of the 14 persons named only five were gentry. Though all these five were JPs, the relationship of the County Committee to the overall Commission of the Peace looks very inferior. Doubtless this will help to explain some of the arbitrary behaviour of the soldiers. When the royalist William Hart was allowed by the County Committee to remain rector of Harford, Major James Pierce was so mad he was said to have advised to local parishioners not to pay their tithes. Though testimony survives of the belligerent acts of Upton Pyne's Sir John Coplestone and of Buckerell's John Searle, the more subtle pressures of many another lay influence can only be surmised.[88]

After 1653 the county had a joint committee of clergy and laymen to vet local sequestrations and admissions. Testimonials in support of incoming clergy often came henceforth from both clergy and laymen who had personal knowledge of their previous ministry or potential.[89] It was a co-operative venture the restored Church might have done well to continue. Augmentations were another casualty of the Restoration, though probably they helped towards the granting of Queen Anne's Bounty 40 years later. A comprehensive scheme to realign some parish boundaries was also abandoned.[90]

From the statistical table given at the end of this chapter it will be seen that there was some appreciable recovery of Anglican numbers after 1655. Whereas Presbyterianism in 1646 depended quite heavily on fellow travellers, by 1660 committed Presbyterians formed about a fifth of the clergy serving officially in Devon. However, the 50 or so across the Anglican/Presbyterian divide who conformed by 1662 left the traditional Church needing only about a decade in which to recover lost ground. Although Independency appears to have increased five-fold across the 14 years so measured, it had no hope of converting the whole county and was doubtless more honourable in defeat than it had been in relative victory. Despite the high proportion of unknowns, and the inevitable wrong categorizing of some individuals, the overall value of the exercise would appear to be vindicated. It sets in proportion the relative loyalty of those who acted as clergymen in this period and shows the extent of the problem which the Presbyterians and Independents faced. If they could not solve it together, how much less likely were they to do so in rivalry.[91]

It was still too soon historically for religious matters to be the subject of public debate, though the Baptists may have gained more than they lost by arguing openly with Francis Fullwood at West Alvington. Not far away, in Dartmouth, Allen Geare and John Flavell offered controversial material for public consideration in their weekday lecture until the young Francis Whiddon of Totnes persuaded them to desist. The pulpit was still generally expected to be used to assert both church and political authority. To some extent the years 1660–2 reversed the roles of persecutor and persecuted, but at least 193 clergy remained in office from 1659 to the end of 1662, despite the quite disproportionate number of vacancies, resignations and deprivations.

The continuing debate on this subject will largely revolve round our reaction to the assertions of George Pierce, the sequestered rector of Tiverton (Pitt portion). He argued that the radicals of his time were like unskilled barbers who drew blood instead of removing a few loose hairs. Their end result, he maintained, was deformation rather than reformation.[92]

What improved understanding of the Commonwealth clergy in Devon has emerged from this study? On the surface the survival powers of Anglicanism suspected by R.N. Worth over a century ago have been well vindicated. The problems of finding adequate replacement clergy were considerable. Despite a modest increase in the number of Presbyterian and Independent clergy right up to 1660, the revival of outright Anglican incumbents after 1655 is surely the more significant statistic. Both Anglicans and Dissenters showed considerable courage when called upon to suffer for their principles.

More hidden from view is the crucial role of the influential laity. Some made cynical attempts to manipulate tithe issues in their favour, others worked deliberately to embarrass those officially appointed, either in London or within the county, by non-episcopal authority. Perhaps the majority of parishes conformed just sufficiently to allow a more or less continuous ministry. If so, this is in itself a remarkable tribute to Devon's traditionalism.

PROBABLE CLERICAL ALLEGIANCE IN DEVON 1646–60

|  | *1646* | *1650* | *1655* | *1660* |
|---|---|---|---|---|
| Anglican | 271 | 262 | 179 | 202 |
| Presbyterian | 39 | 70 | 78 | 87 |
| Anglican/Presbyterian* | 10 | 22 | 46 | 51 |
| Presbyterian/Anglican* | 18 | 22 | 24 | 9 |
| Independent | 6 | 18 | 24 | 27 |
| Anglican/Independent* | 5 | 6 | 4 | 7 |
| Independent/Anglican* | 1 | 2 | 4 | 3 |
| Unknown | 119 | 67 | 110 | 83 |

\* Sometimes a clergyman's allegiance was divided or ambivalent. That cited first indicates an apparent preference at the time.

# Notes

1. W.A. Shaw, *History of the English Church 1640–60* (1900), like much historical work of its time, contains more detailed fact than clear interpretation. For the latter J.S. Morrill (ed.), *Reactions to the English Civil War 1642–49* (1982), 89–110, and G.E. Aylmer (ed.), *Interregnum* (1974), 99–120, offer more recent outlines of the national scene within the time scale under review. See also I.M. Green, 'Persecution of Scandalous and Malignant Clergy', *EHR* (1979), 507–31, and J. Spurr, *Restoration Church of England 1646–89* (Yale, 1991), Ch. 1.

2. A.G. Matthews, *Walker Revised* (Oxford, 1948); J.D. Tatham, *Dr John Walker's 'The Sufferings of the Clergy'* (Cambridge, 1911).

3. J. Walker, *An Attempt towards Recovering an Account . . . of the Sufferings of the Clergy of the Church of England . . . in the late Times of the Grand Rebellion* (1714), 3 vols, hereafter *Attempt*; Edmund Calamy's evidence in support of nonconformist clergy is most accessible in S. Palmer (ed.), *Nonconformists Memorial* (1802–3), 3 vols, hereafter Calamy, *Memorial.*

4. For local church history, see Nicholas Orme (ed.), *Unity and Variety: A History of the Church in Devon and Cornwall* (Exeter, 1991); P.W. Jackson, 'Nonconformists and Society in Devon 1660–89' (unpublished PhD thesis, University of Exeter, 1986); A. Brockett, *Nonconformity in Exeter* (Manchester, 1962). Many early articles in the *Devonshire Association Transactions* were consulted, but because these seldom noted sources, the references that follow here are to primary sources only.

5. Lambeth Palace Library (hereafter LPL), COMM XIIa/5; Bodleian Library (hereafter Bodl.), B.322–9; PRO, E336/28.

6. As regards the more secular situation relating to this subject, see S.K. Roberts, *Recovery and Restoration in an English County* (Exeter, 1985); for a comparative study of other counties, refer to Jim Sharpe, 'Scandalous and Malignant Priests in Essex: The Impact of Grassroots Puritanism' in C. Jones, M. Newitt and S.K. Roberts (eds), *Politics and People in Revolutionary England* (Oxford, 1986); A. Hughes, *Politics, Society and Civil War in Warwickshire 1620–60* (Cambridge, 1987), 66–9, 325–9. For the statistical table, see above.

7. DRO, Chanter 23, 63. Thomas Maynard admitted to North Tawton rectory.

8. Bodl., Walker MS, C.4.310; Calamy, *Memorial*, ii. 73.

9. Viz., Clare (Honiton), Dike (Axmouth), Downe A. (Northam), Downe M. (Exeter), Durant (Cheriton Fitzpaine), Finney (Exbourne), Forward (Ottery St Mary), Garrett (Totnes), Goldstone (Stoke Damerel), Grosse (Bridford), Hughes (Tavistock), Nosworthy (Seaton), Olden (Exeter), Smith Z. (Barnstaple), Trescott (Inwardleigh), Venner (Little Hempston) and Wellman (Luppitt); Bodl., Walker MS, C.2.235, 242; BL, Add. MS 15669, 28 July 1645; A.G. Matthews, *Calamy Revised* (Oxford, 1934), 117, 169, 173, 197, 281, 368, 450, 492, 518; Matthews, *Walker Revised*, 113, 212.

10. G. Hughes (ed.), *Joint Testimonie of the Ministers of Devon . . .* (1648), 34; Matthews, *Calamy Revised*, 440.

11. Matthews, *Walker Revised*, 117, 118; Sharpe, 'Scandalous', 253–73.

12. Bodl., Walker MS, C.2.237.

13. Bodl., Walker MS, C.2.247.

14. Bodl., Walker MS, C.2.311.

15. Bodl., Walker MS, C.2.250, 268, 279, 292, 316; C.4.118; Walker, *Attempt*, ii. 377.

16. Bodl., Walker MS, C.2.219, 418.

17. Bodl., Walker MS, C.2.331, C.8.45; Walker, *Attempt*, ii. 318, 353; Matthews, *Walker Revised*, 122; see above, pp. 210, 217–18.

18. Bodl., Walker MS, C.2.296; Walker, *Attempt*, ii. 193.

19. Bodl., Walker MS, C.4.310; LPL, COMM XIIa/5, 215. Bradstone and Dunterton for example, 'fit to be united'.

20. T. Bedford, *Treatise of the Sacrament* (1939) and *Ready Way to True Freedom* (1638).
21. Bodl., Walker MS, C.8.74; Matthews, *Walker Revised*, 123.
22. Bodl., Walker MS, C.2.335, C.8.64; Walker, *Attempt*, ii. 421.
23. Shaw, *English Church*, ii. 186, 187, 272.
24. See above, p. 221, for an estimate of how many Presbyterians and their sympathizers there were in 1650. Walker's list of subscribers to the Engagement (C.2.39) includes many Presbyterians, ten of whom served then in Devon parishes. Few, if any, would have subscribed willingly, since the decision to truncate Parliament and kill the King was overwhelmingly an Independent and army solution to the political impasse.
25. Viz., Black Torrington, Brampford Speke, Butterleigh, Chawleigh, Chulmleigh, Clayhanger, Cornworthy, Coryton, Countisbury, Dodbrooke, Eggesford, Lynton, Mariansleigh, Newton St Cyres, Northleigh, Oakford, Poughill, Sampford Courtney, Shebbear, Slapton, Stoodleigh and Virginstow.
26. Bodl., Walker MS, C.3.94; LPL, COMM XIIa/5.98.
27. Bodl., Walker MS, C.2.444, 446.
28. Bodl., Walker MS, C.2.354, C.8.45.
29. Bodl., Walker MS, C.8.25.
30. Bodl., Walker MS, C.2.271, C.8.45, 57, 80.
31. Bodl., Walker MS, C.2.296.
32. Bodl., Walker MS, C.8.48; Walker, *Attempt*, ii. 340.
33. Viz., Dove, Elliot, Goch, Helyar, Herniman, Huchenson, Paine, Pyne, Serle, Turner and Wilson.
34. Matthews, *Walker Revised*, 115, 125, 179.
35. Bodl., Walker MS, C.2.219, 424.
36. Bodl., Walker MS, C.2.340, E.8.34. Collins, Getsius, Gove, Sharpe and Travers were the others.
37. Bodl., Walker MS, C.2.433; Walker, *Attempt*, ii. 262.
38. Bodl., Walker MS, C.2.316; Walker, *Attempt*, ii. 356; Matthews, *Walker Revised*, 116.
39. Bodl., Walker MS, C.1.343, C.2.395, C.8.29.
40. Viz., Adams, Bedford, Bourcher, Briant, Burnard, Bury, Carew, Coren, Forbes, Gandy, Hunt, Richard Long, Monck, Newte, John Parsons, Phare, Pierce, Pote, Powell, Reynolds, Scot, Sharp, Shute, Slater and John Travers.
41. Bodl., Walker MS, C.2.411, 422, C.3.304.
42. Bodl., Walker MS, C.2.446.
43. Bodl., Walker MS, C.2.245, 311.
44. Bodl., Walker MS, C.8.25; Walker, *Attempt*, ii. 316.
45. Bodl., Walker MS, C.2.397, 471.
46. Viz., Bartholomew Ashwood (Bickleigh), Robert Hall (Stokeinteignhead), William Huchenson (Kenn) and John Webber (Broadwood Kelly).
47. Bodl., Walker MS, C.2.254.
48. Bodl., Walker MS, C.3.95.
49. Bodl., Walker MS, C.4.367, 368; Shaw, *English Church*, ii. 280.
50. Hughes, *Joint Testimonie*, 33–6; Matthews, *Calamy Revised*, 491.

51. Buckley, Burnard, Ceely, Cresson, Goddard, Gove, Hancock, Hopkins, Pearse, Porter, Preston, Randall, Searle, Squire, Terry, Wilcox and Yeo (East Buckland) all conformed.

52. Viz., Binnore, Cleland, Finney, Hanmer, Herring (Drewsteignton), Horsham, Knapman, Law, Palmer, Syms, Wilkins and Wyne; Matthews, *Calamy Revised*, 56, 121, 197, 247, 259, 278, 311, 317, 379, 442, 530, 538.

53. LPL, COMM XIIa/5, 72, 266.

54. Bodl., Walker MS, C.2.301, 365, 384, 433, C.8.48, E.7.4; Walker, *Attempt*, ii. 241; *DNB* (1885–1900) xxiii, 354 identifies Dr Gurnall.

55. LPL, COMM II, 486; Matthews, *Walker Revised*, 111.

56. Bodl., Walker MS, C.2.290, 344, C.4.154, C.8.50f.; Frances B. Rose-Troup, 'Biographical Sketch of Reverend Christopher Jellinger MA', *DAT* xxxii (1900), 249–70. See above, p. 216.

57. LPL, COMM XIIa/5, 24, 45, 149; I. Gowers, 'Puritanism in the County of Devon 1570–1641' (unpublished MA thesis, University of Exeter, 1971), 32.

58. LPL, COMM VIb/1 fols 5, 8; VIb/2, 37; Shaw, *English Church*, ii. 208–13.

59. Bodl., Walker MS, C.2.337, C.4.118f., 429, C.8.40.

60. Bodl., Walker MS, C.2.244, 261; E.12.82; MS. Bod. 325, fols 65, 135.

61. Bodl., Walker MS, C.2.246, C.6.39–45; Bodl., Rawlinson MS., 711, fols 7–15; DRO, Ottery St Mary parish register Sept 1657. Known subscribers to the Engagement include ten Devon Presbyterians and William Banks of Heavitree, an ally of the Exeter Independent, Lewis Stucley.

62. PRO, SP25/64.452, SP25/92.71, 72.

63. LPL, COMM VIa/1 80, 81; COMM VIa/5 89, 90; Calamy, *Memorial*, ii. 53.

64. Bodl., Walker MS, C.2.246, C.4.210.

65. R. Saunders, *Plenary Possession* (1651).

66. Bodl., Walker MS, C.4.300, MS.Bod. 326 fol. 88.

67. Bodl., Walker MS, C.5.321–8; R.N. Worth, 'Puritanism in Devon and the Exeter Assembly', *DAT* ix (1877), 281–3; Calamy, *Memorial*, ii. 60.

68. F. Fullwood, *Discourse of the Visible Church* (1658), *Some Necessary and Seasonable Cases of Conscience* (1661), *Grand Case of the Present Ministry* (1662).

69. Dr Williams' Library, London, John Quick, 'Icones Sacræ Anglicanæ', Ii 410.

70. Viz., Bickle (Denbury), Farrant (Musbury), Finney (Exbourne), Friend (Little Hempston), Hill (Newton Ferrers), Horsham (Staverton), Mortimer (Sowton), Parr (Rewe), Pitts (Plympton St Mary), Stidson (St Marychurch), Stuke (Ilsington), Tucker (Dittisham) and Thomas Whitehorn (Upton Hellions). The last should not be confused with Otho Whitehorne who did join the Exeter Assembly. In 1655–6 John Nosworthy was moving from Seaton to Manaton. Morse and Way both died before 1660.

71. DRO, 3542D/M1/1; St Thomas the Apostle parish register, 20 August 1657; Bodl., Walker MS, C.4.185, C.5.319; Matthews, *Calamy Revised*, 25, 139, 219, 243, 270, 292, 342, 384, 385, 401, 440, 475, 495, 523, 545; H.W. Watson, 'A Devonshire Village (Feniton) in the Olden Days', *DAT* lxi (1929), 388.

72. DRO, DQS OB 4 Epiphany 1648; Bodl., Walker MS, C.3.31; Quick, 'Icones', Iii 513, 514.

73. Bodl., Walker MS, C.2.246, 354; C.8.40, 58; E.12.85; G. Trosse, *Life of the Late Reverend George Trosse* (1714), 68.

74. Bodl., Walker MS, C.2.235, 246, C.5.322f.

75. Bodl., Walker MS, C.2.324; C.4.166.

76. DRO, DQS OB 1/9, April 1658.

77. DRO, DQS OB 1/9, 15 April 1656, Quick, 'Icones', Ii 415; Matthews, *Calamy Revised*, 426.

78. Bodl., Walker MS, C.2.323, 391, C.3.31, E.7.2–13; Walker, *Attempt*, ii. 356.

79. Bodl., Walker MS, C.1.103, C.4.331; Quick, 'Icones', Iii 463–566.

80. *DNB* xxviii, 85; xxxvii, 27; Matthews, *Calamy Revised*, 279.

81. Bodl., Walker MS, C.2.278.

82. DRO, DQS OB 1/9, 12 July 1653; Bodl., Walker MS, C.2.294, C.4.85, C.5.228; Matthews, *Calamy Revised*, 315; G.H. Radford, 'Thomas Larkham', *DAT* xxiv (1892), 96–146; Calamy, *Memorial*, i. 78, 79.

83. Bodl., Walker MS, C.4.186–208; LPL, COMM VIb/2, 33; W.J. Harte, Presidential Address, *DAT* lxix (1937), 41–72; A. Brockett, *Nonconformity in Exeter* (Manchester, 1962); S. Parr, *Susanna's Apologie against the Elders* (Oxford, 1659). For a modern assessment of this quarrel G.F. Nuttall, *Visible Saints* (Oxford, 1957), 127–30, is much to be preferred to E. Graham et al. (eds), *Her Own Life* (1989), 101–15, which includes in its commentary some serious misconceptions about the Church in Devon at the time.

84. DRO, CC178/Pyworthy 1.

85. PRO, SP29/1/28; Ames Short, *God save the King* (1660), 12, 17.

86. J. Gauden, *Ecclesiae Anglicanae Suspiria* (1659), 117.

87. Bodl., Walker MS, C.4.162, 163, 173, 190, 195, 207, 356; Roberts, *Recovery and Restoration, passim*; A. Everitt, *Community of Kent and the Great Rebellion* (Leicester, 1966), especially Ch. 5; K.M. Beck, 'Recusancy and Nonconformity in Devon and Somerset 1660–1714' (unpublished MA thesis, University of Bristol, 1961), 78, 79. William Fry was the most regularly mentioned of the justices with Joseph Hunkyn, Arthur Upton, John Champneys and John Beare being the others.

88. Bodl., Walker MS, C.2.311, 316; Walker, *Attempt*, ii. 417.

89. LPL, COMM III 3–7; C.H. Firth and R.S. Tait (eds), *Acts and Ordinances of the Interregnum 1642–60* (1911), ii. 970, 979.

90. LPL, COMM XIIc/4, 87–97.

91. Bodl., Walker MS, C.2.422, C.8.48. The assertion by Roberts, *Recovery and Restoration*, 139, that 'religious presbyterianism had been thoroughly discredited (in Devon) after the Scots invasion of 1651, if not before' may summarize the lay situation but cannot easily be supported from the clerical evidence.

92. Bodl., Walker MS, C.2.302, 422, C.4.208, C.8.29; Jackson, 'Nonconformists and Society', Ch. 1.

# Professor J.A. Youings:
# A Bibliography of her Work

IAN MAXTED

This list is arranged in chronological order and omits reviews, letters and contributions to newspapers. It also omits series of publications by societies such as the Devon and Cornwall Record Society for which Professor Youings has acted as general editor.

*1951*

'The Disposal of Monastic Property in Land in the County of Devon with Special Reference to the Period 1536–58' (unpublished dissertation, PhD, University of London, 1951). Summary in: *Bulletin of the Institute of Historical Research*, 24 (1951), 198–202.

*1952*

'The City of Exeter and the Property of the Dissolved Monasteries', *Reports and Transactions of the Devonshire Association*, 84 (1952), 122–41.

*1954*

'The Terms of the Disposal of the Devon Monastic Lands, 1536–58', *English Historical Review*, 69 (January 1954), 18–38. Reprinted in *Essays in Agrarian History*, vol. 1, edited by W.E. Minchinton (Newton Abbot: David & Charles, 1968), 117–4.
'Martin Pateshull and William Raleigh', *Devon and Cornwall Notes and Queries*, 26:4 (October 1954), 121.

*1955*

*Devon Monastic Lands: Calendar of Particulars for Grants 1536–1558*, edited with an introduction by Joyce Youings. (Exeter: Devon and Cornwall Record Society, 1955). xxxvii, 154 pp. Devon and Cornwall Record Society, New Series, Vol. 1, ISBN 0–901853–04–6.
'A Westcountry Manuscript at Rouen', *Devon and Cornwall Notes and Queries*, 26:6 (April 1955), 189.

*1960*

*St Nicholas Priory, Exeter*, historical summary by H. Lloyd Parry; description of building by Harold Brakspear; revised and partly rewritten by Joyce Youings, (Exeter: City of Exeter Museums and Art Gallery, 1960). 32 pp.: ill. ISBN 0–85677–001–9.

'The Council of the West', *Transactions of the Royal Historical Society*, 5th Series, Vol. 10 (1960), 41–59.

*1965*

'Devon Monastic Wool Sales', *Devon and Cornwall Notes and Queries*, 30:3 (July 1965), 70–72.

*1966*

'A Rare Survival: Letter Patent Granting a Pension to a Lincolnshire Nun in 1539', *Archives*, Vol. 7, no. 36 (October 1966), 226–9.

*1967*

'King James's Charter to Tiverton, 1615', *Reports and Transactions of the Devonshire Association*, 99 (1967), 147–63. Also published separately ISBN 0–85214–020–7.

'Landlords in England: The Church', in *The Agrarian History of England and Wales, Vol. 4: 1500–1640*, edited by Joan Thirsk, (Cambridge: Cambridge University Press, 1967), 303–56. Reprinted with new introductory material in *Rural Society: Landowners, Peasants and Labourers, 1500–1750*, edited by Christopher Clay, (Cambridge: Cambridge University Press, 1990), ISBN 0–521–36883–9, pp. 7–10, 71–121.

*1968*

*Tuckers Hall Exeter: The History of a Provincial City Company through Five Centuries*, (Exeter: University of Exeter and Incorporation of Weavers Fullers & Shearmen, 1968). xiv, 258 pp., plates: ill. ISBN 0–900771–48–8.

*1969*

'Recent Books on the History and Topography of Exeter and its Region', *Advancement of Science*, 26 (September 1969), 52–3.

'The Economic History of Devon 1300–1700' in *Exeter and its Region*, edited by Frank Barlow, (Exeter: University of Exeter for the British Association, 1969), 164–74.

*1970*

'Devon's First Local Historians', *Devon Historian*, 1 (1970), 5–8.

'Tuckers Hall Exeter: Some Early Gild Ordinances', *Devon and Cornwall Notes and Queries*, 31:8 (Winter 1970), 235–8.

*1971*

*The Dissolution of the Monasteries*, (London: Allen & Unwin; New York: Barnes & Noble, 1971), 264 pp. Historical Problems: Studies & Documents, 14. ISBN 0–04–942089–5, 0–04–942090–2 Pbk (Allen & Unwin); 0–389–04454–7 (Barnes & Noble).

*1972*

*Local Record Sources in Print and in Progress, 1971/72*, (London: Historical Association, 1972). 24 pp. Helps for Students of History, no. 85. Compiled for the Local History Committee of the Historical Association. ISBN 0–85178–159–8.

*1974*

*Early Tudor Exeter: The Founders of the County of the City*, (Exeter: University of Exeter, 1974). 28 pp. Inaugural lecture, University of Exeter, 1st March, 1974. ISBN 0–900771–96–8.

*1977*

*Local Record Sources in Print and in Progress 1972–76*, (London: Historical Association, 1977). 44 pp. ISBN 0–85278–218–7. Supplement to *Local Record Sources in Print and in Progress, 1971/72* , (1972).

'Obituary: Eleanora Mary Carus-Wilson', *Economic History Review*, 30:2 (1977), iii–v.

*1979*

'The South-Western Rebellion of 1549', *Southern History*, 1 (1979), 99–122.

*1980*

'Drake, Grenville and Buckland Abbey', *Report and Transactions of the Devonshire Association*, 112 (1980), 95–9.

*1984*

*Sixteenth Century England*, (London: Allen Lane, 1984). 444 pp. ISBN 0–7139–1243–X. Also issued as part of the *Pelican Social History of Britain*, (Harmondsworth: Penguin, 1984) ISBN 0–14–022231–6, 0–14–013820–X. Reprinted 1986, 1988, 1991.

*1985*

*Raleigh in Exeter 1985: Privateering and Colonisation in the Reign of Elizabeth I*, edited by Joyce Youings, (Exeter: University of Exeter, 1985). x, 117 pp. Exeter Studies in History; 10. Papers delivered at a conference at Exeter University on 3–4 May 1985 to mark the four hundredth anniversary of the first attempt to settle people in North America. ISBN 0–85989–252–2.

Professor Youings also contributed to *Raleigh in Exeter*: 'Did Raleigh's England need Colonies?', 39–57.

'A New Maritime History of Devon', *Devon and Cornwall Notes and Queries*, 35:7 (Spring 1985), 280.

'What is Social History?', *History Today*, 35 (March 1985), 41–2.

*1986*

*Ralegh's Country: The South-West of England in the Reign of Elizabeth I*, (Raleigh: North Carolina Department of Cultural Resources for the America's Four Hundredth Anniversary Committee, 1986). xiv, 74 pp.: ill., map. ISBN 0–86526–207–1.

*1987*

'Billmen, Bowmen and Hackbutters: The Elizabethan Militia in the South-West', in: *Security and Defence in South West England before 1800*, edited by Robert Higham (Exeter: University of Exeter, 1987), ISBN 0–85989–209–3, pp. 51–68. Exeter Studies in History, 19. The Harte Lecture for 1986.

'Raleigh's Devon', in *Raleigh and Quinn: Papers Presented at the International Sir Walter Raleigh Conference, Chapel Hill, North Carolina, 27–28 March 1987*, edited by H.G. Jones, (Chapel Hill: North Caroliniana Society Inc., 1987), 69–85.

*1989*

'Raleigh's Country and the Sea', *Proceedings of the British Academy*, 75 (1989), 267–90. Raleigh Lecture in History.

'Tudor Barnstaple: New Life for an Ancient Borough', *Reports and Transactions of the Devonshire Association*, 121 (1989), 1–14. Presidential address.

*1991*

'Dissolution of the Monasteries', 'Valor Ecclesiasticus (1535)' and 'Western Rebellion of 1549' in *Historical Dictionary of Tudor England*, edited by Ronald H. Fritze, (Westport, Ct: Greenwood Press, 1991), ISBN 0–313–26598–4, pp. 143–4, 523–4, 540–1.

'John Hooker and the Tudor Bishops of Exeter', in *Exeter Cathedral: a Celebration*, edited by Michael Swanton, (Exeter: Dean and Chapter of Exeter, 1991), ISBN 0–9503320–5–4, pp. 202–7.

*December 1992*

'Introduction' (with Michael Duffy), 'Three Devon Navigators' and (with Peter Cornford) 'Seafaring and Maritime Trade in Sixteenth-Century Devon' in Michael Duffy, Stephen Fisher, Basil Greenhill, David Starkey and Joyce Youings (eds) *The New Maritime History of Devon*, volume 1 (Conway Maritime Press in association with the University of Exeter).